£12.50
£3.95

*The Jordan Valley
Life and Society
below Sea Level*

The Jordan Valley
Life and Society below Sea Level

written and photographed by
Rami G. Khouri

Published in association
with the Jordan Valley Authority

Longman
London and New York

Longman
London and New York

LONGMAN GROUP LIMITED
Burnt Mill,
Harlow, Essex

© Longman Group Ltd, 1981

All rights reserved. No part of this publication may be reproduced, stored in a retrieval system, or transmitted in any form or by any means, electronic, mechanical, photocopying, recording or otherwise, without the prior permission of the Copyright owner.

First published 1981
ISBN 0 582 78318 6

British Library Cataloguing in Publication Data
Khouri, Rami G.
 The Jordan Valley
 1. Jordan – Economic development
 I. Title
 330.95695   HC497
ISBN 0-582-78318-6

Library of Congress Cataloging in Publication Data
Khouri, Rami G., 1948–
 The Jordan valley.
 Bibliography: p.
 Includes index.
 1. Jordan Valley-Economic policy. I. Title.
HC415.26.K49   338.95694   81-12378
ISBN 0-582-78318-6   AACR2

Printed in Hong Kong by
Wah Cheong Printing Press Ltd

Contents

	page
Preface	vii
List of Maps	ix
Chapter 1 Journey to the Valley	1
Chapter 2 Cornerstone of National Development	13
Chapter 3 Twelve Thousand Years of Agriculture	21
Chapter 4 The Genesis of Planning	43
Chapter 5 The Hazards of Implementation	68
Chapter 6 The Promise Fulfilled	88
Chapter 7 Integrated Development: the bold experiment	99
Chapter 8 The New Realism	136
Chapter 9 The Business of Farming	178
Chapter 10 The Last Frontier	213
Bibliography	228
Index	232

Acknowledgements

I am deeply indebted to all those people who have given me so much of their time, hospitality and knowledge during my research. They all know who they are, even if I do not list every one of their names here, and I am most grateful for their co-operation. Above all, I want to thank the farmers and residents of the valley with whom I spent so much time and drank so many cups of tea, and from whom I have learned so much. I have appreciated their thoughts and experiences, and will always value their friendship. I would like to express special thanks to the three generations of the Kawar family who have demonstrated that if the developmental history of the valley has been erratic, its tradition of hospitality, generosity and hard work has been an enduring constant. To the farmers and residents of the valley, this book is dedicated. The Jordan Valley Authority and all its personnel have been most co-operative and gracious. The assistance and thoughts of His Highness Crown Prince Hassan have been much appreciated and my thanks are due to the Jordanian Armed Forces for providing a helicopter for aerial photography. I must also note the professionalism of Mr Robert Coombs and his colleagues at Longman, with whom working on this book has been a pleasure, and the exemplary efficiency of Mrs Hadia Goussous Odat, who typed the manuscript under pressing circumstances and never missed a smile. Finally, I would like to record the patience and understanding of my wife Ellen, whose quiet bewilderment at why I had to spend so many days and nights in the Jordan Valley was never quite fully tempered by the many boxes of fresh vegetables that I invariably brought back with me. These people, and many others, have made this book possible. Any errors, however, are my own responsibility.

Preface

The intensity, scope and full implications of the changes now taking place in the Jordan Valley are so vast that it would require a far more audacious man than I to attempt to document them all in a small book such as this. Only at the end of the 1980s could a thorough analysis of the Jordan Valley development effort be attempted, and a valuable exercise that would be indeed. This book, unlike the Jordan Valley itself, is a modest endeavour, designed to meet the needs of the visitor, the student, the planner, the journalist, the development aid official, the resident in Jordan, the tourist, the academic professor, the farmer, and anyone else who has been to the Jordan Valley and wants more information on the whence and the whither of that enchanting patch of earth. I have paid more attention to the genesis of the valley's development drive than to its future promise, in the belief that conceiving, designing and implementing a project takes far more effort than operating it once it has been completed. Because the full development of the valley is another decade away, this book has taken the completion of Stage I projects as the most appropriate cut-off point. Others in the future may wish to assess the valley development effort in more judgemental terms than I have. Certainly, that sort of evaluation is necessary, but it has not been part of this book's scope. I have tried to chronicle, in broad terms, the intentions and constraints that have gone into the development of the Jordan Valley in the 1970s, while looking backwards and forwards to place that endeavour in its full temporal context. Those readers requiring more detailed information on various aspects of the Jordan Valley can refer to the bibliography at the back of the book. Better yet, they should spend some time in the valley, because that is the only way to truly appreciate the full dimension of the excitement, the human effort, the technological progress and the economic advances that make the Jordan Valley one of the most noteworthy development projects anywhere in the Third World.

List of Maps

	page
Jordan, showing neighbouring countries	x
The Jordan River Basin	14
Jordan Valley Commission Irrigation Development Plan 1975–82	100
Jordan Valley Authority showing stages of development	111
Jordan Valley Commission, Health Facilities and Centres of Population	118

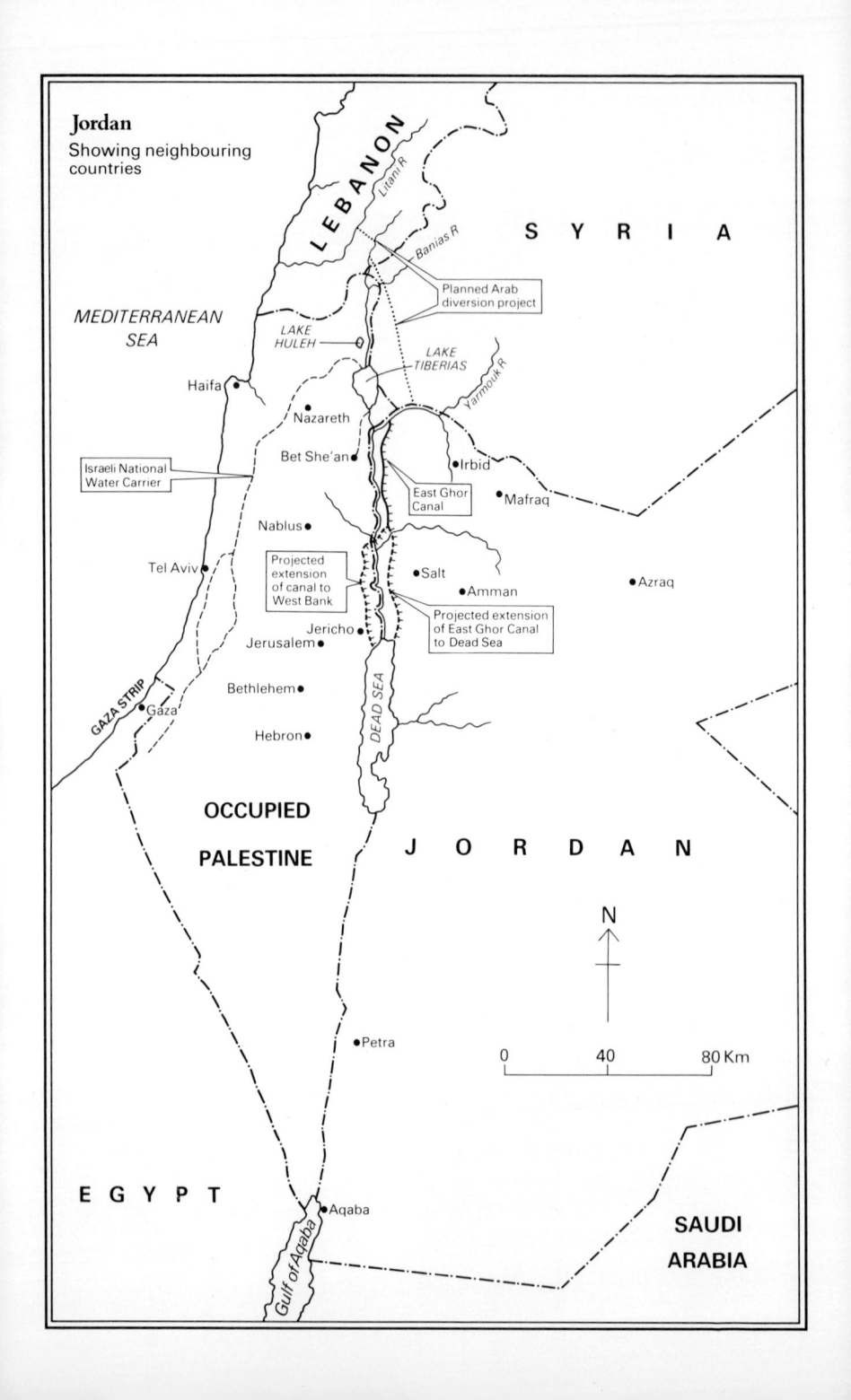

Jordan
Showing neighbouring countries

- LEBANON
- Litani R
- Banias R
- SYRIA
- Planned Arab diversion project
- LAKE HULEH
- LAKE TIBERIAS
- Yarmouk R
- MEDITERRANEAN SEA
- Haifa
- Nazareth
- Bet She'an
- Israeli National Water Carrier
- Irbid
- East Ghor Canal
- Mafraq
- Nablus
- Tel Aviv
- Projected extension of canal to West Bank
- Salt
- Amman
- Azraq
- Jericho
- Projected extension of East Ghor Canal to Dead Sea
- Jerusalem
- Bethlehem
- DEAD SEA
- GAZA STRIP
- Gaza
- Hebron
- OCCUPIED PALESTINE
- JORDAN
- N
- 0   40   80 Km
- Petra
- EGYPT
- Aqaba
- Gulf of Aqaba
- SAUDI ARABIA

Chapter One

Journey to the Valley

The people of Jordan woke up on the morning of Wednesday, 20 December, 1978, hoping the new day would bring rain. But it did not. The winter had been the driest in recent memory; rainfall in November and early December was less than half the annual average. Domestic water-pumping by the municipality of Amman had already been cut back to once a week. The winter wheat crop was just about doomed. In a few weeks, the highest religious authority in the country, the chief justice, would issue an appeal for mass prayers for rain. People went to sleep already praying silently for rain the next day, and woke up hoping to see thick clouds moving into Jordanian skies from the western hills and the Mediterranean Sea. In the winter of 1978/79, they hoped in vain. Except for a few scattered days, the clouds never came. The rains failed.

The evening of Wednesday, 20 December, 1978, was cool and dry, a typical winter night following the day's crisp sunshine. At Amman airport, the flight from Cairo arrived late, landing well past midnight. It was nearly 2 a.m. by the time all the passengers cleared customs and immigration formalities and emerged from the arrivals terminal to be greeted by a sleepy crowd of taxi drivers, a few policemen, airport officials and a handful of Jordanians meeting passengers off the plane. Like most planes on the busy Cairo–Amman route in the late 1970s, that night's flight carried a few businessmen, some students, a group of foreign tourists and a contingent of Egyptian workers – a handful of the one million Egyptians who left their country every year seeking work in the Arab oil-producing states. Though Jordan had no oil, its booming free-market economy absorbed tens of thousands of foreign workers to fill the gaps created by the departure of over a quarter of a million Jordanian workers for high-paying jobs in the Gulf. The Cairo passengers emerged from the arrivals terminal into the quiet midnight chill of a sleeping capital. Some were met by friends or business colleagues. Others drove home with family members. A few took taxis to their hotels. But nobody was there to meet Abu Khalaf.

In fact, Abu Khalaf did not have a clear idea himself of why he was in Jordan, beyond that work was available here for Egyptian labourers such as himself. Abdul Nasser Mahmoud Mustafa, better known as Abu Khalaf ("father of Khalaf"), had left behind his wife, three children, sister and mother in Kandeel, his village 300 kilometres south of Cairo on the banks of the Nile. He had lived in Kandeel all of his forty-seven years, a landless farmer, the archetypal Egyptian *fellah*, scraping a living as a casual labourer on small farms that hugged the Nile valley. When he found work, he could earn about 40 Egyptian piasters a day (about 200 Jordanian fils, or 65 US cents). In 1976, he decided to set off in search of higher-paying work elsewhere. He heard from a friend in the village that there was good work to be had in neighbouring Libya. He travelled to Libya and stayed there for twenty months, working as a manual labourer in a quarry, and then with a contracting company, before returning to Kandeel in 1978 after Egyptian-Libyan relations turned sour. He stayed at home for seven months, working the land whenever work was available, bringing in just enough money to feed and clothe the family. In the summer of 1978, his cousin Ahmed Mahmoud left Kandeel to travel east, to seek work in Jordan. He found a job, and wrote home that there was plenty of work in Jordan, where formalities were few and Egyptians were quickly and easily hired. Abu Khalaf noted his cousin's news. Several months later, he bade his family farewell, travelled to Cairo on a sunny December morning, and caught the next evening's flight to Amman.

He arrived at Amman airport with a cardboard suitcase full of his clothes, a few pictures of his family, and a slip of paper on which a friend back in Kandeel had written the address of his cousin Ahmed Mahmoud in Amman. At 2 a.m., however, he could hardly try to find his cousin. So he took a taxi from the airport and went to the Hussein Mosque, in the heart of downtown Amman, and slept there that night. The next morning, he took another taxi and found the bakery in the Ras Al 'Ain district of Amman, the point of reference from where he was told he could locate his cousin, who shared a nearby room with four other Egyptian labourers. He was led to Ahmed Mahmoud's room, to be told he was at work painting houses. He waited all day until Ahmed Mahmoud returned to his room; they rejoiced that evening, welcoming Abu Khalaf to Jordan. He endeared himself to his cousin even more by giving him letters and a taped cassette, bearing the news and voices of his family back in Kandeel. Ahmed Mahmoud was ecstatic, and insisted that Abu Khalaf stay with them until he found work.

The next day was a Friday, when demand for day labourers was slack. On Saturday, Abu Khalaf went to the square in front of the Hussein Mosque in downtown Amman. He milled around with the hundreds of other Egyptian, Jordanian, Syrian and Asian workers who also came to find work, mostly in the construction business where demand for manual workers on a daily basis was high. Abu Khalaf was hired with several others to work on a new hotel project in Amman, near the Sports City. He worked for five consecutive days at JD 2 ($6.60) per day. The contractor then hired him on a monthly basis, paying him JD 60 ($198) per month. Abu Khalaf slept on the construction site, visiting his cousin every Friday. At the end of three months, the owner of the hotel asked him to stay on and work as a full-time guard. He could bring his family, and stay for many years if he wished. But Abu Khalaf refused. He would have to spend too much money to support his family in Amman, and he would never consider having his wife work in Jordan. No, he thought, the family stays in Kandeel; I'll work on my own in Jordan, and send them as much of my monthly earnings as I can.

View of Zerqa Triangle area

He returned to the downtown labour market and slept in Ahmed Mahmoud's room once again while he sought new work. Three days passed; he was not hired, and returned to his cousin's room every evening slightly dejected, wondering whether he had made a mistake in coming to Jordan without having lined up a sure job ahead of time. On the fourth day, he was hired with four other Egyptians. They were driven for about an hour, sitting in the back of a pick-up truck, until they reached the worksite, a barren piece of land located in a warm, open valley west of Amman. The five workers spent two days building four large dome-shaped houses made of hard plastic. They were each paid JD 5 ($16.50) for two days' work, but the owner of the farm asked Abu Khalaf to stay on and work there on a full-time basis, as a guard and labourer. "How much would the pay be?" Abu Khalaf asked.

"JD 75 a month," the farmer replied.

Where would he live? Abu Khalaf inquired.

In a room that they would build for him, right on the farm.

Could he go home to his family in Kandeel every year during the Moslem month of Ramadan, to fast there and celebrate the feast?

"Yes, of course", replied the farmer, a young Jordanian named Abdulsalam Shaker, recently returned from university studies in the United States.

Abu Khalaf agreed. Since the summer of 1979 he has been working full-time at the Shaker farm, sending half his salary home to his family every month, and living on the other half himself. Abu Khalaf's journey from Kandeel to the Jordan Valley had been improbable and circuitous, but far from unique.

Abdulsalam Shaker was born and raised in Amman, but his family had always been on the peripheries of the Jordan Valley. His mother's parents were Turkish; she was born in Haifa, in Palestine, where her father was the Turkish customs' director. Abdulsalam Shaker's father was born in Sidon, in south Lebanon, where his father had been the Turkish governor of that region. The Shaker family eventually moved to Amman, where Abdulsalam was born in 1953, about the time when his uncle Walid Shaker bought 3,000 dunums of land in the Jordan valley. Abdulsalam graduated from high school, and was promptly rejected for admission at the University of Jordan. He was accepted instead at Louisiana State University, where he had intended to study chemical engineering. Within two months, he had changed his major field of study to beef cattle production, after

Flower nursery in Mashare' in northern Valley

pondering the potential for such work in Jordan, where most red meat is imported. He graduated in 1976, and to gain experience he worked for fourteen months on a cattle ranch in Louisiana. He returned home in 1978 and immediately found work on a new cattle station that the Jordanian government had recently established at Wadi Dhuleil, north-east of Amman. He worked thirteen-hour days, but quit after four months, frustrated with the government bureaucracy and determined to set up his own cattle ranch in Jordan. He quickly realized, however, that a 300-head cattle farm would cost him about JD 100,000, which was far beyond his own means.

How was an energetic twenty-five-year-old Jordanian would-be cattle farmer to raise JD 100,000? Abdulsalam Shaker remembered once reading about a new method of raising grass as feed for cattle, using water instead of soil as the growing medium. The method was known as hydroponics, and was still being developed by various companies in Europe and the United States. He read up on the subject, then visited Glendale, Arizona, to see at first hand the work of a company that had developed its own hydroponics system. He discovered that hydroponic farming could triple or quadruple the yields of vegetables and grasses grown by conventional methods. By controlling the environment in which plants grew, and providing optimum temperature, humidity and nutrients, a skilful farmer could get enormous yields from small areas of land. Could this system be used in Jordan, he thought, to produce high-priced vegetables and plants that had an almost insatiable market both in Jordan and in nearby Arab states? He studied the subject further, obtaining information from companies and university researchers in the United States, West Germany, Spain and England. Finally, he decided that hydroponic farming was how he would make enough money to finance his cattle farm. And when he thought of farming, he remembered the 3,000 dunums that his uncle Walid had bought in the Jordan Valley twenty-five years ago. Most of that land had been sold by Walid's sons, who retained only 100 dunums for themselves and the family. He approached one of the sons, Nimr Shaker, and proposed a 50-50 partnership to establish a hydroponics farm in the Jordan Valley. They would provide the capital equally, Nimr would provide the land, and he would manage the farm. They agreed, and in late 1978, while Jordan was in the middle of one of its worst droughts in recent memory, Abdulsalam Shaker ordered materials from four different Italian companies to set up a four-unit hydroponics farm that he designed himself. Each unit was a dome-shaped hothouse made of fibreglass-reinforced plastic, measuring 288 square metres, complete with a water-and-fans cooling system and automatic temperature and humidity controls to maintain an optimum growing climate all year round.

On 1 May, 1979, he passed by the Hussein Mosque in downtown Amman to hire five labourers to help him erect the four hothouses. One of the workers, a hard-working Egyptian he knew only as Abu Khalaf, accepted his offer to stay on and help run the farm. Together, they started planting potted houseplants in the first unit in early November 1979, and the first crop was sent to market in Amman one month later. Abdulsalam Shaker had decided to start with the houseplants unit because he calculated this would be the biggest money-maker; it would let him cover the JD 42,000 ($140,000) capital cost of establishing the farm within the first year of operation. He decided to use a semi-hydroponic system for the houseplants, growing them in a compost medium imported from the Netherlands. He designed a true water-based hydroponic system to grow lettuce in two of the plastic hothouses, and the fourth house is a strawberry unit with seven imported varieties that produce fruit during eight months of the year.

New projects under way include a unit for growing carnations for export to the Gulf states, sprinkler-irrigated, open-field corn cultivation in the summer, and exporting houseplants to Saudi Arabia. During the first year of operation, the houseplants unit has earned $18 for every $1 invested. The potential profits to be made from a well-managed large farm are such that Abdulsalam Shaker plans to lease land to investors in Amman, who would provide the capital to build new plasticulture units but leave their management to him. He has already started growing houseplants for a major wholesaler in Amman on a contract basis. The wholesaler provides the pots, seeds and fertilizers, while he grows the plants in his plastic houses and delivers them to the wholesaler against a fee of 250 fils per pot per month. One plastic house thus generates a gross income of JD 21,000 ($70,000) per year, and net profits of some JD 15,000 ($50,000) a year, while the wholesaler gets his pots at JD 1.300 ($4.30) each, compared to the JD 1.500 ($5) he was paying before.

The Shaker farm is located in an area in the southern part of the Jordan Valley, near Karameh, that had been a wild, untouched frontier for hundreds, perhaps thousands, of years. The East Ghor Canal stopped about fifteen kilometres short of it, so it never developed as the northern half of the valley did in the early 1960s. It enjoyed no underground springs, wells or side wadi flows, as did the southern region near the Dead Sea, and thus it remained a wasteland.

Its transformation into a highly profitable farming area started on 8 June, 1968, when the South Korean contractor Cho Suk Construction Company turned over to the Jordan Valley Authority the $15 million project extending the East Ghor Canal another eighteen kilometres to the south, and providing a pressure pipe irrigation network covering 36,500 dunums of idle land. The irrigation system brought year-round water to the Shaker family land, and transformed it instantly into a potentially valuable farm in an area that enjoyed a unique natural advantage over competing agricultural regions in Africa, Asia and Europe. Water was the key. Once it was available, Abdulsalam Shaker provided the capital and management, and Abu Khalaf provided the labour. What had brought them to the valley from their different corners of the world and backgrounds to work together and establish a high technology, market-oriented intensive farm generating a 1,800 per cent return on investment? Water provided by the extension of the canal was obviously the decisive factor. It held out the prospect of profitable farming, in

General view of Zerqa Triangle area

which Abdulsalam Shaker saw the means to establish his cattle farm at Azraq, and Abu Khalaf saw steady employment to support himself and his family in Egypt. Within one year of the canal's extension, both men were working in the valley, attracted by the age-old incentive of making money, supporting their families and slowly improving their standard of living.

Behind the simplicity of the water-farming-income-people equation lies a 12,000-year-old history of land, life and agriculture in the Jordan Valley, which is only now reaching close to its awesome productive potential. In the past decade, it has been the story of the Jordan Valley Commission and the Jordan Valley Authority, and their slow, persistent attempts since 1971 to nurture the kind of large-scale indigenous development that had evaded governmental authorities for the last seventy-five years – and human history for the last 10,000 years, since somebody first planted a seed near Jericho and waited for it to germinate and grow into a stalk of wheat. This is where humanity made the transformation from roving hunters to settled agriculturalists, livestockers, village dwellers and city builders.

The Jordanian government's effort in the past decade to fully develop the valley is only the latest of hundreds of similar attempts throughout recorded history to foster permanent, productive societies on the basis of the area's agricultural potential. Before this century, the impetus had always come from farming communities within the valley that cared only to provide their own sustenance from the land. If some surplus produce was available for export, life improved a bit from that small margin of additional income.

By the early 1970s, however, the previous 12,000 years of history in the valley had become largely irrelevant. The destruction and human displacement caused by the 1967 Arab-Israeli war threatened not only the agricultural productivity of the valley itself, but also the very fabric of the Jordanian economy as a whole. The political developments of the previous fifty years had transformed the valley from an isolated inward-facing farming frontier into the strategic core of a precarious nation-state struggling to stand on its own feet. Ultimately, its success or failure would depend largely on two factors: the availability of water and land for farming, and the willingness of Jordanians to commit money and time to develop an indigenous agricultural sector that could provide the stable underpinning for a balanced national economy. The challenge boiled down in its simplest form to water and people, the two variables that had always governed the development or stagnation of the Jordan Valley, and later, of the young state's brittle economy. After the 1967 war, when the valley was almost emptied of its 60,000 pre-war population of farmers, bedouin livestockers and itinerant labourers, the Jordanian team of young planners spotted an opportunity to rebuild a new kind of rural society, to stimulate a fresh, deeper commitment by the farmers of Jordan to both the development of the Jordan Valley and the long-term improvement of their standing of living. Because the valley was the country's only important area for irrigated agriculture, it received special attention from the national planning team. Within an eighteen-month period in 1971 and 1972, a comprehensive social and economic development plan was formulated, designed both to rehabilitate what had been destroyed and to lay the foundation for sustained growth in the longer term.

The original three-year valley plan (1973-75) coincided with the three-year national development plan, but went an important step further by introducing the concept of integrated, comprehensive regional development. Whereas previous projects in the valley had provided dams, canals, roads and scattered social services, the new plan deliberately fused the infrastructural needs of farming with the human requirements for housing, schools, health services, drinking water, electricity and other village-based services. Implementing both the agricultural and human services projects simultaneously, the planners in Amman thought, would provide an unprecedented package of incentives to draw farmers who had left back into the valley, as well as to attract new residents to take up both the farming and non-farming jobs that would be created by the full exploitation of the valley's 360,000 dunums of cultivable land. At full development, the population would reach 150,000. In 1971, when the plan was being conceived, there were fewer than 5,000 people living in the valley (compared to 60,000 before the 1967 war), with a few thousand others braving the chaos of the war zone to go down in the daytime to water their precious citrus groves. The plan aimed to attract nearly 100,000 new residents into a rural area that probably had worse social and economic services than any other part of the country. It hoped to reverse the pervasive trend in Third World countries of rural peasants and farmers gravitating into burgeoning cities looking for paid employment. It introduced the concept of regional planning, of fully exploiting the economic resources of a given region, providing employment for the indigenous population and activating a pattern of social development and incentives that would anchor the rural population to its prospering part of the country. If it worked in the valley, where the agricultural base was probably greater than the productive potential of any other region of Jordan, the integrated development concept would be applied elsewhere in the country.

The success or failure of the novel programme would be felt far beyond the edges of the valley itself. Its implications for Jordan's ability to feed itself and offset massive imports with exports of fresh produce were profound. If the country was ever to make a valiant stab at self-sufficiency, it could only do so on the basis of a strong agricultural sector. For all practical purposes, this meant the Jordan Valley – the main area in the country with significant potential for increased food production. Political implications also came into play. Jordan's long-term viability depended on its people's commitment to an enduring concept of nationhood. During the tumultuous decades of its birth and adolescence, between 1926 and 1956, Jordan balanced gingerly on an erratic foundation of domestic, regional and international uncertainty and conflict. Its own self-perception as a nation-state had often been clouded by demographic upheavals, inter-Arab ideological rivalries, global strategic competition, and a delicate domestic economy chronically kept afloat by injections of foreign aid. The attachment of the Jordanian man and woman to the soil, to the ideal of permanent nationhood, was untested. The 1967 war only proved that the valley's residents would flee the area at the first sound of gunfire, and would only return when the government restored security. The new plan for the valley included an unwritten but clear political dimension – it would test the commitment of the Jordanian national to the land, to investing in an economy in the middle of a war zone, to relocating home and family to a growing, changing rural area, to risking substantial money in a traditionally erratic sector of the economy, to working hard and producing food instead of relying on a soft government job in Amman.

The three-year plan that was formulated and approved in 1972 grew into a series of longer, bigger programmes. By the end of the 1970s, the Jordan Valley Authority was working on a long-term plan to exploit all the 360,000 dunums of cultivable land between the Dead Sea and the Yarmouk River, to develop the southern extension of the valley from the Dead Sea south to Aqaba, and to provide the Amman-Irbid plateau area with domestic water from the valley. Its work expanded into a $1.5 billion package of agricultural and social service projects that would require nearly two decades to be fully implemented. The first group of projects in the initial plan was dubbed Phase 1, and included the eighteen-kilometre extension of the East Ghor Canal completed in June 1978. The arrival of Abu Khalaf and Abdulsalam Shaker into the valley is part of the first wave of new residents, workers and investors envisaged in the minds of Jordanian planners ten years ago.

This book is a brief summary of what has happened in the Jordan Valley in the 1970s, or up to the completion of Phase 1 projects. To understand and fully appreciate the significance of the changes taking place in the valley today, one must place contemporary events in their proper historical context. This means going back to the earlier decades of this century, to review previous formal planning efforts, and also back into the days of antiquities, to review the cycles of prosperity and deterioration that swept through the valley. Little has changed in the last 12,000 years. The willingness of a farmer to plant a seed and wait to harvest it still depends on whether the endeavour allows him to support a family, feel safe within a community of his peers and anticipate with some certitude that his children's future will be no worse than his life has been, and might even be slightly better. The novelty in the current development effort is its scope. It is the most ambitious attempt ever to exploit the valley's productivity, while tying together human and agricultural services. It is a bold experiment in social engineering, and as such it has unleashed forces of

The Jordan Valley

Water gushes out of "riser" (foreground) from where farmer decides how to apply it to his land

change that were not always anticipated. It has aroused passions for and against it. But it has undeniably ushered in a new era of development and metamorphosis in the Jordan Valley that is most meaningfully reflected in the lives of its inhabitants. This book is an attempt to document the background and achievements of the Jordan Valley Authority's activities, and some of their consequent effects on the amorphous mass of people that has moved in and out of the valley, or hovered on its periphery, for the last half a century. It is a chronicle of resources – people, water, land, capital, labour, technology – and how they have converged on a unique 100 kilometre-long strip of land for twelve thousand years.

Chapter Two
Cornerstone of National Development

The 1970s were years of brisk, often uncontrollable, growth for the economy of Jordan. The country started the decade trying to revitalize itself after the 1967 war turmoil, and entered the 1980s trying to control the forces unleashed by its geographic and political proximity to the oil behemoths of the Gulf, to build a self-sustaining economy based on productive industries and agriculture. Inadvertently, almost imperceptibly, the Jordan Valley gravitated to the vital core of Jordan's economic aspirations. In many ways, the entire Jordan Rift Valley, from the Yarmouk River in the north to Aqaba in the south, is both the linchpin and litmus test of Jordan's ability to develop a viable economy and a coherent social and political structure in the long term. There are three crucial national factors riding on the fate of the Jordan Valley development programme.

1   In terms of sheer agricultural output, the valley offers the best prospect for a significant increase in irrigated farming, given its combination of soil and water, and its advantage in producing winter crops at least two to three months before other parts of the Middle East. Because it lies between 200 and 400 metres below sea level, the valley acts like a natural hothouse. Tropical winter weather allows vegetables to be planted in October and November, and harvested as early as December–January, when the market demand for fresh produce is intense, and prices are correspondingly high. Winter temperatures in the valley average 15°–22°C between November and March, but rise to an average of 30°–33°C in the summer, when days of 40°C are common. The average annual rainfall is 380 mm per year in the north, but less than 100 mm a year in the South Shouneh area. Frost and snow are extremely rare. The mean monthly humidity is 35 per cent in summer, 84 per cent in winter.

The Jordan River follows a meandering course from Lake Tiberias in the north until it flows into the Dead Sea in the south, a distance of 104 kilometres. Its main tributary is the Yarmouk River, whose average annual flow is 438 million cubic metres (ranging between 240 Mm^3 and 870 Mm^3 a year). The Zerqa River, the second most

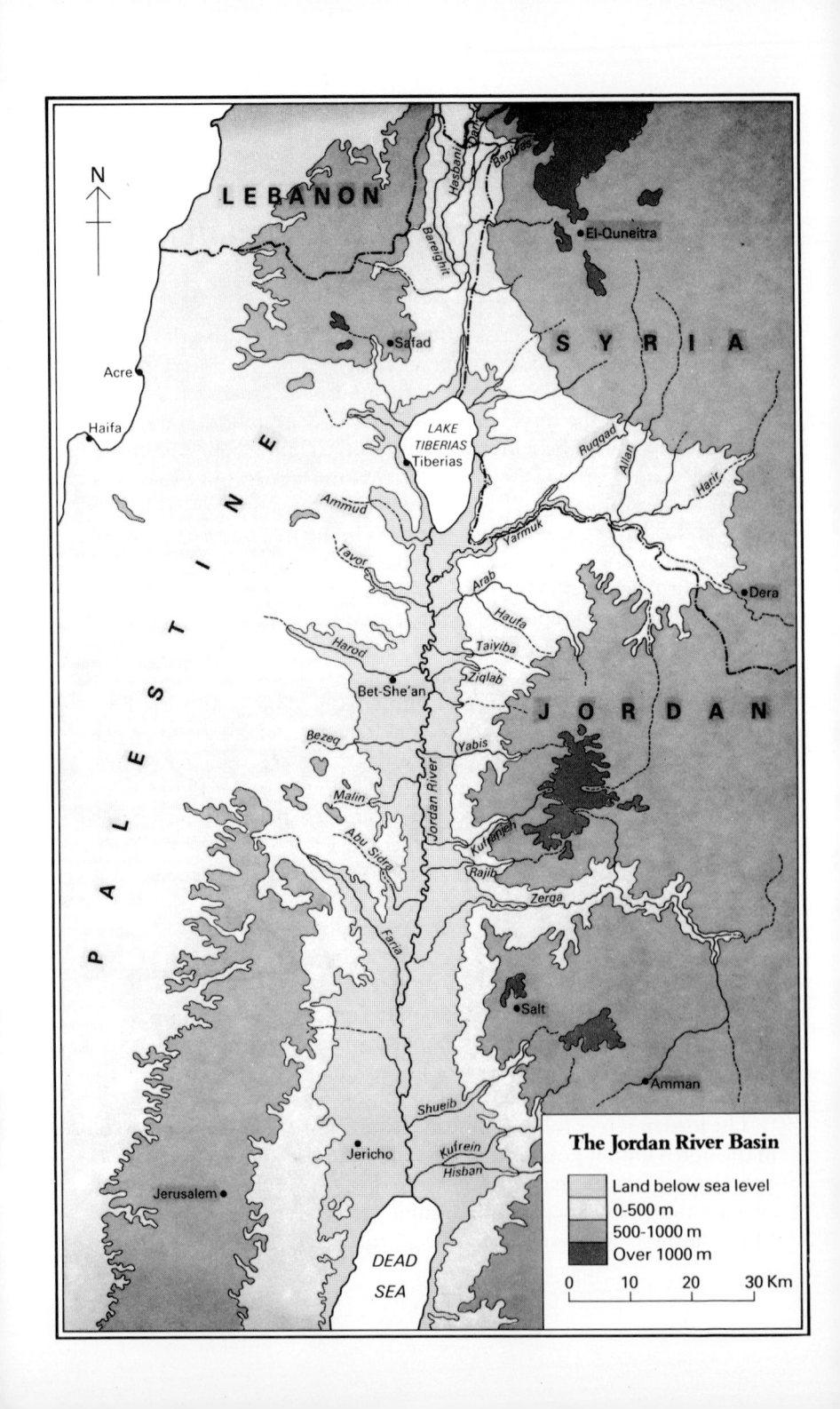

The Jordan River Basin

- Land below sea level
- 0–500 m
- 500–1000 m
- Over 1000 m

0 10 20 30 Km

important tributary, has an average annual flow of 85 Mm³. Nine other side wadis flow into the valley from the eastern hills, combining with the Yarmouk and Zerqa to provide a total average annual flow of 636 Mm³. The maximum recorded annual flow of the valley's rivers and wadis was 1,190 Mm³, while the minimum was 312 Mm³. The Jordan River itself is set down in a 30–60 metre-deep gorge, flanked by its flood plain, called the *zor* in Arabic. The *katar*, an eroded zone of uncultivable land, separates the *zor* from the rest of the valley floor, the *ghor* which stretches eastwards between 4 and 16 kilometres until it reaches the foothills leading up to the Jordanian plateau. The *ghor* slopes down from the hills to the Jordan River at a rate of 15 to 25 metres per kilometre. The hills on both sides of the valley reach an altitude of 900 metres above sea level, and help protect the valley from extreme winter weather, thereby giving it its three-month headstart in harvesting winter vegetables.

By harnessing all the valley's water resources, efficiently irrigating the full 360,000 dunums of top-quality land and generally improving such agricultural practices as seed selection, application of fertilizers and chemicals, land levelling and improvement, crop rotation and irrigation, the 1975–82 valley plan aimed to achieve the following production targets:

(produce)	(tons)	
	1975	1982
vegetables	129,400	460,500
cereals	3,750	31,800
fruits	46,800	150,400
fodder	1,710	850,000

These targets have changed with every new study and introduction of new cultivation techniques. For example, the extensive use of drip irrigation and plastic hothouses by private farmers since 1975 has altered the JVA's original idea of applying sprinkler irrigation throughout the valley. Because land is privately owned, and there is no formal co-ordination among the farmers, the valley's crop pattern tends to follow free market forces. If there is big demand for winter tomatoes, the farmers grow more winter tomatoes. If the price of cucumbers goes up sharply one year, the next year will see a big increase in cucumber cultivation. The government does not impose a cropping pattern on the farmers, and therefore its output targets should be viewed more as a realistic projection of the valley's potential than a strict forecast of actual cultivation and production.

The maximization of agricultural production is obviously important to create jobs and to support related industries and services. But it is also crucial in Jordan's overall economic picture. In 1972, when the valley plan was taking shape, the country imported JD 27.6 million ($91 million) of foodstuffs, out of a total imports bill of JD 95.3 million ($316 million). Jordan's total exports that year were just JD 12.6 million ($42 million), or less than 46 per cent of its food imports alone.

In 1979, food imports of JD 100.6 million ($332 million) were still more than Jordan's total exports of JD 82.5 million ($272 million). The country's overall trade balance had deteriorated badly in the 1970s. Jordan imported goods and services in 1979 worth JD 589.5 million ($1.945 billion) and exported JD 82.5 million ($272 million), leaving a trade gap of JD 507 million ($1.673 billion). The trade gap alone was larger than the central government's entire budget in 1979, and only JD 91 million ($267 million) less than the country's gross domestic product (at factor cost).

If the feverish investment programme of the government and the private sector precluded a healthier trade balance in the short run, Jordan has to increase its productive capacity in the long term if it is to avoid a crushing balance of payments deficit. This could only be done in two areas on a significant scale: agriculture and minerals. Over $1 billion has gone into three big mineral projects to produce fertilizers for export (phosphates, potash and chemical fertilizers). These should bring in over $600 million a year in export revenues by the end of the 1980s, when agricultural exports, almost entirely from the valley, will both increase total exports and reduce food imports.

Assuming cropping intensity throughout the valley will increase from 1.06 to 1.31 (i.e. a cropped area of 350,860 dunums divided by a cultivated area of 266,700 dunums, reflecting the use of the same land for more than one crop per year), the 1976–82 plan envisaged total production in the valley at full development rising from 170,264 tons in 1975 to 1,109,524 tons in 1982. The latest feasibility study for Stage II projects (Maqarin dam and irrigation works) anticipates an output of 1,066,000 tons by 1990, from 359,990 dunums, with another 66,000 tons of milk production and 2,000 tons of beef and veal production.

In 1979, foodstuffs accounted for JD 21.2 million ($70 million) of Jordan's total exports of JD 82.5 million ($272 million), taking second place behind phosphate exports of JD 26.3 million ($87 million). The JVA programme aims to more than quadruple the valley's crop contribution to gross domestic product, from JD 7.3 to JD 32.5 million ($24 million to $107 million) at 1975 prices, though recent innovations in production techniques are likely to surpass this target.

2 When it was initiated in 1972, the Jordan Valley development programme aimed solely to harness local water resources for irrigation and domestic applications in the valley. By 1978, however, when Jordan was into the third consecutive year of drought, the National Planning Council was forced to eye the valley's water resources in a national context. Underground and surface water sources throughout the country were being fast depleted, as rising demand was catching up with limited supplies. By tapping all possible water resources, Jordan could realistically get about 900 Mm^3 a year, though less than two-thirds of this, or around 550–600 Mm^3 a year, is now available for use. Demand has risen steadily to more than 500 Mm^3 a year in 1980, and there is a precarious balance between supply and demand in Jordan today. The capital region around Amman is already short of water, and has started drawing 10 Mm^3 a year from the Azraq Oasis, 100 kilometres to the east. Within the 1980s, Jordan will suffer from a devastating water shortage if present consumption trends continue and new supplies are not tapped; the only significant new sources of water are in the Jordan Valley. In 1977, in an emergency situation, the government made plans to draw nearly 15 Mm^3 of water a year from the King Talal Dam to Amman, but these were scrapped when the Zerqa River water was found to be too polluted by industrial wastes to be used for domestic consumption. In 1979, the JVA was asked to study the practicality of supplying the Amman-Irbid northern half of the country with water from the Jordan Valley's water resources, notably the Maqarin Dam, which was still in the design stage. It was decided later the same year to allocate a net depletion of 60 Mm^3 a year of Maqarin water to help meet north Jordan's water needs in the 1980s and 1990s. Two American engineering firms, Stanley Consultants and Boyle Engineering Corporation, designed a water conveyance, storage and treatment system to deliver 15 Mm^3 of water a year from the Maqarin Dam to the Irbid region, and 45 Mm^3 a year from the East Ghor Canal at Deir Alla to Amman. The project, estimated to cost $200 million, will need nearly three years to build. Construction is expected to get under way in 1981. Water to Amman will be pumped up 1,350 metres, in a 35 kilometre-long system of underground steel pipelines. The water will be diverted from an intake structure on the East Ghor Canal, just north of Sawalha, to a treatment plant at Zai, near Salt, and on to a 246,000 cubic metre terminal reservoir south of Sweileh. From there, it will be distributed via the existing network of the Amman Water and Sewage Authority. The JVA has allocated a gross 120 Mm^3 of water per year for use in north Jordan, at full development of the Maqarin Dam, of which 60 Mm^3 would be recycled back for irrigation use in the valley, leaving a net contribution of 60 Mm^3 of water per year to north Jordan cities.

The diversion of 60 Mm^3 of water a year will reduce the amount of water available for irrigation. The JVA therefore foresees a reduction in its irrigated area at full development, from 360,000 to 300,000–330,000 dunums. The ultimate nature and extent of irrigated farming, however, will depend on how the application of new technology, such as drip irrigation and plasticulture, affects water use and productivity. More efficient water use systems could permit the irrigation of more than 330,000 dunums of land. The fact remains, though, that the development of the Jordan Valley has become crucial to providing water for more than three-quarters of the entire population of the country.

3   The success or failure of the integrated, comprehensive development concept now being put to the test in the Jordan Valley will also have important repercussions in the rest of the country. In the 1970s, the idea of "regional development" took root in the minds of the Jordanian planning team headed by Crown Prince Hassan. The valley's development plan was the forerunner of this idea – by which a geographical area of the country would be planned as a unified, almost self-contained entity whose economic growth would be wedded to the social and infrastructural services needed by its indigenous population. In this way, the productive potential of an area would be achieved according to a coherent, long-term plan that takes into account the need for social services of a local population that might otherwise emigrate to the capital region of Amman, with its better services and greater job opportunities. Regional planning, the theory goes, would reduce or even reverse the rural-to-urban population drift, achieve maximum productivity from provincial areas' economic resources, and raise the standard of living in rural Jordan to close the gap with the more developed cities. As a planning

concept, "regionalism" was formally adopted in the late 1970s. The Jordan Valley has been its first practical test. Integrated development plans are being formulated for several other regions of the country, notably Aqaba region in the south, Irbid region in the north and the Greater Amman region, which alone accounts for 1.2 million of Jordan's 2.3 million people. The initial emphasis on regional planning is being followed up by a parallel effort to turn over more executive and fiscal authority to regional bodies working within the boundaries of the country's five governorates. Ultimately, the central government aims to revitalize both local government and socio-economic development momentum by turning over greater decision-making powers to elected councils, municipal authorities and the executive staff of the regional governor's office.

The political corollary to this is clear. By directly taking part in decisions affecting their own areas and lives, Jordanians in provincial regions should feel a greater sense of political participation and responsibility. The precise mechanisms for such regional action will be put into place gradually during the early 1980s, parallel with the adoption of regional development plans such as the one being implemented in the Jordan Valley.

These three aspects of the Jordan Valley development project – increased food production, providing water to the Amman–Irbid area, and putting into practice the untested concept of regional planning – have transformed it into a far more important effort than just the rehabilitation drive that was first envisaged in the chaotic post-war days of 1971. In the long run, Jordan's very coherence and viability will be influenced greatly by the changes now taking place in the Jordan Valley: the willingness of private sector investors to put large amounts of capital into farming, of workers to move into the valley with their families, of a rural population to tie itself down to the soil, to take a stand on a patch of land it calls home. Will the valley become the prototype of a successful rural development strategy that is applicable in other parts of the country, the region, or the world? It is too early to judge, despite several visible trends that have been unleashed already by the ten-year-old effort. These include, most strikingly, the movement of people into the valley, sharply increased access to social services, rising agricultural production and a high rate of private sector investment. The JVA estimates that for every $1 it is spending on infrastructural works, private sector farmers are investing another $5 in the business of farming. Between 1973 and 1979, the total number of children enrolled in schools in the valley increased by

61 per cent, from 12,028 to 19,345. The population of the valley reached 85,000 by November 1979 – compared to less than 5,000 in 1971, and a pre-1967 war population of some 60,000. The average number of cars and trucks using the main highway in the valley increased from 875 vehicles per day in 1973 to 2,096 per day in 1978. Between 1976 and 1979, irrigated farmland increased from 186,590 dunums to 242,860 dunums, of which 93,970 dunums were under a pressure pipe (sprinkler) system. Cropping intensity of the land has risen from 106 to 120 (that is, for every 100 dunums of cultivated land, 120 dunums are cropped, by growing more than one crop a year on the same land).

The statistical record only reflects that part of the Jordan Valley that is quantifiable: how many tomatoes are grown, how many plastic houses are erected, how many schoolchildren are registered, how many housing units are built. Below the surface, the more profound chronicle is about human beings making rational decisions about their future, their livelihood, the welfare of their families and, ultimately, the depth and durability of their nation. If the Jordan Valley has emerged suddenly as the cornerstone of the overall development of Jordan today, the saga of the valley itself must be recounted in centuries and millennia.

Chapter Three

Twelve Thousand Years of Agriculture

For all its contemporary importance, the development of the Jordan Valley today is certainly not novel. Human beings first planted seeds in the valley earth and waited for them to sprout into produce as early as 9,000 years ago. Foodstuffs from the valley were exported to nearby states at least 5,000 years ago, while irrigation networks were built in the Bronze Age, more than 4,500 years ago. The growth and development of villages and larger urban centres has been taking place for at least the last 5,000 years.

Like the rest of Jordan, the valley has a rich archaeological history that has barely been investigated in any real depth. The most systematic archaeological survey of the valley floor, between the Dead Sea and the Yarmouk River, was conducted in 1975–76 by the Jordanian Department of Antiquities, the University of Jordan and the American Center of Oriental Research (ACOR) in Amman. It turned up 224 different antiquities sites, many of which had been occupied during more than one era.

The most fertile, best irrigated and most extensively used area of the valley throughout history seems to have been the central stretch between Wadi Kufranjeh and Wadi Zerqa. A quarter of the 224 antiquities sites identified by the survey lie in this area: in sharp contrast to the barren history of the area to the south, between Wadi Zerqa and Wadi Nimrin. This part of the valley was rarely exploited until the East Ghor Canal was built in the early 1960s, thereby revolutionizing age-old patterns of settlement and socio-economic activity that had always been determined by the location of natural water sources. There is no evidence of a similar major water supply system ever being built or even attempted in the Jordan Valley along the scale of the East Ghor Canal. Smaller systems were constructed throughout history. The Nabataeans had impressive water storage and irrigation networks in Wadi Araba. The Ummayad period saw reservoirs and canals in the northern half of the valley, while the Mamluk era was a high point of agricultural development, thanks to the efficient use of water to irrigate sugar cane fields and drive sugar

Main canal at Wadi Yabis

mills. But all these were local ventures, depending on water from the side wadis. Nobody had ever tried building a major canal system such as was finally done in the 1960s and '70s, to break people's historical pattern of dependence on the side wadis and springs. For the first time since the dawn of humanity, the East Ghor Canal took water to where the people lived and farmed. It brought water – and therefore life – to previously uninhabited and uncultivated parts of the valley, which quickly flourished because of the rich soil that had been virtually untouched during the past 400,000 years of recorded history. First in the north and then in the south, the East Ghor Canal caused a radical break with traditions and practices dating back 9,000 years, when human beings first mastered cultivated agriculture somewhere near Jericho, but staying close to side wadis or underground springs to obtain their water.

The archaeological evidence indicates that the valley's history, like its twentieth-century experience, includes widely fluctuating periods of prosperity and paucity, war and peace, development and stagnation. It reached its peak in the Mamluk era, in the thirteenth, fourteenth and fifteenth centuries AD, and its low point in the

Ottoman era, in the sixteenth, seventeenth, eighteenth and nineteenth centuries. Unlike the rest of the country, however, the valley's archaeological evidence only dates back to about 10,000 BC. Artifacts dating back 400,000 years have been found in all parts of the Jordanian desert and hill country, and even in the foothills of the Jordan Valley. Flints from the Middle Paleolithic era, from around 20,000 BC, have been found at the site of the Arab Potash Company township, just off the Dead Sea's southern end. The valley floor's oldest artifacts are very small stone tools, mostly crude blades for making composite tools. These date back only to about 10,000 BC, and are found at Jericho, near the Zerqa River basin and at Wadi Kufrein. Archaeologists are divided on the reason for this sudden cut-off. Two theories are presented. The first believes that a northern extension of the Red Sea once covered the entire valley, and formed a continuous body of water from Lake Tiberias in the north to present day Aqaba in the south. A large inland lake formed around 100,000 BC, stretching from Lake Tiberias to just south of the Dead Sea. This inland water body was called Lake Lisan, and it lasted until around 20,000 BC, when it also began drying up and shrinking. By 10,000 BC, it had broken up into two inland water bodies, Lake Tiberias and the Dead Sea, and two dry valleys, the Jordan Valley and Wadi Araba. The Jordan River formed between Tiberias and the Dead Sea, while the side wadis flowing into it from the eastern and western hills forged their own paths to the new Jordan River. The combination of dry land on the newly formed valley floor and the availability of year-round river water attracted the first human settlers into the valley, according to this theory, around 10,000 BC.

The second theory believes that human beings had lived in the valley hundreds of thousands of years ago, but their remains have been covered over by successive layers of earth that have accumulated by soil erosion from the hills to form the valley floor that exists today.

In the Bekaa' and Orontes valleys in Lebanon, the northern geological extensions of the Great Rift Valley which reaches its lowest point at the Dead Sea, drillings have turned up hand axes that indicate a human presence there as early as 500,000 years ago. Therefore could not the floor of the Jordan Valley also have accommodated human settlements or nomadic activity at the same time?

Evidence found along the foothills, just above the valley floor, dates back to 400,000 BC. Could this have represented villages that flourished along the banks of the lake or inland sea that existed in the place of the valley we know today? In geological terms, the valley floor is a relatively recent deposition of earth, hardly used and still very rich, and an important reason for the large agricultural potential of the area today. Whether it happened 10,000 or 500,000 years ago, the valley floor was slowly formed and built up by the continuous erosion of soil that moved down into the valley from the eastern and western hills. There are also theories stating that the size of the valley floor expanded and contracted, as the water bodies in the area alternately dried up in drought years and expanded in wet ones. In fact, this is still happening today, as the Dead Sea becomes larger or smaller depending on the amount of rainfall in the area. In the 1970s the Dead Sea was drying out and dropping its level at the rate of about half a metre per year. In the unusually wet 1979–80 winter, the water level rose by 1.2 metres. This may have been the Dead Sea's swansong, however, because the long-term trend is for it to keep shrinking. Having been denied most of the 900 million cubic metres of inflowing water a year from the Jordan River and 14 side wadis that it needs to maintain a steady level, the Dead Sea is slowly evaporating and shrinking. It also suffers from the afforestation of its catchment area in Jordan, Israel and Syria, which deprives it of rainwater that would otherwise flow into its rivers and wadis. In another 1,000 years or so, it will become mud flats and then totally disappear. This is already happening off the Lisan Peninsula in the south, where the dropping water level has turned the area immediately west of the peninsula into mud flats that can be traversed on foot by using special mud shoes. If political boundaries between Jordan and Israel did not exist, people could walk across the Lisan, just as they used to do a hundred years ago.

According to data compiled by the United States Geological Survey (USGS) in 1978, the historic low point of the Dead Sea's water level was 399.4 metres below sea level, registered in 1818. The highest ever recorded was −388.6 metres in 1896. Since then, the water level dropped steadily, and reached a new record low of −400.8 metres in 1979, after a four-year drought. The data shows that the Dead Sea's water level rises and drops in approximate ten-year cycles, corresponding to wet and dry weather periods in the area comprising Jordan, Syria, Lebanon and Palestine/Israel. It is likely that the same pattern of expanding and contracting water bodies obtained in the area hundreds of thousands of years ago, making it all the more difficult for historians and archaeologists to judge precisely

Yarmouk River runs through gorge where Maqarin Dam will be built

when the Jordan Valley was formed, and subsequently inhabited. Perhaps systematic drillings could unearth traces of human activity in the valley from more than 10,000 years ago. Until this is done, however, it is safer to assume that the valley we know today has remained geologically stable and constant for the last 10,000 years.

The first archaeological evidence of human activity dates from the 10,000–6000 BC era, and was found all across the southern end of the valley, from Jericho in the West Bank of the Jordan River to Rama, Wadi Nimrin and Wadi Shu'eib in the East Bank. Jericho is generally accepted to be the world's oldest continuously occupied human settlement, where people first made the changeover from being pickers of wild plants and hunters of wild animals to settled cultivators of agricultural produce and domesticators of livestock. From 14,000 to 8000 BC, humankind started a slow, gradual transition period which came to be called the Neolithic Revolution when it reached its peak between 8000 and 5000 BC. This was the domestication drive, as people settled down in one place, built simple dwellings, and started growing their food and raising animals to be slaughtered and eaten. Simultaneously in the great river basins of the

Middle East – in Egypt, Mesopotamia and the Jordan Valley – people were being pushed off the deserts and into the more hospitable valleys, where water and land could support life. Somewhere around 6000 BC, the deserts of Syria, Iraq, Egypt, Arabia and the Sahara were all formed. The desert of Jordan, east of the Irbid–Amman–Aqaba highway, was considerably wetter in past centuries. There is evidence of huge lakes in the heart of today's desert areas. Some of these at Jafr and Azraq may have been as large as 40 kilometres in diameter. The oldest archaeological evidence in Jordan, basalt and flint bifacial handaxes, shows that Paleolithic sites existed throughout the eastern desert 400,000 years ago, suggesting that the area was much wetter than it is today. Epi-Paleolithic sites (14,000–8000 BC) are also scattered throughout the eastern desert, indicating there was enough water, wildlife and vegetation to support a population of primitive people who lived by animal hunting and plant gathering.

The desert was last occupied in the Early Neolithic era (8000–6000 BC), during which climatic changes made the area warmer and drier, and forced the inhabitants to move westwards into the valley, towards the only perennial sources of water in the vicinity. After 6000 BC, we find no permanent villages or towns in the desert, but only Roman forts, Ummayad palaces and lodges, Ottoman outposts and nomadic pastoral activity. By this time, domesticated agriculture had also taken root in the valley, at Jericho and Ghassul, where there is evidence of wheat and barley cultivation and sheep and goat domestication. There are even earlier hints of a settled lifestyle in the valley, when primitive agriculture was practised around Jericho about 10,000 BC, as evidenced by sickle blades from that time. But what did those early Jericho residents harvest? Did they cut down wild plants, or grow their own crops? Housing structures start to appear in Jericho at this time, and an urbanization process had also gotten underway simultaneously east of the Dead Sea, near Bab Al Dthraa'. People started cultivating grains and cereals and trying their hand at livestocking, though others continued to live by gathering plants and hunting animals. At Bab Al Dthraa', just above the Lisan Peninsula on the road to Kerak, excavations by the American School of Oriental Research and the Smithsonian Institution have turned up carbonized seeds from among the world's earliest farming communities. People were tying themselves down to the soil, working out elementary social systems and trying their hand at primitive architecture. The Cradle of Civilization was taking shape.

While these first farming communities developed between 10,000 and 5000 BC, the southern part of the Jordan valley began to dry up, and people started moving north, setting in motion an historical process of demographic movement and change that persists to this day. Since the Stone Age, the valley has always experienced a dynamic, even turbulent, pattern of development. Settlements and villages sprang up, flourished and died off, either by military conquest, natural disaster or climatic changes that would affect local water supplies. The southern part of the valley, where the first settled societies established themselves around the Wadi Kufrein and Wadi Shu'eib area, was much wetter five centuries ago than it is today. Few people today would choose to live there, preferring the more hospitable and pleasant northern valley above Wadi Yabis, where temperatures are slightly cooler and rainfall is more plentiful.

The early farmers relied on side wadis and springs for their water supplies, and not on the Jordan River itself, which is set down in a 30–60 metre-deep gorge (called the *zor* in Arabic, as opposed to the *ghor*, which is the entire valley floor). The technology available to farmers five and ten centuries ago precluded their drawing up water from the Jordan River gorge to meet their domestic and agricultural

Government veterinarians examining bedouins' herds in northern part of Valley

needs. People relied instead on the side wadis, and the East Bank of the valley was historically more active than the West Bank because it has more substantial and more numerous wadis feeding into the Jordan River. By the Late Neolithic and Early Chalcolithic periods (4750–3750 BC) Jordan's desert had dried out and been emptied of its inhabitants. Only the Jordan Valley and the nearby hills sustained life, with all population centres in the valley located near side wadis. These were small, open farming communities with few built structures. Primitive architectural attempts were mostly clay or stone-lined circular pits, which may have been covered with simple reed roofs. Pottery makes its first appearance in Jordan in the Late Neolithic era, around 4500 BC, east of Bab Al Dthraa'. The ware was well-fired and of simple shapes, such as cups and bowls.

At about this same time, more enterprising valley residents started trying their hand at building larger structures. In the first foothills just 50–100 metres above the floor of the valley overlooking Ghassul and Damiyah, hundreds of dolmens pay silent tribute to humankind's first would-be architects and builders. The dolmens are simple structures, usually composed of two vertical stone slabs about one metre apart, covered with a larger third slab and sometimes closed off on one side by a fourth slab. They represent humankind's first attempt at large-scale building, and Jordan is the only place in the Middle East where they are found. They are the forerunners of similar, but larger and more elaborate, structures built one or two thousand years later at Stonehenge, England. Like the mystery that surrounds the exact purpose of Stonehenge, the significance of the Jordan Valley dolmens perplexes historians to this day. Were they humankind's first attempt at building homes? Were they temples, or places of worship? Were they tombs to house the dead? Other dolmen fields are located in the hills east of Jerash and around Irbid, and span the years from 4500–1000 BC.

Bones from domestic animals, mostly sheep and goats but also some cows and pigs, have been found throughout the valley, as have seeds of wheat, barley, fig, flax, chickpeas, lentils, grapes, dates and olives, though the last two may have been imported into the valley from the nearby hills. The site of Ghassul, north-east of the Dead Sea, was a fully developed village in the late Chalcolithic period (3750–3300 BC). Recent pollen studies suggest that marshes existed there, providing water for an unfortified farming community in an area that is now dry and inhospitable. Polychrome frescoes have been discovered in the remains of some old houses at the site. The best

Typical mud-brick houses found throughout Valley

example was a colourful painting depicting what seems to be a religious procession in front of a shrine, suggesting that the room in which it was found may have been part of a larger stone and mud brick sanctuary. The Jordanian Department of Antiquities, with help from UNESCO and other international sources, has saved a large section of the painting, which is exhibited at Amman's archaeological museum. The Ghassul frescoes are thought to be the second oldest of their kind in the world, after the Catal Huyuk paintings discovered in Turkey, dating back to 5750 BC.

Underneath the floors of some houses, excavators discovered child burials, though no evidence has yet been unearthed of where the community's adults were laid to rest. Further south in the valley, however, at Bab Al Dthraa', several large cemeteries housing thousands of different kinds of tombs have been discovered from approximately the same period, between 3300 and 2150 BC.

The cemeteries help archaeologists estimate the size of the villages that existed there. Some archaeologists believe that Bab Al Dthraa', judging only by the number of tombs, may have accommodated as many as 25,000–30,000 people in the Early Bronze era (3300–2150

BC). Others who have studied the area's agricultural potential believe the city only supported around 5,000 people at its height, and that the large cemeteries were also used by other villagers and nomads in the region.

Archaeological evidence, mainly seeds, confirms that Bab Al Dthraa' was an important agricultural centre during the third and fourth millennia BC. At the start of its urban development, around 3200 BC, it grew almost equal amounts of wheat and barley, which was irrigated by the local wadi flows and spring water. Five hundred years later, according to a study of 700 soil and seed samples recently completed by an American archaeologist, Mr David McCreery, barley became the dominant crop; and by 1500 BC, wheat was virtually abandoned in favour of barley growing. This could have resulted from a gradual rise in the soil's salinity, causing the farmers to favour the more salt-resistant barley plant, as happened in Mesopotamia over a similar span of time. This could also explain why the city of Bab Al Dthraa' faded away and eventually died out. Or the increased barley cultivation and the phasing out of wheat may have reflected the traditional pattern of consumption of developing areas. As people get richer, they tend to eat fewer cereals and more proteins and sugar foods such as meats and fruits. The residents of Bab Al Dthraa' may have planted more barley to feed their domesticated animals, which included sheep, goats, donkeys, pigs and a few cows and camels. Wild animals included gazelle and ibex, both of which are clearly pictured on local pottery. Besides wheat and barley, the farmers of Bab Al Dthraa' also grew olives, grapes, figs, flax, date palms, chickpeas, beans, peas and the jujube-producing *zizyphus* shrubs. Two peach pits have been found in the area, but do not provide enough certain evidence on their own that peach trees were grown there. They could have been imported into the valley from the eastern hills, as were almonds and pistachios. Bab Al Dthraa' was one of the earliest exporting regions of the valley, sending its distinctive large-seed, irrigated flax to Arad and Hebron, across the Dead Sea in southern Palestine, around 3000 BC. Egyptian texts from the same era mention imported dates, olives and wine from Palestine, which may well have come from the western edge of the valley or even from middlemen in Arad and Hebron who trans-shipped food imports from Bab Al Dthraa'.

In the Early Bronze I–III era (3300–2300 BC), major sites were located on hilltops and included fortifications, for obvious defensive purposes. Recent surveys indicate that Bab Al Dthraa' was one of a series of fortified towns stretching southwards in the valley. Before 3000 BC, people in the valley were not concerned about military defences, and never bothered to fortify their communities. But in the third century BC, fortified cities started to appear, some with 8 to 10 metre-thick walls, including Tell Saa'adiyyah, Bab Al Dthraa' and Tell Handakook, in the East Bank, and several others in the West Bank.

Judging by the number and location of Early Bronze Age sites discovered so far, this was one of the valley's high points in history. Small city-states dotted the entire valley, from the Yarmouk River in the north to Aqaba in the south. The normal arrangement seems to have been for a fortified city-state to be associated with a cluster of nearby open villages and nomadic camps. Bab Al Dthraa' is a fine example of such a city, with its wall, towers and large cemeteries. At least five such fortified towns have been identified along the edge of the southern Ghors, in the Wadi Araba-Dead Sea region. All are located on spurs of land overlooking the valley floor, and all are on or near one of the side wadis leading into the valley from the eastern hills. The fortified cities were probably built after residents of open farming villages found it too demanding or dangerous to keep defending themselves against attack from foreign invaders, or perhaps just from roving bands of bandits or hostile nomadic tribes. The bulk of the smaller village sites that supported most of the southern valley's population in the Early Bronze Age have not been discovered. The most promising theory is that most of the villages and nomadic camps associated with the fortified cities were located in the side wadis, and only sought out the safety of the cities in time of danger or attack. The wadis were also the most logical, indeed, some archaeologists say, the only possible, communication routes connecting the eastern highlands with Wadi Araba and the Red Sea, the south Palestine area to the south-west and Sinai and Egypt. Some contend that a major Early Bronze Age trade route passed from Syria to the Red Sea and Sinai via Gilead, Amman, Moab, and Tafileh, then down Wadis Hassa and Feinan into Wadi Araba and westwards to Sinai and Egypt. This is given some credence by a 1979 archaeological survey of thirteen sites that the Jordan Valley Authority had chosen to develop in Wadi Araba and the southern Ghors. The survey showed that ancient peoples in that area chose exactly the same sites to live in that the JVA had earmarked for its development projects, based on the same criteria of availability of water and good farmland, with all the water coming from the side wadis and springs.

The Jordan Valley

Overlooking Arda Intersection area
Late afternoon, view overlooking Arda Intersection area

In the succeeding Early Bronze IV era (2300–1950 BC), the people moved back in large numbers on to the valley floor, where they lived in large, sprawling, unfortified farming communities near the side wadis. The abundance of basalt rock saddle querns, used to grind grain, indicates that farming activity flourished in many small communities.

By the Middle Bronze I–III era (1950–1550 BC), however, many sites are once again fortified cities on top of hills, such as the Citadel in Amman, and Tell Saa'adiyyah and Pella in the valley. By this time, most of the sites have also moved towards the central and northern parts of the Jordan Valley, confirming the drying up of the southern region.

Major cities in the Late Bronze I–II era (1550–1200 BC) include Tell Deir Alla, Pella and Tell Mazar, which had mud houses and were considerably more advanced than the hill country. Recent research indicates that Jordan flourished during the Late Bronze period when major cities such as Pella, Deir Alla and present day Amman traded with Egypt, Greece, Cyprus, Syria and Iraq. Fine bronze instruments that may have been produced in the Jordan Valley include daggers, swords, tripods, strainers and cups. What appear to be the first written records in Jordan, inscribed clay tablets, were discovered at Tell Deir Alla. The city that existed at Tell Deir Alla was totally destroyed about 1200 BC, though it is not clear whether this was the result of warfare or a natural disaster, such as an earthquake.

The Iron Age I A–C (1200–918 BC) that followed left evidence of a small site in the southern Jordan Valley (Rashidiyeh West), and several large communities in the north (Tell Deir Alla, Pella, Tell Al Ma'ajajeh). Smelting operations were taking place at Tell Deir Alla, while domestic mudbrick architecture was also developing. International imports have dropped off by this time, and iron is used with bronze to produce weapons and domestic implements. Iron IC sites in the valley (Tell Nimrin, Tell Deir Alla, Tell Mazar) produced very few artifacts. This was a period of strong foreign influence in the valley, and one of the few times in history when it was politically separated from the hill country to the east. The Philistines had invaded Jordan about 1150 BC, moving into the northern and central part of the valley from their territory along the Mediterranean coast, with their heartland at Gaza and Asqalon. They were more developed than the Israelites, Ammonites and Moabites, whose little kingdoms controlled the hills on both sides of the valley, and they dominated the region by the grace of their more advanced iron culture. The

The Jordan Valley

Philistines, whose name was to be immortalized in the name of the Roman province of Palestine, ruled the valley for 150 years. They were defeated by David, who went on to establish a Jerusalem-based Israelite state.

The short-lived Israelite Kingdom split up into two states in 922 BC, and the Egyptians invaded the area soon after in 918 BC. These two events loosened the Israelite control that had been imposed on the Ammonite, Moabite and Edomite kingdoms to the east. From 918–332 BC, these three native Arab kingdoms flourished while the wider Middle East region was successively dominated by the Assyrians, Babylonians and Persians. This seems to have been a peaceful time in the valley, as most of the people farmed on the valley floor, and only a few fortified hill cities existed. In the southern Edomite Kingdom, copper was mined and smelted in Wadi Araba, at the site now known as Khirbet Nahas, or "Copper ruins". In the northern valley, development appears to have slowed down during the Persian era, when only sixteen sites were inhabited, according to the available evidence. The Edomites drifted further west of Wadi Araba to settle in Palestine, making room for a new tribe that moved into southern Jordan from the Arabian Peninsula: the Nabataeans.

The Greek armies defeated the Persians in 332 BC, and Jordan became part of the Greek world until 63 BC. In the south, the Nabataeans were to remain independent of Greek rule, but the rest of the country was quickly Hellenized, including the valley, where twenty-five Greek sites have been confirmed.

By the Roman-Nabataean era (63 BC–324 AD), the Roman General Pompey had conquered Syria and Palestine and federated the existing Greek cities into the league of ten cities called the Decapolis. One of these was Pella, in the north-eastern foothills of the valley near the modern village of Tabaqat Fahl. Pella is typical of human settlements in the Jordan Valley: rising and ebbing with the circumstances of history, flickering out completely at times and being resurrected at others, engaging in farming and some international trade, sometimes being at the centre of political life in the region, at other times remaining an unobtrusive sideline observer of history, usually casual in its military concerns though having to fight off the occasional would-be conqueror, and sometimes falling under foreign domination. Archaeological research taking place there now jointly by a Wooster College (Ohio) team headed by Professor Robert Houston Smith, an Australian team from the University of Sydney headed by Basil Hennessy and the Jordanian Department of Antiquities is trying to compile a sustained record of Pella's occupation. Flints from the Stone Age have been found very near the site, but not on it. Stone artifacts and Neolithic–Chalcolithic pottery from around 5000 BC have been dug up at Pella, which sits atop a large mound just east of the valley floor, at about sea level altitude. One of the reasons it may have been such a popular site throughout so many ages is its cool climate. It never freezes, while the Wadi Jurum spring provides plentiful water all the year round.

It is certain that Pella was continually occupied from the Late Neolithic era (4750 BC) to the Middle Ages (fourteenth to fifteenth centuries AD), but its fortunes fluctuated widely in between. It reached its height in the Byzantine era, in the fifth and early sixth centuries AD. The relatively large Canaanite city, around 1500–1600 BC, was restricted to the central mound, and probably had 5,000 people. The Roman city expanded southwards into the wadi, and the Byzantine city was six times the original Canaanite community, and may have had 20,000–25,000 people. While the city proper had its delineated limits, the territory controlled by Pella must have extended down into the floor of the valley, about one kilometre to the west, perhaps reaching to the Jordan River itself, five kilometres away. This, too, would have changed with the times, reflecting Pella's prosperity, industriousness, military strength and economic priorities. It always needed to control the valley floor to grow its food, but in more prosperous times, such as in the Roman and Byzantine periods, it would also have been a large importer of food and basic goods. The ten cities of the Decapolis were essentially trading centres, and there is no reason for Pella to be an exception. It is certain that Pella's authority never extended to the other side of the Jordan River; that area would have been under the control of Beth-Shan, the only Decapolis city west of the river, located ten kilometres to the northwest.

Pella's location put it away from the main trade routes. The Romans constructed the Via Nova highway in AD 111, linking Aqaba with their great city of Bosra, in southern Syria, and followed by establishing many military outposts, camps and watchtowers to protect this vital route and the urban centres to its west. Pella was well off this important artery, and probably was more oriented to the valley and the west than it was towards the highlands to the east. For one thing, the people of Pella could see the valley floor from their hilltop homes, and spent a good deal of time going into the valley to work their farms.

View of main road in northern part of Valley

The main north–south road that passed through the centre of the Jordan Valley was a secondary highway, more important for intra-valley transport than as part of an international road network. Pella was in between the Via Nova and the valley road, and connected to both. Milestones have been found along an ancient road connecting Pella to Jerash via Ajlun, while the second main road out of Pella would have linked it with Beth-Shan.

Throughout history, the only easy, natural and commonly used international route passing through the valley was the northern one, connecting the Mediterranean port of Haifa with Beisan (Beth-Shan) in northern Palestine, and from there through the northern edge of the valley to southern Syria and on to Damascus. This was the easiest east–west route that avoided the Lebanese mountains and connected the Mediterranean ports and coastal cities with the inland trading centres of the Fertile Crescent. Another important route passed through Wadi Araba, connecting Gaza with Petra and Aqaba. The Dead Sea, with its steep eastern cliffs, prevented the development of a major international road through the centre of the valley, from Aqaba to the Yarmouk River basin, though secondary roads have

Spring flowers

always linked the valley with the hills on both sides. Roman roads connected Amman and Salt with Damiyah, which has always been an important crossing point of the Jordan River, and also linked the valley with Jerash and Umm Qais, two other cities of the Decapolis. Driving from Amman to the valley via Salt, a motorist today can see the old Roman road markers on the left-hand side of the road between Sweileh and Salt. Pella, however, remained away from these main routes, and seems to have enjoyed a relatively quiet, provincial life for most of its history. There is not much obvious evidence of military structures, such as a thick city wall. In Roman and Byzantine times, Pella exhibited simple architectural forms, which is perhaps not surprising for a provincial city off the beaten track. From the middle of the first century and for about 100 years, the Decapolis cities competed with each other to produce the most sophisticated buildings, monuments and urban complexes, vying to replicate the architectural splendour of Rome itself.

Pella's handsome civic complex, located below the central mound near the wadi, dates from this time, and must have been built around AD 50–70. The people's aesthetic sensitivities declined in the late

Roman and early Byzantine years. Old buildings were reused, and new construction lacked the grandeur of the early Roman architects.

Archaeological evidence is still being gathered to piece together the full record of Pella's successive inhabitants. The most recent discoveries, unearthed during the 1980 digging season, include the remains of a first century AD theatre on the edge of Wadi Jurum, a 380 cubic metre-capacity cistern that was used during the Byzantine period (perhaps when the spring waters became temporarily unusable) and a large colonnaded room that was used as a camel stable in the early years of the eighth century. A powerful earthquake brought down many of Pella's buildings then, as evidenced by the grotesquely twisted skeletons of six camels and their male driver found amid the stable's fallen stones.

A rich collection of Late Bronze Age pottery provides the first firm evidence that Pella was an important city with links with Egypt some 3,500 years ago. It was then called Pihilum, and is mentioned in ancient Egyptian records as a powerful Jordanian principality. The 100 pots discovered in three tombs near the main mound include red and white painted ceramic jugs, burnished bowls, alabaster juglets, much coarse pottery and a gold pin and a scarab of the Egyptian eighteenth Dynasty, from 1500 BC.

A large earthquake in the first half of the eighth century destroyed much of the city, and ushered in a long period of decline. Many people abandoned Pella, perhaps after a whole series of earthquakes made life difficult and dangerous. The city became sparsely populated after most residents fled and never returned. From 750 onwards, Pella experienced several lean centuries with a small population of poor, simple people who lived frugal lives.

The Islamic conquests of the seventh century had broken down the traditional trade patterns of Roman and Byzantine times; some cities could not make the adjustment to the new economic and political order, and entered a period of decline. Or did the nearby spring of Wadi Jurum dry up or somehow turn bad, perhaps becoming too warm? One ancient text tells about the water of Beth-Shan becoming poisonous. Perhaps Pella's spring water started coming out of a vein in the hills that had too many minerals and chemicals, and was not to the people's liking. Whatever the reasons, Pella began its long, slow decline.

After Jordan was conquered by the Islamic armies between AD 630 and 636, the Ummayads ruled the area from their capital in Damascus for almost a hundred years. Jordan continued to prosper, being close to the centre of power, and the valley was no exception. Many small farms were scattered throughout the valley floor, and used irrigation systems that were first installed in Roman times. Water reservoirs and channels were common.

The big Byzantine cities, including Pella, continued to be occupied during the Ummayad years, but deteriorated quickly thereafter. When the Abbasids moved the Islamic Caliphate to Baghdad in AD 750, Jordan reverted to being a neglected sidelight to historical events, away from the main power centres and trade routes.

The Abbasid, Fatimid and Seljuk-Zengid era (AD 750–1174) was a period of general decline for Jordan. Archaeological evidence from these centuries is poor throughout the country. Only fifteen Abbasid sites have been identified in the Jordan Valley, and most of these were in the process of dying out and being abandoned. The entire valley was in the midst of one of its periodic ebbs, with few permanent communities, little productive activity and insignificant construction or public works. This was, however, the quiet before the storm.

The Ayyubid-Mamluk era (1187–1516) was perhaps the Jordan's Valley's finest hour. The Ayyubid leader Saleh Al Din (Saladin) defeated the Crusaders at the Battle of Hattin in 1187, and Jordan was firmly back in Arab hands. The uniting of Egypt and Syria under the Ayyubids and the Mamluks returned Jordan to a pivotal geographic location in the middle of two great civilizations, and set off a general revival of socio-economic activity that would last until the Ottomans conquered the area in 1516.

Under the Mamluks, the Jordan Valley reached the peak of its agricultural development. Irrigation innovations sparked a large-scale sugar industry based on growing sugar cane. Sugar mills, driven by water, processed the sugar cane in many parts of the valley, but were concentrated in the northern area above the Dead Sea. This must have been a "wet phase" in Jordan's climate, because there is not enough water in the valley today to irrigate large sugar cane plantations and also power so many mills. This may have been one of the few times in history that farmers drew water from the Jordan River itself, as well as the side wadis, to irrigate plantations that must have covered nearly the entire valley floor. The valley had at least twenty sugar mills, according to the evidence to date, some of which were still being used in the late 1960s. Aqueducts and simple stone canals diverted the water from the side wadis and let it fall sharply to maximize the energy required to run the sugar mills. The water may have been recycled to irrigate the fields after it passed through the mills. Many of the mill sites have turned up the remains of specialized industrial sugar pots that were produced in the valley.

There were also a few major sites south of the Dead Sea where sugar was grown and processed. Sugar mills have been found at Safi and Feifeh, the former giving the name to the area now known as Tawahin Al Succar ("the sugar mills").

Most of the settlements in the Mamluk era were on the valley floor, and were generally big, sprawling villages without any fortifications or obvious military structures. The population and productivity of the valley increased markedly in these three centuries, an era that has left behind traces of 107 separate sites – the most of any period before the second half of the twentieth century. At its peak, the valley exported sugar to other parts of the Arab World. This was one of those rare moments in history when all factors synchronized to achieve maximum production from the unique combination of human and natural resources that converged in the valley. Favourable political conditions, climate, population density and markets combined to prompt farmers, food processors and merchants to achieve optimum productivity during the fourteenth century. But then, just as suddenly as it had began, the prosperity of the Mamluk era started to decline. A Mongul invasion from Asia had been turned back in 1260, and a second invasion, led by the feared Tamarlane, was repulsed in 1401, but only after it left great destruction in its wake throughout Syria and Jordan. Damascus was burned, as were most other big cities in the area. Mamluk coins stop appearing in Jordan after 1399, reflecting a new period of disarray and decline. From 1400 onwards, the Mamluk central government was weak and started losing control of provincial areas, including the Jordan Valley. Poor administration followed, and large-scale industries and public services started to deteriorate. This was aggravated by a series of natural disasters, including the spread of the Black Plague of Europe and a gradual reduction in the amount of rainfall, signalling the end of the valley's bountiful "wet phase".

When the Ottoman Turks invaded Jordan in 1516, they inherited an already deteriorating situation, and made it worse by imposing high taxes on agriculture, land, commerce and other forms of wealth. This was the final burden: the valley virtually collapsed, and from 1600 onwards, it was almost deserted.

When the first European and American explorers arrived in the nineteenth century, they found a hot, empty valley and assumed that nobody could possibly live in such an inhospitable area. It must have been an unwelcoming sight after almost 300 years of virtual abandonment. Left alone, the valley would develop into regions of barren earth where no water passed, interspersed with patches of thick sagebrush-like vegetation near the foothills, wadis and sources of ground water. Wolves, snakes, wild boars, leopards, alligators and lions inhabited the valley and no doubt scared off many would-be settlers, who congregated around the relative safety of places that could be watered by simple earth canals from the side wadis. It is easy to imagine today what the valley must have looked like in the last century. The roads leading into the valley, from Salt, Irbid and Na'ur, all have well marked, fenced-off mine fields on both sides, just as they enter the flat valley floor. These areas are thick with wild plants, trees and bushes, and are probably the only untouched plots of land in the valley that exhibit the area's natural shrubbery. Such vegetation covered large expanses of territory during the last four centuries, and was a fine source of food for animals.

Nomadic bedouins have always used the valley as a winter home, attracted there by warm weather and food for their herds of goats, sheep and camels. It is difficult to determine the exact extent and

Mamluk sugar mill in Arda Intersection area

importance of nomadism in the valley throughout history. Traces of obvious domestic campsites have been found that date back to 5000 BC, and it is logical to assume that seasonal nomadic activity was always a part of the valley culture. Dr Adnan Hadidi, Director General of the Jordanian Department of Antiquities, suggests that this is the case, that nomadism and urbanism probably co-existed in the area throughout history – as they still do today.

The traditional pattern of movement of people and animals has them wintering in the valley, growing their winter and spring crops, then moving up into the nearby hills to escape the summer heat that reaches 40°C in June, July and August. This regular movement of people into and out of the valley makes it all the more difficult to pinpoint the exact extent of settlement and the nature of human activity. Some people lived in the valley all the year round, as we can deduce from their buildings. At Pella, for example, there are remnants of three large Byzantine houses with one metre-thick walls designed to cool the interiors in summer. But did some of the inhabitants of Pella live there only half the year, when they were tending to their winter and spring cultivation, and move back up into the cooler hills in the summer? Did the Nabataean farmers in Wadi Araba migrate from their capital of Petra down to their sophisticated farms for the growing season from October to May, and return to the hills for the summer? The Nabataeans constructed extensive water gathering and distribution systems in the southern part of the valley. A good example is at Telah, south of the Dead Sea. A dam caught the water of Wadi Telah and directed it through a 500-metre stone canal to a large pool set against the hills, from where irrigation channels fed an enormous area on the floor of the valley that was divided into smaller plots by stone walls. Could the Nabataeans have used such a system in July? There was unlikely to be enough water from the wadi at that time of year. Did they therefore leave the hot valley in summer and retreat to their cities in the hills, like their descendants do to this day?

Chapter Four
The Genesis of Planning

However wild, hot, inhospitable and dangerous the Jordan Valley may have been during the last one hundred years, particularly at the end of the nineteenth and the start of the twentieth century, its agricultural potential was always quick to be appreciated. Ironically, it was usually foreigners – visitors, travellers, officials or occupiers – who had visions of the valley as a vast garden, housing hundreds of thousands of people and feeding several hundred thousand more. And it was usually not very far from appreciating what the valley could become to drawing up a formal plan to transform it into an agricultural wonderland. There have been dozens of plans to develop the Jordan Valley during this century, but the plethora of plans was always matched by a paucity of implementation. The general idea of developing the valley along the lines of today's JVA programme is not at all new; the novelty is in actually executing the plans.

The concept of a "development programme" was introduced into the Jordan Valley in the early part of the twentieth century. Throughout the nineteenth century, a handful of daring and hardy European and American travellers visited the valley, noted its seemingly contradictory combination of harsh and pleasant environment (depending on what time of year they came), and recorded what they saw of existing agricultural practices. Some travellers came to conduct semi-formal "surveys" of a political or military nature, others were motivated by a fascination for history and archaeology, while others yet were simply eccentric travellers and explorers, wishing to visit areas that few other Westerners had seen. The Jordan Valley was a prime candidate for such a journey.

The nineteenth-century explorers mistakenly decided the valley could never support life, a theory that was not disproved until the 1930s when the American archaeologist and Biblical scholar Nelson Glueck carried out the first detailed exploration of the Jordan Valley. He surveyed ninety different antiquities sites, and showed that the area had been continuously occupied throughout history. But he found only a handful of permanent villages in the valley in the 1930s,

The Jordan Valley

Aerial view of Sawalha village showing main road and main canal

which included some former Turkish slaves from East Africa, and some bedouin tribes.

By the post World War I era, foreign powers were looking to be involved in the Middle East. The new factor that would emerge, and dominate thinking about the valley for the next sixty years, was a desire to implement structured development plans, systematically to exploit the area's agricultural potential. The plans being implemented today had their genesis in the minds of European officials as early as 1914, but only after a series of Western travellers had made exploratory visits to the area in the nineteenth century.

One of the more famous early visitors was the Anglo-Swiss explorer John Lewis Burckhardt; he is credited with "rediscovering" the Nabataeans' mountain-ringed capital city at Petra, which had been "lost" to the outside world from 1200 to 1812. Dressed as an Arab and passing himself off as a Muslim, Burckhardt made several trips to the Holy Land in the early 1800s, which he documented in his book *Travels in Syria and the Holy Land*, published posthumously in London in 1822 by the Association for Promoting the Discovery of the Interior Parts of Africa.

Aerial view of new citrus groves in Deir Alla area in central Valley

Burckhardt passed through the valley on one trip in early July 1811. On 2 July he recorded in his diary the presence of "a luxuriant growth of wild herbage and grass," though he added that "the greater part of the ground is a parched desert, of which a few spots only are cultivated by the bedouins". He notes that the valley "affords pasturage to numerous bedouin tribes," some of whom live there all year, while others only winter in the valley. He specifically identifies the bedouins of Nazareth and Nablus, two important Palestinian cities in the hills and plains to the west, as among those who spend their winters in the valley, but added that they are joined by "those (bedouins) of the eastern mountains," the hills of Jordan.

He ran into "several encampments of stationary bedouins, who cultivate a few fields of wheat, barley and Dhourra", the latter being the Arabic name for corn or maize, which is one of the summer crops grown today in the valley, and one of the few cultivated crops that would have been growing in the brutal July heat. The bedouins, Burckhardt noted, "are at peace with the people of Szalt, to many of whom the greater part of them are personally known".

The British and American navies both sent small expeditions to survey the Jordan Valley–Dead Sea area in the 1840s, though the military significance of these trips is not clear. The British group, in *H.M.S. Spartan* under the command of Lt. Molyneux, made a five-week boat journey from Lake Tiberias, down the Jordan River and into the Dead Sea in August and September 1847, though the commander of the force paid for the experience with his life. Upon returning to Jaffa on 3 October, 1847, he became feverish, and died the same day, probably from malaria which he contracted in the valley.

The next year, the American Navy sent an expeditionary force commanded by a Lt. W.F. Lynch, who was more fortunate than Lt. Molyneux, and returned home to write his *Narrative of the United States' Expedition to the River Jordan and the Dead Sea*, which was published in Philadelphia in 1850.

Some of the most systematic surveying of this part of the world was done in the 1860s, by two expeditions led by officers of the Royal Navy, Col. Sir Charles Warren and Capt. Claude Reignier Conder. Their three-volume *Survey of Western Palestine* was published in London in 1884 by the Committee of the Palestine Exploration Fund. In July–August 1867, they took their men, provisions, animals and guides and crossed into "East Jordan" via the Jordan Valley, which they found to be a "country well cultivated by black bedouins" in the area of Wadi Nimrin. At Wadi Kufrein, slightly further south near the Dead Sea, they noticed many "rivulets" that passed through "dense masses of underwood," and were carried off for irrigation purposes. The bedouins had cut well defined walkways through the thick shrubbery. On 19 July, 1867, the explorers noted: "We went down at sunrise to look for ruins, but the growth of underwood was too great to allow of our proceeding far on either side of the paths."

One year later, the team once again set out to explore East Jordan, but this time took only a few provisions for a brief trip. They crossed the Jordan River in the north on 24 February, 1868, and stayed in East Jordan for ten days, returning to the western bank of the river on 5 March. They spent most of their time in the valley, which they visited in winter this time. They found a completely different terrain that sprang to life in the rainy season, with "vast meadows abounding in grasses and flowers". But they cautioned the unwary traveller not to be deceived by the lush environment, because "when the hot winds spring up in May, the grasses, like tinder, are broken up and blown away, and nothing remains but a barren waste."

They encountered bedouins who sometimes rushed at them with

spears, commanded by handsome sheikhs with magnificent swords. Finding the strange foreigners to be peaceful explorers, the bedouins invited them for festive meals and offered them all the hospitality the Arabs are renowned for. One sheikh in the northern part of the valley told them he feared that if the rains continued unabated, "the corn crop would be damaged by a worm eating at the roots." At Tell Saa'adiyyah, they found "the ground cultivated to the water's edge", and between Wadi Rajib and Wadi Zerqa, "irrigated and cultivated land" was much in evidence.

A decade later, an archaeologist of the American Palestine Exploration Society, a certain S. Merrill, spent the three years from 1875 to 1877 travelling in the area east of the Jordan River. He published his findings in 1881, in a book entitled, appropriately, *East of the Jordan*. One fine winter day in Wadi Yabis, 12 March, 1876, Merrill wrote in his diary: "All nature is alive here; trees, shrubs, grass, flowers are growing with all their might. The air is thick with the steam of rank, luxuriant vegetation. . . . It is not an exaggeration to say that the air here has been filled with the roar of insects." He also recorded the lighter side of life in the Jordan Valley in the late

Western tourists enjoy floating on Dead Sea at Sweimeh

nineteenth century, telling us that he ran across a band of gypsy musicians with "one of the largest monkeys I have ever seen."

And so it was in the valley more than a hundred years ago: a few settled bedouin communities grew wheat, barley and corn, irrigated by the plentiful flow of the Yarmouk River and the side wadis; tribal sheikhs and their armed followers on camels or horseback rushed at unannounced trespassers; nomadic bedouin tribes descended into the valley to spend the winter, returning to the hills of Salt or Nablus in the summer to graze their animals and trade with the city merchants; the threat of malaria always lurking, ready to kill local or foreigner alike; and the perennial cycle of nature changing the face of the earth several times a year, from lush greenery in the winter and spring to desolate, scorched barrenness in the summer.

The political climate in the nineteenth century was less turbulent. The Ottoman Turks controlled the area from the provincial seat of government at Salt, in the eastern hills just above the valley. Their control over the valley, however, was always tenuous, restricted to occasional trips to collect taxes or discuss some new matter of state with the tribal sheikhs. The valley was a neglected corner, while more important developments – and the attention of the Ottoman rulers – focussed on political and military ties between Istanbul and the nascent Arab political forces stirring in Beirut, Damascus, Aleppo, Jeddah and Mecca. Arab nationalists were crystallizing their thoughts in various capital cities, while Ottoman leaders searched for means of consolidating their control over the more distant Arab provinces under their rule. The idea of building the Hijaz railway was translated into action at the turn of the century, as Ottoman garrisons had to quell isolated rebellions in different parts of the Arab World. By the early years of the twentieth century, the inhabitants of the Jordan Valley were only grudgingly keeping pace with fast-moving political events all around them, more content to perpetuate their centuries-old pattern of growing cereals in winter and spring, and migrating with their herds to the nearby hills in the summer.

The first formal, if rudimentary, development plan for the Jordan Valley was an irrigation and hydro-electric power scheme designed by a certain Mr Georges Franghia, who was Director of Public Works in Palestine under the Ottoman Empire around 1910. He had already designed an irrigation scheme in 1909 for the Konia region of south-central Turkey. By 1913, he had turned his attention to harnessing the water resources of the Jordan Valley to irrigate the western side of the river and drive a hydro-electric power plant. He

General view overlooking Deir Alla area

prepared a neat diagram of his proposed system, which would locate a 12,400 effective horsepower station just north of the town of Tiberias, and an optional 8,600-horsepower station at Mejame' Bridge, on the Jordan River fifteen kilometres south of Lake Tiberias. He suggested that if the power station were located at Mejame' Bridge, the Yarmouk River would have to be diverted into Lake Tiberias, and the principal supply canal would have to be enlarged to provide a flow of 100 cubic metres per second in the Tiberias–Mejame' section. Without the diversion of the Yarmouk, the principal supply canal that would run the entire 121 kilometre length of the western side of the River Jordan would have an initial flow of 65 cubic metres per second. His diagram gives the water level of the Dead Sea as 432 metres below sea level, which is about 25 metres lower than all other accepted readings of the time. The lower level of the sea also accounts for the length of the 121 kilometre-long canal that would provide irrigation water for the valley. The length of the Jordan Valley today, from the Dead Sea to Lake Tiberias, is about 104 kilometres.

The outbreak of World War I, during which the Ottoman Turks lost control of the Arab World, put an end to the pioneering ideas of

Mr Franghia. His concept for a canal running down the entire length of the valley would reappear many times during the next fifty years, but it would not be until the early 1960s that the Jordanian government would build such a canal – on the eastern bank of the river, initially running only halfway down the valley, and without any provisions for power generation.

The next attempt to channel the excess waters of the Jordan and Yarmouk rivers to irrigate dry areas of the valley was launched in 1920, and also centred on the western side of the Jordan River.

In the wake of World War I, the British and French governments formally divided up the Middle East into zones of influence and responsibility that were legally enshrined in the mandates they were given by the League of Nations. The British were responsible for Iraq, Palestine and Transjordan, while the French governed Lebanon and Syria. On 23 December, 1920, the two European powers signed a separate convention in Paris "on Certain Points Connected with the Mandates for Syria and the Lebanon, Palestine and Mesopotamia," in which they officially called for a joint survey of the water resources of the Jordan and Yarmouk rivers, for irrigation and power-generation purposes. Article 8 of the convention stated:

"Experts nominated respectively by the Administrations of Syria and Palestine shall examine in common within six months after the signature of the present convention the employment, for the purposes of irrigation and the production of hydro-electric power, of the waters of the Upper Jordan and the Yarmouk and of their tributaries, after satisfaction of the needs of the territories under the French mandate."

The principal beneficiary of any water harnessing projects that might ensue from the joint surveys was, in the minds of the Europeans, the territory called Palestine, lying west of the Jordan River. The convention stated clearly:

"In connection with this examination the French Government will give its representatives the most liberal instructions for the employment of the surplus of these waters for the benefit of Palestine. . . . To the extent to which the contemplated works are to benefit Palestine, the Administration of Palestine shall defray the expenses of the construction of all canals, weirs, dams, tunnels, pipelines and reservoirs or other works of a similar nature, or measures taken with the object of reafforestation and the management of forests."

There is no evidence that such a study was ever carried out, probably because the Administrations of Syria and Palestine had

The Genesis of Planning

King Talal Dam

King Talal Dam in 1977, before it was filled with water

more pressing matters to worry about than irrigating the Jordan Valley.

Another Franco-British protocol signed on 3 February, 1922 gave the government of Palestine the right to build dams to raise the levels of lakes Tiberias and Huleh, if owners and tenants of the flooded farms were adequately compensated. A mixed commission would settle compensation disputes, but this commission was never established.

The next systematic attempt to formulate a development plan for the valley was a scheme presented in London in October 1922 by a Mr E. Mavromatis, entitled "Preliminary Scheme for the Irrigation of the Valley of the Jordan." It was the most ambitious valley scheme designed to that date, though it was a general proposal lacking many specific details. Mavromatis went so far as to build a 2 metre-long, three-dimensional scale model of the entire Jordan Valley, from the swamps above Lake Huleh, north of Tiberias, to the Dead Sea, which he photographed and included in his fifteen-page report (which also includes Mr Franghia's diagram of his irrigation scheme).

The Mavromatis plan included the following main components:

   A main dam on Lake Tiberias where the Jordan River originates;

   Two principal earth-dug supply canals "of navigable dimensions" originating at the Tiberias dam, serving both banks of the river, and following the contours of the mountains, valleys and ravines;

   A powerhouse near the Mejame' Bridge on the west bank of the river, fed from the main supply canal by a masonry branch conduit with sluices to regulate its flow, at a maximum flow of 35 cubic metres per second. Its output would be 8,400 effective horsepower, which would be sufficient for the needs of Jerusalem and unidentified "other districts of Palestine." Electricity could also be produced from the Yarmouk River if future power demand required; the plan outlines a possible future hydro-electric station at Himmeh, with an output of 12,600 horsepower, fed by a supply canal from the river;

   A diversion canal to send the entire flow of the Yarmouk River into Lake Tiberias after having passed through the Himmeh powerhouse;

   Increasing navigability of the Jordan River from its first 30 metres to its entire length, "by rectification in its bed" and augmenting the flow of water into the river in summer from Lake Tiberias by opening the dam at the lake's outlet.

The Genesis of Planning

King Talal Dam

Mavromatis envisioned two main canals on the west bank, one higher than the other, and one on the east bank, hugging the edge of the eastern hills. The main canals on both sides of the river would reach about ten kilometres past the Dead Sea. Secondary distribution canals would branch off the main canals, and the third class canals, as he called them, "would be dug by the villagers themselves, who are accustomed to work of this kind, and can lead the waters to those places which they wish to irrigate first."

He also made provision for a series of drainage canals, at a lower level than the secondary supply canals. Communications throughout the valley would be via well-kept metalled roads running alongside the main canals, and, in future, via agricultural electric railways. Land above the main supply canals would be irrigated by the use of "small retaining dams in the ravines to conserve the waters of the torrents and springs."

Mavromatis did not specify how much land would be irrigated, leaving this for more detailed design studies that were never undertaken. He included plans to irrigate the flatlands around Lake Huleh, between Tiberias and the mountains of Lebanon, by building small dams to catch the water from local springs and tributaries. But details of the work, including reclaiming the marshes there, were left for elaboration "in the final plans," which never materialized.

Developing the Jordan Valley remained tangential to both regional and international affairs. A 1928 report published in Jerusalem, *Geology and Water Resources of Palestine*, by Mr G.S. Blake, geological advisor to the Palestine Government, noted the lack of serious study of the topic:

"The employment of the water of the Jordan which is the biggest source running to waste amounting to between 1,000 and 2,000 million gallons a day, and the irrigation by these waters of the upper terraces, consisting of good soil washed down from the hills covering areas on each side of the Jordan of 200 square kilometres, has not yet been seriously considered."

Another report published in 1928 and entitled *Irrigation and Water Supply*, was a survey of irrigation potential in Palestine prepared by an Englishman named Cyril Q. Henriques. It was prepared in 1927–28 as an expert's report submitted to the Joint Palestine Survey Commission. While it dealt only with the Palestinian side of the Jordan River, it did give further evidence of conditions in the valley in the late 1920s. It noted: "All authorities combine in classifying the soil of the Hulah Plain as some of the most productive in the world. Also all medical and sanitary authorities combine in condemning the climate as being as malaria-impregnated as any in the world." Henriques says he does not treat that part of the Jordan Valley lying south of Beisan, because of "its inaccessibility, want of detailed information about it and lack of time and money to collect it." He adds that "also this area is too hot for settlement by the methods at present employed". He obviously did his fieldwork in the summer.

He did point out, however, that the 30,000 dunums in the Yarmouk Triangle, bounded by the Jordan and Yarmouk rivers and Lake Tiberias, is well suited for irrigated agriculture. The two most promising means of providing the needed water would be to store the Yarmouk River's excess winter flow, or to use the "practically unlimited" water of Lake Tiberias, which could be pumped up about 20 metres before flowing down by gravity in open channels onto the plain.

By the 1920s others had started looking at the rushing waters of the Jordan and the Yarmouk solely as a means of power to drive hydro-electric plants, urgently needed to supply the growing population of Palestine with its electricity requirements. In March 1926, the British High Commissioner for Palestine signed an agreement giving a seventy-year concession to the Palestine Electric Corporation, run by an enterprising Jewish engineer named Pinhas Rutenberg, to use the Yarmouk and Jordan waters to produce electricity for both Palestine and Transjordan. Rutenberg had secured a previous thirty-two-year concession in September 1921 to use the waters of the Auja basin, in western Palestine, to provide electricity. By 1944, the Auja and Jordan-Yarmouk concessions were providing 173 million kilowatt hours of power a year. The Jordan-Yarmouk concession was to prove a nagging obstacle that would have to be dealt with by more ambitious planners who wanted to use the waters of the Jordan and Yarmouk rivers to irrigate the entire valley.

By the early 1930s, a decade after the Emirate of Transjordan had been formally established in 1921, the developmental momentum in the young country started to pick up; formal government institutions, such as ministries and technical departments, came into being and began to address the socio-economic development of the small, sparsely populated country. For the first time, the state appointed a Director of Development, an Englishman named M.G. Ionides. By the end of the decade, he was to provide the first comprehensive survey of the Jordan Valley's water resources and irrigation potential

The Jordan Valley

View of main canal

for the lands lying east of the river, complementing the many surveys of the western side of the valley that had been prepared in the previous decade.

In August 1936, the British government had appointed a Palestine Royal Commission to investigate the causes of clashes that had broken out in April between indigenous Palestinian Arabs and the increasing numbers of Zionist-inspired Jewish immigrants and settlers. The Commission spent three months in Palestine at the end of 1936, and published its report on 7 July, 1937, in which it recommended that a full survey of Transjordan be carried out and "a scheme be prepared for its irrigation and development".

A hydrographic survey of Transjordan was planned and finally funded in October 1937, and fieldwork started by the end of the year. While it was under way, the British-appointed Palestine Partition Commission, headed by Sir John Woodhead, paid a three-month visit to Palestine to investigate the practicalities of partitioning the disputed territory into two states, one for the Palestinians and the other for the Zionists. The Commission paid a brief visit to Transjordan in June 1938, and commented out of hand that

"Transjordan offers small scope for intensive settlement on the land . . . we are convinced that the additional agricultural population which the land can support is small." Officials in Jordan thought otherwise. Director of Development M.G. Ionides was pushing ahead with the national hydrographic survey that had been initiated the previous winter. He stressed the importance of the perennial streams found all along the Jordan Valley, and argued that these could only be fully developed comprehensively if a contour survey of the valley terrain were available. Such a survey was initiated in early spring 1938 by the Department of Lands and Survey, with the fieldwork in the valley under the charge of a Mr V. Serbinovitch. The hard work in the valley in the oppressive summer heat was accelerated in June, and would have been completed in December. But the unruly political climate in the area took its toll yet again. The surveyors' field camp was attacked in mid-August, and Serbinovitch and two assistants were killed. The attackers have been described as "bandits", though some reports say they were Palestinian nationalists who mistook the field party for a new Jewish settlement. The rest of the field party fled in fear, and the contour survey was interrupted, but later completed.

Ionides' four hundred-page report, entitled *The Water Resources of Transjordan and their Development*, was published in Amman on 5 March, 1939. It would prove to be a prophetic document, identifying the valley as the country's potentially most productive agricultural area, but also pinpointing the need for strict control of water resources to prod the confidence of the farmers themselves in their ability to make a living on the land. Ionides estimated there were 260,000 dunums of irrigated farmland in Transjordan, of which 186,395 dunums were in the valley, between the Dead Sea and the Yarmouk River, according to tenuous land registration statistics. Irrigation water came largely from perennial streams in the valley. Most of the 239 million cubic metres of stream flow available every year for irrigation in the entire country was already being used, but much of it was wasted due to lack of control, few progressive irrigation systems and quarrels among bedouin tribes and individual farmers. He suggested that only by instituting a system of water control "can landowners feel sufficient confidence in the regularity of their water supply to justify them in spending money on improvements, and until the present owners are prepared to do so, it will not be possible to attract outside capital".

"In the Jordan Valley, there is little dry farmed land, and

JVA underground pressure pipes being installed in 1978

agriculture depends upon irrigation. It is here that the only opportunity for rapid and economic development is to be found, depending upon government works which are, in the case of water distribution, essential."

He estimated that the "dozen or more" small streams that flow into the valley between Wadi Arab in the north and Wadi Hassa in the south provide about 157 million cubic metres of water a year, much of which was already being diverted for irrigation via simple earth canals dug by the farming bedouins. But this was highly inefficient use of the water, most of which evaporated or was absorbed into the earth before it reached the cultivated areas. Ionides suggested five different possibilities to develop the valley's water resources: controlling existing side wadis, preventing absorption losses by building impervious concrete canals to replace the earth channels, pumping water from the Jordan River, pumping from underground wells, and building a canal to divert the water of the Yarmouk River into the farming lands east of the Jordan River.

He thought the first option was the most immediately attractive. By improving the design of the existing earth canals and building some regulatory structures on the side wadis, at least 105 million cubic metres of water a year could be tapped for irrigation (the remaining one-third of the 157 million cubic metres being lost by absorption and evaporation). Such a scheme would deliver water to farmers at a cost of one-twentieth of a mil per cubic metre. (The Palestine pound, the legal currency in Palestine and Transjordan then, was divided into 1,000 mils, and was worth about $5 in the late 1930s. One cubic metre of water costing one-twentieth of a mil would have been the equivalent of about .025 US cents.) If concrete channels were built to replace the earth ones, the cost of the works would have risen to about one-third of a mil per cubic metre (.16 cents).

Sprinkler irrigation in use at JVA demonstration farm in northern valley

Ziglab Dam

Ionides identified the Yarmouk River as "the sole substantial supply of *new* freeflow water in Transjordan". He proposed building a canal to divert the Yarmouk's water into the valley. One plan would use Yarmouk and Zerqa river waters, with side wadi flows, to irrigate 150,000 dunums of land. Using concrete irrigation channels, he estimated the cost of works at 5–6 Palestinian pounds ($25–30) per dunum, and half that sum if earth channels were used.

A second, more modest, plan would combine Yarmouk waters with flows from Wadi Arab and Wadi Ziglab to irrigate 40,000 dunums of land in the northern valley, between the Yarmouk River and Wadi Ziglab. He put the capital cost of such a project at 70,000 Palestine pounds ($350,000).

He thought the most profitable and sensible course for the government would have been to build the Yarmouk canal and control the existing side wadi earth-channel irrigation systems (105 million cubic metres) to provide the valley with an assured 138 million cubic metres of water every year, at a total capital cost of 120,000 Palestine pounds ($600,000).

Ultimately, he thought, the valley could support 300,000 dunums

Work on southern extension of main canal in 1977

of irrigated land, using 14.5 cubic metres per second of Yarmouk and Jordan River waters, or a total annual supply of 460 million cubic metres. He said the only practical way to store the waters of the Jordan River would be in Lake Tiberias.

When Ionides wrote his report in 1939, he put the total population of Transjordan at "325,000 souls, whose livelihood is almost exclusively agricultural and pastoral". He already saw signs of "land hunger" in the country, and looked to the valley as the only place where agricultural development would make any sense, the rest of the country being too dry.

While officials in Transjordan were starting to focus for the first time on fully tapping the water resources on their side of the Jordan River, more ambitious projects were being conceived in the minds of others. A few years before Ionides produced his plan, a Jewish corporation, the Palestine Land Development Company, had asked a firm of British consulting engineers to study the possible development of 42,000 dunums of land in the lower Huleh Basin that it held as a concession. The study was done in 1935, and proposed draining the entire Huleh Basin (the marshes and the lake) to provide 104,000 dunums of irrigated land. But this plan could not go ahead without first reaching agreement with Mr Rutenberg, whose 1926 concession to produce electricity specifically prohibited any other water-use or irrigation scheme in the area.

By the early 1940s, it had become obvious that no easy solution was to be found for the clash between native Palestinians and the hundreds of thousands of Jewish immigrants who were pouring into Palestine, intent on establishing a country in a land already inhabited and cultivated by the Arabs. The Jewish leadership and its friends in the West, primarily in the United States and Great Britain, went to great lengths to try and show that there was plenty of room in the region to accommodate both the Palestinians and the immigrant Zionists, who mostly came from East Europe and the Soviet Union. Inevitably, their attention turned to the Jordan Valley, with its untapped water, power and agricultural resources. Assorted plans were proposed before and after the state of Israel was created. Some were primarily aimed at settling Jewish immigrants, others at resettling displaced Palestinian refugees. They were invariably grandiose, and politically controversial.

The first plan came from the American development engineer and land reclamation authority Walter Clay Lowdermilk. He had visited Palestine in the late 1930s, on behalf of the US Department of Agriculture, to investigate the economic potential of the area. In 1944, he published his book *Palestine: Land of Promise*, in which he proposed harnessing the waters of the Jordan, Yarmouk, Zerqa, Banias, Hasbani and Dan rivers to irrigate the Jordan Valley, large sections of Galilee and northern Palestine. The Litani River in southern Lebanon should be diverted to form an artificial lake in northern Palestine, from where the water would be pumped to irrigate the Negev Desert, in southern Palestine. A canal dug across northern Palestine, bringing Mediterranean sea water into the Dead Sea, would replenish the loss of Jordan River water that would go to irrigate the valley, and generate one billion kilowatt hours of electricity during the 400-metre drop from the Mediterranean to the Dead Sea. Lowdermilk thought big. He suggested his land reclamation and power project would provide "farms, industry and security for at least four million Jewish refugees from Europe, in addition to the 1,800,000 Arabs and Jews already in Palestine and Transjordan." He envisaged irrigating 800,000–1.2 million dunums of land.

He foresaw the establishment of a powerful body to oversee his plan, to be called the Jordan Valley Authority, or JVA. The

Lowdermilk plan excited many Zionists, who went so far as to form a society to drum up support in the West and to promote Jewish immigration to Palestine. On the basis of the plan, the World Zionist Organization invited the American engineer James B. Hays to Palestine in late 1944 to take a closer look at Lowdermilk's proposals, and to come up with more specific plans. Hays worked independently of the British mandate government in Palestine, and came up with his proposals in 1945, which were published in book form in 1948. He suggested diverting the headwaters of the Jordan, Hasbani and Banias rivers via a channnel built high in the mountainsides west of Lake Huleh, first to Haifa and then to southern Palestine. The Huleh area itself would be irrigated by other springs to the east and west. A channel would bring sea water from the Mediterranean to the Jordan Valley, to generate 660 million kilowatt hours of hydroelectric power. Half the waters of the Yarmouk River would be diverted into Lake Tiberias, to prevent it from drying up from the loss of the headwaters of the rivers Jordan, Banias and Hasbani. The Jordan Valley itself would be irrigated by the small amount of water that would still flow in the Jordan River, and from underground springs and wells. Hays thus envisaged irrigating a total of 2.5 million dunums with some 2 billion cubic metres of water per year, at a cost to farmers of 2.25 mils per cubic metre (1.125 US cents). He thought his project would assimilate 1.75 million immigrants into the area.

In early 1946, political commissions looking into the Palestine conflict once again proposed water projects for the valley. The Anglo-American Committee of Inquiry had asked the mandatory government of Palestine to present it with a thorough survey covering political, economic and social aspects of the territory. This was compiled in December 1945 and January 1946, presented to the committee in February and published in April 1946. In discussing irrigation methods for 28,000 dunums of land along the banks of the Jordan and Yarmouk rivers between Lake Tiberias and Beisan, the survey proposed two alternatives. Water could be pumped from the rivers and distributed by gravity through small concrete channels, or a large dam across the Yarmouk River and a system of gravity canals could take the water to the farmlands. The advantage of this plan, the survey said, "is that the barrage would also serve as the headworks of a canal commanding, on the Trans-Jordan side of the river, a greater area than in Palestine."

Here, then, was another appreciation of the potential for irrigated farming in the Jordan Valley east of the river, the latest in a series of

The Jordan Valley

Typical one-room concrete house found throughout the Valley

dams-and-canals proposals that had surfaced intermittently during the past thirty years. The reality, however, was far more simple. The valley in the late 1930s and 1940s was mostly used to grow wheat, barley and corn. Bedouin sheikhs and their men fiercely protected their water rights on the side wadis, which they tapped via crude earth canals to irrigate their fields of cereals. A few adventurous farmers tried planting tomatoes and cucumbers in the summer, and would send any surplus produce on the backs of donkeys to be sold in Salt. The valley's population fluctuated wildly, depending on the season, as nomadic livestockers moved in and out of the area with their herds of sheep, goats and camels. The only permanent structures were a handful of mud brick houses. The basic shelter was the dark brown or black bedouin tent, housing year-round as well as seasonal inhabitants. While grandiose proposals were being published in London and Jerusalem to criss-cross the valley with hundreds of small channels fed by massive dams and diversion works to the north, the bedouin farmers went about their business as best they knew how: ploughing the land and sowing the seeds of wheat or barley in

November or December, watering it for the next five months, and harvesting the crop in the late spring and early summer.

In 1949, the government of Jordan once again turned its attention to the valley. It commissioned the British consultants Sir Murdoch MacDonald and Partners to formulate a development plan for the area based on the 1939 report of Ionides. The MacDonald report was published in December 1950, and envisaged using Lake Tiberias as a storage reservoir for the flood waters of the Jordan and Yarmouk rivers. It presupposed an agreement between Israel and Jordan for common use of Tiberias as a reservoir, from where two canals would irrigate both banks of the Jordan Valley. A four-stage plan was proposed, ultimately to irrigate 650,000 dunums between Tiberias and the Dead Sea.

All the proposed water harnessing, irrigation and power-generating plans for the valley before 1948 stemmed from the grandiose, entrepreneurial instincts of visionary individuals, or from governmental authorities who realized that only in the Jordan Valley was there enough untapped water and land to induce a big increase in agricultural output. After the Arab-Israeli war of 1947–48, however, a new factor entered the equation: the Palestinian refugees. About 450,000 Palestinians, driven from their homes and villages before, during and immediately after the 1948 war between Jewish-Zionist and Arab forces, fled eastwards, either settling in eastern Palestine, in the area known today as the West Bank, or crossing the Jordan River and huddling in the Hashemite Kingdom of Transjordan, as the former Emirate came to be known after achieving independence from Great Britain on 25 May, 1946. The sudden influx of so many refugees into the eastern bank of the river, coupled with the annexation of the West Bank into the expanded Hashemite Kingdom of Jordan, radically altered the complexion of what had hitherto been a quiet, relatively isolated corner of the world. The capital city of Amman was only a large village of 30,000 people in 1948. Overnight, Jordan found itself with triple its former population, responsible for that part of Palestine that was not occupied to form the new state of Israel, and trying to cope with the rigours of day-to-day life while simultaneously having become a front-line state confronting an aggressive, trigger-happy enemy. King Abdullah was assassinated in Jerusalem on 20 July, 1951, further aggravating the delicate internal situation. King Talal assumed power in early September, to be followed by King Hussein, who ascended to the throne on 2 May, 1953 when he reached his eighteenth birthday. In these fragile years of

The Jordan Valley

Farm tool in one hand and schoolbook in the other . . . a typical Valley teenager at North Shouneh

the early 1950s, Jordan's ability to survive as a nation-state was an open question in many people's minds. British support was vital to meet annual budgetary requirements, and American aid followed soon after in the form of a $2 million technical assistance grant. A retrospective report, written in 1962 by the head of the United States Agency for International Development (AID) programme in Jordan, would recall that in the early 1950s "little thought could be given to long-range, careful planning for Jordan's ultimate viability, for the good reason that Jordan apparently had no long-range future. It had, in fact, only a doubtful chance of surviving from one fiscal year to the next." A survey by the new Amman office of the US Foreign Operations Administration, the forerunner of US AID, noted that Jordan in the early 1950s was a country with its finances in chaos, general unemployment, only small industrial establishments, tourism discouraged by war and regional unrest, agriculture little changed since biblical days and totally insufficient to support the country's new population of 1.5 million, narrow and rough roads "more suitable for animals than for automotive equipment," an educational system disrupted and fragmented, with no schools or teachers at all in many rural areas, malaria prevalent in low-lying areas of the Jordan Valley, malnutrition a problem throughout the entire country, and, above all, a lack of water that precluded irrigation of any magnitude, and caused livestock to die of thirst in drought years. But all was not hopeless, because "foremost on the positive side was, of course, the population, a cheerful people not afraid of hard work and not unaccustomed to working with foreign advisors. Mainly farmers, they lived in small villages or settlements near, hopefully, a perennial source of water. They planted their crops in the fall, before the winter rains, and prayed that enough rain would fall at the right time. When it did, the yield would be good, because the soil itself is rich; when the rains failed, as they do on an average of one year in three, or were deficient as they have been in the last eight years in ten, there was no money in the village, and little enough food. There was nothing to do but replough the hardened earth and hope for a better season next year."

Hope alone, however, would not help Jordan stand on its own feet. What was needed was a hard-nosed, realistic development strategy based on whatever indigenous resources the young and dishevelled country could muster. That meant, for all practical purposes, the Jordan Valley. As Ionides had pointed out in his report more than a decade before, "there seem to be no opportunities whatever for irrigation development in the hills which can even remotely compare with those of the Ghor". The situation was the same in the early 1950s, and would remain so in the 1980s.

Chapter Five

The Hazards of Implementation

On a cloudy winter day in 1951, the chief of the Water Resources Branch of the United States' Point Four aid team in Amman, Mills Bunger, was flying over Jordan when bad weather diverted his plane into a flight path over the Yarmouk River valley. At one point, through a brief break in the clouds, Bunger looked down and saw a spot where several streams converged and fed into the Yarmouk River. A bit downstream from that point, the valley suddenly widens and deepens, forming a massive natural reservoir – a perfect site for a dam to trap the river's winter flood waters. Bunger and his staff visited the site on the ground, (called Maqarin, the Arabic word for the point at which several tributaries converge to form one river), and started work on a detailed plan to store the Yarmouk's excess winter water for irrigation and power generation. The Jordanian government and the United States Point Four programme mentioned the plan to officials of the newly formed United Nations Relief and Works Agency (UNRWA), which had been established after the Arab-Israeli war to help Palestinian refugees cope with their post-war difficulties. UNRWA immediately adopted the proposal, seeing in it a means of providing gainful employment for some of the hundreds of thousands of Palestinian refugees in Jordan, many of whom had settled in emergency camps in the valley. UNRWA allocated $40 million out of its $200 million budget for the proposed project, which was initially called the Bunger Plan. It envisaged a 480 foot-high dam on the Yarmouk River at Maqarin, storing 500 million cubic metres of water. A canal would lead to a diversion dam at Addasiyyeh, feeding into a main canal along the eastern side of the valley. A second canal would run the length of the West Bank, fed by a diversion dam on the Jordan River, south of the Israeli border. The works would irrigate 435,000 dunums of land in the valley and 60,000 dunums in Syria. The Maqarin and Addasiyyeh dams would generate 28,500 kilowatts of electricity, for use by Jordan and Syria. The entire project was estimated to cost $60 million, and would need about seven years to be completed. Experts suggested that over 100,000 people could live and work in the valley upon full implementation of the projects. One of the main attractions of the plan was that it did not rely on Tiberias as a storage reservoir, and therefore could be implemented without securing the agreement and co-operation of Israel.

In June 1953, and with an eye to implementing the Bunger Plan, Syria and Jordan concluded an agreement on joint exploitation of the Yarmouk River basin. Syria would use the higher springs of the river for irrigation schemes within its territory, while the balance of the waters would flow downstream into Jordan. Both countries together would build the Maqarin Dam and four related hydro-electric power stations, with most of the output going to Syria.

By the autumn of 1953, however, after two full years of planning, the Yarmouk River scheme fell victim to political pressures. As Jordan's King Hussein tells it in his autobiography written in 1962, *Uneasy Lies the Head*: ". . . the Israelis protested in Washington and to the United Nations: they preferred a scheme which would benefit all countries in the area, and even laid claims to a share of the Yarmouk waters. Incredibly, the free world stood behind this frustration of a strictly internal project, which as long ago as 1956 would have enabled a hundred thousand or more refugees who had lost their homes because of the Israelis to earn their own living and regain their self-respect." The Bunger Plan was killed.

By this time, the United States had become involved in the question of regional water projects in the Jordan River basin. Soon after the demise of the Bunger Plan, American officials working under the State Department's Ambassador Eric Johnston, the special envoy of President Eisenhower, sought to devise a new plan to placate all the parties to the disputed waters of the Jordan. The Israelis had started working on their National Water Carrier scheme (the All Israel Plan) immediately after the armistice agreements were signed with Syria, Jordan, Lebanon and Egypt in 1949. By early 1951, they began draining the Huleh swamps, and in 1953 were working to divert the Jordan's waters at a point above Lake Tiberias, from where they would be pumped via a canal to southern Israel. Syrian forces were sent to the worksite, along the demilitarized zone, forcing the Israelis to change their plans and move the main pumping station from north of Lake Tiberias to its western shore. It was against this tense background that President Eisenhower sent Ambassador Johnston to the area to negotiate a water sharing plan acceptable to all the states bordering on the Jordan River basin.

UNRWA had pinned high hopes on resettling many Palestinian

refugees in the valley, where they could continue to earn an agricultural livelihood, as most of them had done in their native villages in Palestine. Israel had protested that the Bunger plan was a unilateral Jordanian development of the waters of the Jordan and Yarmouk rivers, to which it had riparian rights. Its protests in Washington succeeded. The United States withdrew its intended funding for the Bunger Plan, and UNRWA was left alone with the Jordanian government in seeking out other means to support Palestinian refugees while simultaneously tapping the full productive capacity of the Jordan Valley. To overcome political disputes, UNRWA asked the Tenessee Valley Authority (TVA) to supervise the formulation of a regional development plan that took into consideration the water rights of all states concerned, namely Israel, Jordan, Syria and Lebanon. Such a plan was produced for the TVA in 1953 by the consultants Charles T. Main of Boston, Massachussetts, using data culled from the several previous plans for the Jordan River basin. The Main Plan, as it was first known, recognised the "watershed priority" principle embodied in the Ionides and Mac-Donald reports: that the waters within a catchment area should not be diverted outside that area until all the requirements of those within the catchment area have been satisfied. The Main Plan was the first truly unified, regional development plan for the entire Jordan River basin. It was taken by Ambassador Johnston and presented to the Arabs and the Israelis in 1953 as a set of proposals to be used as a starting point for negotiations. It was immediately dubbed "the Johnston Plan", by which name it has been known ever since, even though a formal plan document as such never existed.

Its main elements were: a dam on the Hasbani River in Lebanon, with a canal feeding a power plant in northern Israel and the water being used for irrigation in the Galilee area; dams on the Banias and Dan rivers, feeding 120 kilometre-long canal to irrigate Galilee farmlands; drainage of the Huleh swamps; building a dam at Maqarin with a capacity of 175 million cubic metres; building a dam at Addasiyyeh to divert Yarmouk waters into Lake Tiberias and the proposed East Ghor Canal; raising the small dam at the outlet of Lake Tiberias to increase the lake's storage capacity; and building two principal canals on the east and west banks of the Jordan River, to irrigate the valley between the Yarmouk River and the Dead Sea.

The Johnston Plan allocated 45 million cubic metres of water a year to irrigate 30,000 dunums of Syrian land, 774 million cubic metres for 500,000 dunums in Jordan and 394 million cubic metres for 420,000 dunums in Israel. The Arab countries objected that the water allocations were unfair, and the Arab League appointed a technical committee of engineers to review the Johnston Plan. The committee noted, among other things, that the plan allocated 819 million cubic metres of water a year to the Arab states, while the amount of water flowing into the Jordan River from these states was estimated at 1,283 million cubic metres. In March 1954, the committee came up with an Arab counter-project, whose main points included changes that would use half the Hasbani River dam waters to irrigate farms inside Lebanese territory; use some of the Banias River waters to irrigate Syrian lands; build a dam at Maqarin and a diversion dam at Addasiyyeh with a hydro-electric power plant at the latter, whose waters would flow into Lake Tiberias for storage before being released to irrigate the valley lowlands; build irrigation canals on both sides of the valley; and form an international body to oversee the fair allocation of regional water resources to all the concerned states.

The Israelis also objected to the Johnston Plan, claiming that its water allocations were insufficient and that Lebanon's Litani River should be included if one aimed for a truely regional water-sharing system. The Israelis presented a counter-proposal, which was prepared by the American engineer Joseph Cotton, who was then a consultant to the government. The Cotton Plan envisaged using half the Litani waters to produce power in Israel and replace diverted Jordan River water in Lake Tiberias. It would also divert Jordan River waters outside the watershed to irrigate Negev lands, as originally proposed in the All Israel Plan of 1951.

A significant principle had been established by this time: both the Arabs and Israel agreed on all riparian states' rights to use the water of the Jordan River system, though the Arabs insisted that the water should remain in the catchment area, while the Israelis wanted to divert it south-westwards to irrigate the Negev.

In early 1954, Johnston and Arab League officials discussed the proposed Arab changes, which increased water allocations to the Arab states by fifteen per cent over the Johnston Plan's quotas. But Johnston insisted on providing Israel with 394 million cubic metres a year, and negotiations continued for most of 1954. The Israelis, meanwhile, were implementing various elements of their National Water Carrier plan, which had been developed in the early 1950s by the same Joseph Cotton, on the basis of the original Lowdermilk and Hays proposals of the 1940s. This revolved around using Tiberias as Israel's main storage reservoir, after raising its level by 1.5 metres and diverting more than 300 million cubic metres of water a year to the Negev. Israel was taking water from the Jordan River, storing it in Lake Tiberias and pumping it for use in areas totally outside the Jordan River basin. The Israeli plans posed a serious threat to Jordan, which relied heavily on Jordan-Yarmouk River waters to irrigate the valley floor.

Back in June 1953, Jordan had commissioned two American consultants, Harza Engineering Co. of Chicago, Illinois, and Michael Baker Jr., Inc. of Rochester, Pennsylvania, to start work on a master plan for the Yarmouk and Jordan River valleys. Six months later, Baker and Harza turned in their preliminary Appraisal Report, which recommended developing an intensive irrigation project covering 460,000 dunums on both banks of the Jordan River Valley, 296,000 dunums on the east bank and 165,000 dunums on the west bank. The importance of the Baker-Harza report was that it was the first accurate study of precisely how much water would be needed to irrigate the valley floor. It showed that more land was cultivable than had been previously thought, and with lower water requirements as well.

Johnston took the Baker-Harza plans, the Cotton Plan and the Arab counter-proposals, and prepared a revised set of proposals on unified regional exploitation of the Jordan River system. He presented these new ideas to both sides in early 1955. This Unified Plan, as it was named, presumed that water would be diverted outside the Jordan River basin only after in-basin users had satisfied their water needs. The plan envisaged a dam on the upper Yarmouk to store 300 million cubic metres of water and to generate 150 million kilowatt hours of power a year. Yarmouk floodwaters would be stored in Lake Tiberias to irrigate Jordanian lands via a canal from Tiberias to Addasiyyeh. A study would also be made on the feasibility of building a large storage dam on the Hasbani River in Lebanon, for use of the water in that country. The Unified Plan allocated 720 million cubic metres of water a year to Jordan, 35 million cubic metres to Lebanon and 132 million cubic metres to Syria, with all the rest going to Israel. Therefore, Israel's allocation would vary every year, according to rainfall and run-off, but only after the specified allocations of the three Arab states had been assured. Israel's average annual supply of water from the Jordan River basin would be about 400 million cubic metres, according to the plan. But Israel insisted on receiving an assured supply of 550 million cubic metres a year, 400 million cubic metres of which would be diverted to the Negev.

It also wanted the states concerned to supervise the water-sharing project themselves, while the Arabs insisted on a strong international body to supervise implementation of the Unified Plan.

Thus by the autumn of 1955, agreement in principle on unified regional water development gave way to political disputes once again, which were complicated by an American desire that its proposed financing be linked to resettling of Palestinian refugees as part of the project, to which the Arabs objected. Neither the Arabs nor Israel formally endorsed the Unified Plan, though both sides' technical committees had agreed on its principles. After the Johnston talks collapsed inconclusively, both sides reverted to unilateral plans to tap the water resources of the Jordan River basin.

Israel fell back on its Lowdermilk-Hays-Cotton plans, based on diverting Jordan River water north of Lake Tiberias to flow by pipeline to meet the needs of central and southern Israel. The Huleh swamps were drained by 1956, and the system of north-south pipelines comprising the National Water Carrier was completed in the mid 1960s.

Jordan and Syria, for their part, focussed again on implementing their 1953 agreement on exploitation of the Yarmouk River. They deferred building the large Maqarin Dam because of financial constraints, and went ahead with partial diversion of the Yarmouk's flow to irrigate valley lands in the east bank of the Jordan River. Throughout the 1950s, the Israelis and the Arabs exchanged warnings and gunfire about the other tampering with the waters of the Jordan River basin. A few times, the matter reached the United Nations Security Council, and on other occasions tension would grip the region as border clashes erupted over unilateral diversion of the vital water resources. But work went ahead on different projects in all parts of the river basin.

Israel's unilateral diversion of Jordan River basin waters into its National Water Carrier system triggered angry calls for action throughout the Arab World, which were met by fresh pan-Arab proposals to tap the headwaters of the Jordan in Lebanon and Syria, before they ever entered Israeli territory.

In 1959, a Lebanese plan proposed diverting the Hasbani into the Litani River, which flowed totally through southern Lebanon. The Arab League's technical committee adopted the plan, which would have tapped 200 million cubic metres of water a year if both the Banias and Hasbani rivers were diverted northwards into the Litani. But denying Israel this water also meant depriving Jordan of *its* rightful share of the headwaters of the Jordan River basin. In November 1960, Jordan put forward a counter-proposal by which the waters of the Hasbani and Banias rivers would be diverted eastwards via a long open canal across south-western Syria, into the Wadi Raqqad and then into the Yarmouk River. A storage dam at Nahila, in Syria, would hold these diverted waters, while the joint Syrian-Jordanian Yarmouk Project of 1953 would be implemented in full, notably building the Maqarin Dam. This scheme would have diverted Arab water into Syria and Jordan before it could be tapped by Israel. The Arab League adopted the pan-Arab scheme, but it was never implemented.

Israel still pressed ahead with its own water projects, further angering Arab states for whom water was a strategic commodity in an arid part of the world. A special Arab Summit Conference convened in Cairo in January 1964 and appointed a new technical committee to come up with yet another pan-Arab scheme to counter the Israelis. This was quickly done; the proposed works included implementing the Hasbani-Banias diversion scheme outlined in 1960, and raising the level of the newly built East Ghor Canal to accept new supplies of water that would reach the valley from the diverted Jordan headwaters in Lebanon and Syria. This plan, like its predecessor four years previously, was also never implemented, mainly because of inter-Arab differences.

It became clear in the late fifties and early sixties that formal regional water-sharing schemes among Jordan, Syria, Lebanon and Israel would have to await a more propitious political climate. The Johnston negotiations, nevertheless, had established two important principles. All concerned parties agreed on the principle of riparian rights, by which every state was entitled to a share of river waters running through its territory or along its border, though they disagreed on the exact amounts allocated to each. And they proceeded with unilateral diversion projects based on a loose adherence to the water rights specified in Johnston's 1955 Unified Plan. The feeling both in the area and among involved American officials was that if an Arab-Israeli peace settlement one day allowed the implementation of a regional water project, the parties would inevitably return to the Unified Plan's principles and water quotas, at least as a starting point to resume negotiations.

By June 1955, Jordan had in hand the final Baker-Harza report on a master plan to irrigate the Jordan Valley, using the waters of the Yarmouk River. The massive eight-volume report represented two years of intensive fieldwork, and included the first comprehensive soil

Farmer demonstrates how plastic row tunnels can easily be handled by one person

analysis and land classification ever done for the entire valley, on both sides of the river. Its importance was that it gave the Jordanian government technical data that was imperative for any coherent attempt to develop the valley's agricultural potential.

The Baker-Harza master plan aimed to break the historical pattern of subsistence farming and pastoral nomadism by making efficient use of the Yarmouk, Jordan and side wadi waters to maximize agricultural production and raise the standard of living of valley residents by a big increase in family incomes. When the plan was presented in mid-1955, less than half the valley's arable land was irrigated, and about half of that went to produce cereals. There were 3,825 "farms", supporting a total (farm and non-farm) population of 57,000 people. The typical farming family's income was $190 a year, and the total annual net farming income of the entire valley was a mere $725,000.

The Baker-Harza master plan aimed big – in line with the long-known potential of the Jordan Valley's land, water and human resources, not to mention its climatic advantage and favourable geographic location relative to nearby markets. "The project represents major land and water resources which are now largely unused and wasted," the report noted, echoing Ionides' thoughts fifteen years previously. Its aims were to irrigate 514,000 dunums of land on both sides of the river, using 760 million cubic metres of water a year, half from the Yarmouk and the balance from the Jordan River, the side wadis and smaller springs. It recommended farm units of a minimum size between 15 and 26 dunums, depending on the soil quality, which would be irrigated for four hours every fifth day. Therefore, 26,875 new farm units would enter service at full development, supporting a farming population of 160,000, with tens of thousands of others working in non-farming jobs. The valley's total net agricultural income would rise from $725,000 a year to $14.2 million a year.

The premises of the Baker-Harza study were that Lake Tiberias would be used as a storage and regulating reservoir for Yarmouk water, supplementary storage dams would be built on the Yarmouk itself, and a gravity canal distribution system would deliver the water to farms throughout the valley. Its main features included: the Maqarin dam, with a gross capacity of 47 million cubic metres; a diversion dam at Addasiyyeh to direct water into Tiberias and into the East Ghor Canal; a feeder canal from Tiberias to the East Ghor Canal; the East Ghor Canal, running the length of the east bank, with an inverted siphon leading to a West Ghor Canal; a pumping system for 104,000 dunums of land above the main canals; and a system of laterals and drains for the individual farms. It was anticipated that building all the irrigation works would require twelve years, at a cost of $109 million.

Between 1940 and 1960, farming advanced in the valley thanks largely to two factors: the influx of agriculture-oriented Palestinian refugees, and the entrepreneurial impulses of prominent landowning Jordanian families. The area under cultivation increased, as farmers moved into the profitable new field of vegetable production. But reliance on the perennial flows of the side wadis remained dominant, and the business of farming continued to be held hostage to the vagaries of nature and rainfall. Technical proficiency and agricultural services were poor, as most people cultivated their land in the traditional manner they had learned from their fathers and grandfathers. The transition from subsistence farming to efficient, market-oriented agro-business was slow and erratic, but it had started to happen in the late 1940s. One of the pioneers of the Jordan Valley's transformation was Fayez Kamal, whose life story is something of a chronology of Jordanian agriculture. Like everybody else born in Salt

Wadi Jurum weir . . . typical of side wadi waterworks to control side wadi flows and feed the main canal

in 1918, Fayez Kamal faced an uncertain future. World War I had just ended, the Ottoman Empire was defeated and the British entered Jordan as the mandatory power, entrusted by the League of Nations with seeing the territory through to self-reliance and independence. Unlike most Jordanians, he completed primary school in 1932 and went with his brother Nabil to a missionary secondary school in Ramallah, Palestine. Upon graduating in 1935, he decided to attend an agricultural college, and secured the support of the British High Commissioner in Transjordan to enroll at the Khaddouri agricultural college in Tulkaram, also in Palestine. He graduated in 1939, but could not continue his studies in the United States as he had planned because of the outbreak of World War II. Therefore the twenty-one year-old would-be farmer stayed in Salt, and spent his days working with his father Issam, after a brief but frustrating four-month stint with the government's agricultural department in Amman at a salary of JD 12 ($40) per month.

Issam Kamal was a prominent Salt merchant, farmer and spirits maker. He owned large vineyards in the hills around Salt, and produced wine, cognac and the favourite Arab drink *arak*. He had once

The Jordan Valley

Typical plastic hothouse
Seedlings produced at vegetable nursery in South Shouneh

tried to make champagne, but failed and gave it up. In the early 1930s, Issam Kamal started buying up large tracts of land in the Jordan Valley, only about thirty kilometres down the dirt mountain track from Salt. At one point, he had owned 20,000 dunums, much of which he arranged to be cultivated by bedouin sharecroppers who wintered in the valley. The sharecroppers planted wheat and barley, and took eighty per cent of the crop, while Issam Kamal took twenty per cent. He had to pay an annual land tax of JD 800 ($2,500), while deriving an average annual income of JD 100 ($330) from his valley holdings. Those were the days when 120-kilogram wheat bags sold for 600 fils ($2), a goat cost 300 fils ($1) and a sheep 600 fils ($2). A few sharecroppers grew small plots of tomatoes and summer cucumbers, which were sent on donkeys to be sold to Salt residents who made and stored tomato paste for use in the winter months. Mostly, though, the Jordan Valley in the 1930s was an isolated, forgotten backwater of bedouins who farmed casually, lived in tents and relied on their goats, sheep, cows and camels for a livelihood. There were only a few exceptions to the rule. In Ghor Al Safi, south-east of the Dead Sea, tomato growing was picking up quickly, reflecting the influence of farmers from Hebron who first crossed into Transjordan as merchants. In the far north, a small religious community of Bahais at Addasiyyeh had grown irrigated vegetables since the 1920s. The Bahais, a religious sect that originated in Iran, believe that religious truth is progressive, not final; that God, the Almighty Father, educates the human race through a series of prophets who have appeared throughout history and will continue to appear to guide the destiny of mankind. These Divine Educators include Moses, Zoroaster, Buddha, Jesus Christ, Mohammad and Baha'ullah, the founder of the Bahai faith who declared his mission in Iran in 1844 and was executed in Tabriz in 1850, at the age of thirty-one. His followers and son Abdul Baha' brought his remains to Acca, in north Palestine, in 1909, and they founded the Bahai shrine at Haifa that remains to this day the world headquarters of the faith. A small community of Bahais soon afterwards settled in Addasiyyeh, where the two dozen Bahai families used Yarmouk waters to irrigate small fields of tomatoes, bananas, citrus, pomegranates, squash and eggplant. Their speciality was the dark "Ajami" (Persian) eggplant that still retains their name today.

Along the side wadis, a few farmers also irrigated small vegetable plots in the 1930s and 1940s, and some who could afford it planted small citrus and banana groves. Wheat and barley were the mainstay of Jordan Valley farming, however, with any excess produce more often than not being sold across the river, in the markets of Jerusalem and Nablus, and sometimes going as far as Haifa.

Fayez Kamal started going down to the valley with his father in the early 1940s, after a phylloxera epidemic wiped out the thriving grapes and wine industry around Salt. In 1940, the impatient Fayez asked his father for some land to cultivate on his own. He was given charge of a 500 dunum piece of land east of Amman, near Sahab village. Fayez travelled to Palestine and bought a steel plough from a Jewish farmer for JD 9 ($30), which he hooked up to two mules and used to plough his 500 dunums. For three years, he successfully planted wheat and barley, out-performing those farmers who stayed with their old wooden ploughs. Where water was available, a few farmers in the highlands planted small vegetable plots, particularly at Fuheis, Wadi Seer, Jerash and Zerqa. By 1944, flush with success, Fayez ordered a second-hand tractor from the United States for JD 300 ($1,000). It was delivered to Amman, where a taxi driver cousin was induced to learn the new business of tractor driving by being given a salary increase from JD 4 ($13) to JD 6 ($20) per month.

All along, Fayez had his eye on the family lands in the valley. His academic training and natural farming instincts convinced him that farming in the *ghor* could be a profitable business. In 1946, he asked his father to plant bananas in the valley on a large scale. He planted 200 dunums of bananas south of Arda Intersection, watered by earth channels from the Zerqa River. The Kamal family farmhouse, an imposing two-storey mud brick structure that still stands and is being used to this day, was built that year. It is the only two-storey mud brick house in the valley.

Two years later, hundreds of thousands of Palestinian refugees streamed across the river as the Palestine war of 1948 ran its course. That year was also historic in that it was the first time in recent memory that frost had ever hit the valley. Fayez and his father Issam woke up early one morning and were horrified to see their young trees covered in frost. The bananas were wiped out, and were quickly pulled out of the earth. Fayez pondered what to do with the huge quantities of manure that remained from the luckless banana plantation. He decided it was time to test the valley's potential for irrigated vegetable farming, and asked his father to replace part of the banana plots with tomatoes. Issam was dubious, and turned down the request. Fayez insisted, and finally threatened to leave for the United States if his father would not allow him to plant tomatoes. The threat

JVA test plots at Wadi Yabis

worked, and Issam told his eager son to go ahead. Fayez planted 50 dunums of tomatoes, using four sharecroppers who would take two thirds of the output. The experiment was an instant success. The tomato plot earned the Kamals JD 5000 ($10,000) after merchants from South Shouneh bought the tomatoes for JD 5 ($16) a box and sold them in the markets of Jerusalem, Amman and Salt. The next year, Fayez's father allowed him to plant 100 dunums of tomatoes, and from then on large-scale vegetable farming went on to embrace other kinds of produce in larger tracts of land.

In 1950, as vegetable farming in the valley spread under its own momentum, Fayez wanted to introduce another new technique: using machinery to grow wheat. He bought a tractor for JD 300 ($1000) from a Palestinian farmer in the West Bank village of Toubas, and drove it himself across the Damiyah bridge. He used it to plant 500 dunums of wheat, which produced 500 140 kg sacks of wheat. But there was one more technological barrier for Fayez to cross, which he did in 1951 when he brought into Jordan the country's first combine harvester. He paid JD 1,650 ($5,500) for a unit that was shipped in pieces from England, assembled in Amman and driven to the valley by a British technician who had come with it to see that it was properly assembled. Two days later, Fayez took over the driver's seat himself, and quickly taught some of his Jordanian farmhands to operate the machine. The mechanization of cereals farming, combined with the Kamals' success in irrigated vegetable production, allowed Fayez to institute a system of crop rotation and thereby achieve higher yields from the rich soil. By the early 1950s, the Kamal farm was exporting fresh fruits and vegetables to Baghdad, earning hundreds of thousands of dinars.

"We never used fertilizers or chemicals until the sixties," Fayez recalls today. "The land was virgin, and rich. It didn't need any help."

The Kamals relied totally on dependable water supplies from the Zerqa River, and perhaps were more fortunate than others whose water was less regular. The success of the Kamal farm, however, was the exception to the rule. A few other big landed families and tribes also irrigated large farms in the 1940s and 1950s, and sold their produce in nearby market cities in Palestine and Transjordan. But most life in the Jordan Valley still depended on cereal cultivation, inefficiently irrigated from the flow of the side wadis, and allied livestocking activity.

The Jordanian central government, in the fast-growing capital of Amman, was preoccupied in the late 1940s with the post-war realities of coping with the influx of half a million refugees to the East Bank and administering the West Bank that would soon be annexed into the enlarged Hashemite Kingdom of Jordan. Few officials had the time — and the national budget certainly lacked the money — to pay attention to fully developing the Jordan Valley. The logic of harnessing the valley's water resources for agricultural development was so obviously compelling, however, that a few simple and inexpensive projects started to be implemented in the closing days of the 1940s. These were basic diversion weirs and small concrete canals on the side wadis, designed to improve the efficiency of the farmers' existing earth channel irrigation networks by reducing water loss and more efficiently diverting side wadi waters to the cereal fields. The works were designed and implemented by the Department of Lands and Surveys' new irrigation section, which was established in 1947 by Mr Nicolai Simansky, a British colonial officer of White Russian origin who came to Jordan after having retired from service in the Sudan. He set up the irrigation section's offices in the valley at Addasiyyeh, renting a small basalt stone house from the Bahai community there to use as an office.

Reservoir of King Talal Dam, which is seen on the far right

Agricultural techniques were primitive. Simple diversion weirs and canals were built by packing mud in between stones, tree branches and shrubs, to direct the water into earth channels that led to the wheat and barley fields, which were flooded three or four times a year. Each heavy rain would wash out the irrigation systems, which had to be ponderously rebuilt.

The first scheme undertaken by Simansky and his young engineers in late 1949 was a concrete diversion weir and a stone and concrete canal on the south bank of Wadi Arab: a project that was outlined originally in Ionides' 1939 study. The diverted water flowed only a short way through the concrete canal, and then fed into the existing dirt channels. Between 1949 and 1956, the irrigation section built similar diversion weirs and concrete canals on most of the East Bank's important side wadis, including wadis Arab, Ziglab, Jurum, Kufranjeh, Zerqa, Rama, Kufrein and Shu'eib. All these works, however, were designed primarily to irrigate farms located above the projected East Ghor canal, whose construction had become imminent in the early 1950s. By 1954, the irrigation section was integrated into the Department of Public Works to form the new Department of Irrigation and Hydro-electric Power.

The next year, after the Johnston negotiations collapsed, and Israel continued its works to divert Jordan River waters, Jordan and Syria initiated studies to implement part of their previous 1953 agreement to exploit the Yarmouk River. While pan-Arab discussions and summits would continue to be held for the next ten years, and several ambitious Arab plans would be drawn up (but never implemented) to divert the headwaters of the Jordan River before they entered Israeli territory, Jordan found itself in the awkward position of having to suspend its long-held aspirations to develop the valley, which, after all, was totally in Jordanian territory. After some preliminary planning, the Jordanian government decided to go ahead with construction of a canal in only the eastern side of the valley, initially to be fed by diverting the free flow of the Yarmouk River. Syrian agreement was obtained once again, after some hesitation in Damascus about a project that would only benefit Jordan. By July 1956, the Department of Irrigation and Hydro-electric Power came up with an initial model plan for the canal, designed by Mr Simansky.

In 1957, and based on the land classification data of the Baker-Harza study, a group of Jordanian and American aid engineers joined forces to design and draw up construction specifications for the first phase of the East Ghor Canal. This was to be a 69 kilometre-long, concrete-lined gravity canal fed by a one-kilometre-long diversion tunnel running underneath the mountain between the Yarmouk River and the village of Addasiyyeh. The canal works were divided into three sections, each approximately twenty-three kilometres long, to irrigate a total of 117,000 dunums. Lateral concrete-lined channels would branch off the main canal to reach the farmlands. The distribution and drainage system would total seven hundred kilometres.

The Jordanian-American team designed the East Ghor Canal so that it could still be fed by a gravity canal from Lake Tiberias, if international politics ever allowed a regional water-sharing project to take shape in the Jordan River basin. A few hundred metres after the East Ghor Canal emerges from the Yarmouk diversion tunnel at Addasiyyeh, it drops sharply down a shute-like structure, from an elevation of -210 metres to -214. At the lower level, it can be fed by a gravity canal from Tiberias. If political conditions ever permit the implementation of decades'-old plans to use Lake Tiberias as a natural storage reservoir for Yarmouk waters to irrigate the Jordan Valley, the existing East Ghor Canal will be ready to play its role.

The United States agreed to finance the construction of the first section of the main canal. The Italian firm Imprese Vanete's low bid won it the construction contract, and it started excavating the Yarmouk-Addasiyyeh tunnel in November 1959, after Jordanian government crews had started digging the main canal. In 1960, the East Ghor Canal Authority was established to take charge of the canal works, as an agreement on further American aid financing allowed the Italian contractors to start work on the lateral canals' distribution system of section one. In the spring of 1961, another agreement with the American government provided financing for section two, and work got under way in May. By September 1961, section one of the canal was completed and entered operation. Sections two and three entered service in April 1964 and June 1966.

A Jordan Valley irrigation canal was finally built, after first being conceived in the mind of an Ottoman engineer named Georges Franghia, exactly fifty years before. A land redistribution scheme was launched in 1962 according to the terms of the East Ghor Law; its aim was to break up very large land holdings and allow more families to live off the rich land, whose productivity and value was significantly increased by the advent of the canal.

While the East Ghor Canal was being built in the early 1960s (under supervision of the new East Ghor Canal Authority), Jordanian planners once again turned their attention to long-term, complete development of the valley. This essentially meant harnessing the area's water resources by building one or more dams on the Yarmouk. Things had not changed very much in the twenty-five years since Ionides had written his report: the Yarmouk River was *still* "the sole substantial supply of new freeflow water in Transjordan," just as it had been in 1939. But while Ionides had envisaged Lake Tiberias as the logical storage reservoir for the Yarmouk's excess winter flow, the political impossibility of reaching agreement with Israel on a regional water-sharing scheme prompted Jordanian officials to think in terms of storing Yarmouk water in dams built astride the river on Jordanian and Syrian territory. In early 1963, the Yugoslav consultants Energoprojekt were commissioned to study the feasibility of building a 90 million cubic metre-capacity dam on the Yarmouk at Mukheibeh, just above the village of Himmeh. In July 1964, six months after the Arab summit had approved the financing and implementation of a pan-Arab plan to divert the Lebanese and Syrian headwaters of the Jordan River into the Yarmouk River, Energoprojekt were called in once again to study the feasibility of one or more larger dams on the Yarmouk. The diversion of the Banias and Hasbani rivers would add 100 million cubic metres a year to the Yarmouk's flow. Energoprojekt's report recommended irrigating 500,000 dunums of land on both sides of the valley by utilizing the net 660 million cubic metres of water a year available to the *ghor* from the combined flows of the Yarmouk, Banias and Hasbani rivers, and the side wadis on both banks of the Jordan River. It recommended building two dams: a 200 million cubic metre dam at Mukheibeh, and a 450 million cubic metre dam at Maqarin. After preliminary design studies for both dams were done, the Arab League decided to give priority to the smaller dam at Mukheibeh, which was named the Khaled Ibn Al Walid dam, after a famous seventh-century Islamic military leader.

To oversee the work and co-ordinate the pan-Arab diversion projects, the Jordan River and Tributaries Regional Corporation (JRTRC) was established in Amman in 1964. It took charge of raising the sides of the East Ghor Canal, to double its capacity from $10m^3$ to $20m^3$ per second (in anticipation of receiving the diverted headwaters from Syria), and later concentrated on building the King Talal Dam and other smaller dams on the side wadis. Energoprojekt

Aerial view of new housing scheme in southern part of the valley

completed the design work for Khaled Ibn Al Walid dam in 1966, when the JD 18 million ($60 million) construction contract was awarded to the Egyptian company Arab Contractors, owned by the prominent Egyptian businessman Osman Ahmad Osman. The earthfill dam would have a gross capacity of 200 million cubic metres, and a live capacity of 150 million cubic metres. It was seen as the first phase of a long-term plan to harness the valley's most important rivers and side wadis. The Yarmouk Project, including the two dams, was assigned top priority, followed by a smaller dam on the Zerqa River and another on Wadi Arab. Three other earthfill dams, each with a capacity of between two and five million cubic metres would also be built on wadis Ziglab, Kufrein and Shu'eib, thereby controlling all the important sources of water flowing into the Jordan Valley by the early 1980s.

Arab Contractors started work on Khaled Ibn Al Walid dam's foundation trench, diversion tunnel, grout gallery and irrigation tunnel in 1966–67. About twenty per cent of the work was completed, and the dam was expected to come into operation in the 1970–71 season. In June 1967, however, the development of the Jordan Valley would once again fall victim to Arab-Israeli hostilities. The June War resulted in the Israeli occupation of Syria's Golan Heights, which included the northern bank of the Yarmouk River, where work was proceeding on the new dam. Israeli occupation of Syrian territory brought all work on the Khaled Ibn Al Walid dam to a halt.

More importantly, the June War shattered the agricultural momentum that had been generated by the East Ghor Canal, the first land redistribution programme and the sustained investment of private capital in land improvement, farm machinery, chemical inputs and orchard planting. The canal had set off an unprecedented developmental spree, which was proving correct the projections of all the planners of the past half a century who had visions of transforming the valley into an agricultural wonderland. The advances that had taken place in the few years since the canal entered service were stunning; but all was now precariously balanced on the knife-edge of war and peace in the Middle East.

Chapter Six

The Promise Fulfilled

The entry into service of the East Ghor Canal in the early 1960s was the turning point in the modern history of the Jordan Valley. The canal quickly transformed the area from one of old-fashioned subsistence cereals farming to large-scale irrigated production of high-value, marketable fruits and vegetables. By assuring existing farmers a steady supply of water and bringing water to previously uncultivated parts of the valley, the canal would prove to be the most important organized, large-scale water system in five hundred years since the days of the Mamluk sugar industry. It provided the first real incentive for people to move into the valley from the highlands, to take up farming or man jobs in such expanding sectors as education, health, transport, retail trade and construction. The land redistribution programme initiated in 1962 started to reorganize the valley's haphazard land tenure into a more coherent pattern. This was based on the Baker-Harza and a World Bank mission's recommendations in 1955 of relatively small farms of 20–40 dunums each, capable of supporting an entire farming family while generating some surplus income for non-farm expenses. Not only did land redistribution reorganize the land into farm units that could be efficiently irrigated by the new canal; it also allowed more people to own and operate farms, thereby setting in motion the "social equity" theme of valley development that would become more prominent and more deliberate in the 1970s and '80s – the need to allow the greatest possible number of people to benefit from the agricultural advances taking place.

Law 31 of 1962, which is still the basis for land distribution, worked as follows:

- An owner of 30–50 irrigable dunums of land could keep them all;
- An owner of 51–100 dunums could keep 50 dunums plus 25 per cent of the area exceeding 50 dunums;

- An owner of 101–500 dunums could keep 62 dunums plus 17 per cent of the area exceeding 100 dunums;
- An owner of 501–1000 dunums could keep 130 dunums plus 12 per cent of the area exceeding 500 dunums;
- An owner of over 1000 dunums could keep 200 dunums.

Subsequent land redistribution laws promulgated in 1968, 1973 and 1977 kept the same basic allotments but increased the minimum farm size to 40 dunums, which is deemed more efficient for sprinkler irrigation. The law of 1962 distributed land in the following order of priority:
1. To farmers who own and cultivate their land;
2. To full-time, professional farmers in the East Ghor Canal project area;
3. To other professional farmers living in the same district, which includes residents outside the canal project;
4. To professional farmers living in other parts of the country;
5. To landless farmers who rent or sharecrop farms within the canal project.

Vegetable nursery in South Shouneh

The 1968 and 1973 laws maintained these priorities, but the 1977 law introduced two new changes. It raised sharecroppers and land leasers into second priority (from fifth), and assigned fifth priority to landowners living outside the country. Another important change in the law had allowed the state to allocate separate farm units to each individual in a family, whereas previously the entire family was considered as one landowner. The change meant that a farmer who had registered his lands in the names of his wife and children could, in theory, receive a farm unit for every member of the family. In practice, this allowed a few landowners to evade the full force and intent of the redistribution law by keeping more land in their family's name, as smaller units registered in the names of wives and children, than they would otherwise have been able to keep had their land been registered only in the name of the head of the family. In 1976, the JVA froze all land sales and transfers for the areas that would come under Stage II irrigation works, thereby largely preventing landowners in the southern part of the valley from evading the purpose of land redistribution by transferring land ownership deeds to their children's names.

The redistribution procedure is relatively simple. The JVA declares an irrigation area, within which all land transactions are subsequently frozen. A three-man evaluation committee (composed of a senior official of the Lands and Surveys Department and two JVA-nominated members) appraises and makes public the value of land, property and water rights for the irrigation area. The landowner has fifteen days within which to appeal the assessed value of his property to a three-man committee headed by a government-appointed Appeals Court judge and including two other JVA-nominated members, whose ruling is final. A third three-man committee, composed of two senior JVA officials and one experienced valley farmer, then chooses those who can buy farm units in the area, according to the priority order specified in the law.

The land redistribution programme for the East Ghor Canal, completed in two stages between 1963 and 1967, covered 96,000 dunums. Before redistribution 5304 farmers owned the land, of whom 4007 exercised their right to obtain farm units in the project area. Through redistribution, some 500 new farm owners had obtained 11,000 dunums of land; these were mostly landless share-croppers or wage labourers working in the valley, over ninety-five per cent of whom succeeded in profitably running their new lands. After the redistribution programme, the average land holding in the canal area had dropped from 43 dunums to 21.3 dunums. Only nineteen people (3.5 per cent of the population) owned farms larger than 150 dunums after redistribution, while ninety per cent of holdings were 90 dunums or smaller. Just over sixty per cent of farmers owned less than one unit (30 dunums) after redistribution, indicating the flexibility of Jordanian officials in implementing the law's unambiguous specification of 30 dunums as the minimum size for a single farm unit. The alternative was to dispossess several thousand small landowners who could not be allocated a full farm unit from excess lands relinquished by the large landowners.

In practice, the redistribution lands in the East Ghor Canal area were bought and resold to new owners for JD 40 per dunum for top quality land; the poorest land was valued at JD 8 per dunum. A new farmer buying land in the irrigation zone paid for it over twenty years, at an annual interest rate of four per cent. Thus the redistribution of lands considerably reduced the average size of land holdings, joint and fragmented holdings and the size-range of holdings, and brought in a modest number (500) of new farmers who could earn a comfortable living in the irrigated canal zone.

The East Ghor Canal quickly stimulated both qualitative and quantitative aspects of farming. Between 1959 and 1965, total agricultural production in all of Jordan more than doubled. Grains and field crops rose from 154,100 to 437,800 metric tons; vegetables increased from 350,900 to 582,500 tons; and fruit production increased from 112,300 to 218,800 tons. While it is difficult to specify exactly how much of the increase came from the valley, the lands in the East Ghor Canal region clearly accounted for the bulk of it. We can ascertain this from comparing the findings of several pre- and post-canal studies. UNRWA conducted a 1953 study entitled *Jordan Valley Agricultural Economic Survey*, and the Jordanian Department of Statistics in 1961 followed with *The East Jordan Valley, a Social and Economic Survey*. These two studies, with the Baker-Harza master plan, are the most reliable pre-canal sources of statistical information. They show that in 1953, the valley's 3,825 farms covered 260,000 dunums, of which 180,000 dunums were partially or totally irrigable though not all this land was actually cultivated. Total agricultural production in 1953 was 61,000 metric tons, and net agricultural income totalled JD 294,015 ($970,000). The 1961 study (covering the 1959–60 crop season) showed 3,341 farms covering 207,941 dunums, including all the farms in the canal area, of which 152,712 dunums were partially or totally irrigated. Total net agricultural income was

JD 466,272 ($1,538,700). Because farm sizes fluctuated so widely before land redistribution, a comparison of per dunum income is more telling than a per farm income analysis. The available data shows that the average net income per dunum in 1953 was JD 1.131 (gross income of JD 4.692 minus expenses of JD 3.561), while in 1960 it had increased to JD 2.242 (gross income of JD 3.757 minus expenses of JD 1.515).

Two post-canal sample studies were conducted by joint Jordanian-American research teams in 1965 and 1966. The first, covering a sample area of 2,450 dunums in the canal area, showed that net income per dunum had risen five-fold to JD 10.9 (gross income of JD 23.9 minus expenses of JD 13). If this per dunum income is extrapolated for the entire 117,000 dunums irrigated by the canal, net income for the canal project would have been around JD 1.265 million ($4.174 million).

The next year's study covered a sample of 120 farm units, totalling 4,063 dunums in the canal area. It showed an average net income per dunum of JD 13.6 (gross income of JD 28.8 minus expenses of JD 15.2). Thus in 1966 the entire East Ghor Canal's 117,000 dunums generated a net income of JD 1.592 million ($5.253 million).

These statistics must be taken cautiously, as they derive from disparate studies that measured different farm areas in years of widely fluctuating rainfall. They also used different methods to calculate net farming income (for example, the 1953 UNRWA study accounted for depreciation and taxes in calculating net income, while the 1961 Department of Statistics study did not). But the overall trend between the early 1950s and the mid-60s is clear: the East Ghor Canal substantially increased irrigated farmlands, total production and net income. The average net income per irrigated dunum of a Jordan Valley farmer increased more than twelve times from 1953 to 1966, rising from JD 1.1 to JD 13.6 ($3.63 to $44.88). The canal increased the area under *intensive* irrigation from 25,256 dunums to 103,000 dunums, according to an unpublished memorandum dated 20 February, 1967, prepared by Mr Abdul Wahab Awwad of the US AID team in Amman. Total agricultural production in the canal area increased from 61,000 to 108,360 metric tons between 1953 and 1966, while net agricultural income in the valley increased correspondingly from JD 294,015 ($970,000) to JD 1.592 million ($5.253 million).

The increased production was due to other factors besides greater area under irrigation, including less idle land, more double cropping, higher yields per dunum, better marketing practices, improved use of fertilizers and other chemicals, and increased availability of credit. The canal's impact proved the Baker-Harza forecasts of the early 1950s uncannily correct. Gross per dunum income in 1964–66 averaged JD 26.35, compared to JD 26.4 projected in the Baker-Harza master plan; net income per dunum was JD 12.2, compared to the forecast of JD 11.3.

The canal started to make a difference in the quality of life of residents who had lived in the valley for a long time, providing some extra income that could be spent on consumer goods or ploughed back into farming operations. After the 1967 war, all this was threatened with oblivion, as most of the valley's population abandoned homes and farms and fled to the safety of the eastern hills.

The post-war dangers of life in the Jordan Valley forced many long-time residents to rethink their priorities, to make the difficult choice between fleeing the area for the safer hills or staying on the family farm in the face of frequent Israeli artillery bombardments. Many remembered the Palestinian experience of 1947–48, when people who fled their homes during bouts of fighting were never allowed to return. Others simply had no alternative to farming as a

A fine crop from greenhouses in southern Valley

livelihood. If this meant braving the occasional battle, then so be it.

"The artillery fell like rain," recalls Abu Ghani, one of those who stayed. If there is an archetypal native son of the *ghor*, it is he – forty-three year-old Fahd Mreiwid Khaled, better known as Abu Ghani, whose ancestors have spent the last five hundred years in the Jordan Valley. His ancestors came to the area from the Arabian Peninsula in the Islamic era after the seventh century, and drifted in and out of the valley for several centuries. Generations later, three brothers (Khaled, Khalloud and Khaldoun) parted ways. Khalloud settled in Jenin, in Palestine. Khaldoun moved to Damascus, and Khaled made the Jordan Valley his home. He settled on a *tell*, a small natural mound, one kilometre west of the village of Deir Alla, in the centre of the valley. Ever since then, the mound has been known as Tell Khaled, and the small village that grew up around it is also called Khaled, attesting to the longevity of a family line deeply rooted in the valley earth. Khaled had a son named Mohammad, who in turn sired Abdullah, whose own son was also called Mohammad, the family tree continued down through the centuries with Sadr, Mheiwish, Fare', Mreiwid and in 1938, Fahd, or Abu Ghani. The entire 180-strong Khaled family lives in the valley, except for one cousin who moved to Jbeiha, near Amman, several years ago.

Abu Ghani lives right on top of Tell Khaled with his three wives and sixteen children, on the same spot where he was born in his family tent more than four decades ago. Like all other bedouins in the valley, the Khaleds grew some winter cereals and raised a four hundred-head herd of sheep, goats and cows. Abu Ghani was more fortunate than other children. Between the ages of six and fifteen, he received a basic education. Initially, this meant studying with the local *khatib*, the learned Islamic figure who delivered a sermon-like talk in the mosque every Friday. Before the first schools were built in the valley in the 1940s, the *khatiba* were responsible for educating those few children who persevered with their studies. Abu Ghani remembers the *khatib* coming to their home to teach the children Arabic, religion, mathematics, history and geography, for which he was paid JD 7 ($23) a month. The young Fahd entered a new nearby government school in the late 1940s, and graduated with a high school diploma in 1955. The next year, his father Mreiwid built a mud brick house alongside the traditional family tents, and it was around this time that Fahd and his brother Amer took over running the family farm, covering the land all around Tell Khaled. Mreiwid had inherited 900 dunums of land from his father Fare', which he passed on in full in the

Houseplants unit of farm in southern valley

mid-50s to his sons Fahd and Amer. Dirt canals from the Zerqa River irrigated cereal fields and small plots of tomatoes, peppers, beans, cucumbers, onions and potatoes. During peak work seasons, the Khaleds would hire six or seven labourers to help run the farm, paying them with one-quarter of the output. The 1948 Palestinian refugee influx provided ample supplies of seasonal agricultural workers, who gradually became entrenched in the *ghor* as sharecroppers.

When the East Ghor Canal was completed, the Khaled lands were redistributed. Of the family's 900 dunums, the two brothers kept 250 between them, relinquishing 650 dunums to the East Ghor Canal Authority against payment of nearly JD 30,000. Abu Ghani had married his first wife, a cousin named Jamila, in 1957; she gave birth to seven children. In 1962 he married his second wife Nabila, who produced five children, and in 1964 he married Widad, his third wife, who has given birth to four more sons and daughters. Three mud brick houses now sit atop Tell Khaled, each housing one of Abu Ghani's wives, though the old family goat's hair tent is still set up and used every summer. Working his 100 dunums, Abu Ghani has

The Jordan Valley

Spraying insecticides in Arda Intersection area

comfortably provided for his family, adding more rooms to his three houses, sending eight of his children to school so far, as each reaches school age, and marrying off two of his eldest daughters.

"The artillery fell like rain," says Abu Ghani, remembering the 1967 war and its aftermath. His brother Amer took his family and stayed in Jerash for a year, preferring the safety of the hills. But Abu Ghani stayed on Tell Khaled.

"We were not afraid, because we are only afraid of God," he says. "If you have to die, it is better to die in your own home, on your own land."

In the summer of 1968, he took the family to spend some time in Salt in a rented house, while he went every day to the valley to take care of the farm. "We felt like strangers in Salt, and returned to the valley after a month. Life in the *ghor* is like sitting in Jerusalem," he says, betraying veneration for both his family home and the Holy City. Later that year, he took a job with the Agricultural Marketing Organization and started drawing a monthly salary to supplement his farm earnings. He now works at the Arda grading and packing centre, where he stays two weeks before returning home for a week off.

New housing scheme for farmers and government employees in North Shouneh

Unlike other *ghor* natives, he is not afraid that his children will become so educated that they will leave the family and never return to the valley.

"If you don't have a pen in your hand today, you don't live properly," Abu Ghani comments about his children's education. "We don't need all the children to work on the farm; we have enough labourers these days. And I'm not worried if they leave Khaled to work elsewhere. If they find a good job that takes them somewhere else, I'm happy for them."

For Abu Ghani and his family, the JVA projects offer the prospect of a better future. He wants to buy two housing units for his oldest son, Ghani, and the younger Ibrahim and Sadr. Paying for the houses in instalments is a big attraction for him, and he thinks the price is right. The new cement room he added to his house on Tell Khaled in 1976 cost him JD 470 ($1,550); he figures a new house would cost him at least JD 800 ($2,640) per room. Thus a JVA-built house at JD 3,100 ($10,250) strikes him as a good buy, especially at payment terms he could never arrange himself to build his own home, and with the access to services that are available in the new villages. The Khaleds do not have electricity or drinking water in their home. Free domestic water is trucked in by the JVA, while the family pays for irrigation water that reaches its farm through the original East Ghor Canal distribution network of lateral concrete channels. A government clinic in the village of Khaled takes care of most medical needs, charging 300 fils ($1) per visit. A midwife from Sawalha, five kilometres away, comes to Tell Khaled to deliver all the babies.

Abu Ghani contracts with eight sharecroppers on a 50-50 basis to operate his 100-dunum farm, while he works at the Arda centre. Seasonal labourers, mostly local bedouins, help out during peak periods by spraying, picking and packing the vegetable crops. Brother Amer has built plastic hothouses on seven of his 150 dunums of land, but Abu Ghani looked into using plastic and found it too expensive. He is also dubious about sprinkler irrigation. "Few people will succeed with sprinklers," he predicts, "because they will either drown or dry out their plants." All in all, Abu Ghani says, it's easier to keep using the same old surface irrigation system that the Khaleds have practiced around their family *tell* for five hundred years.

For Abu Ghani and his family to remain in their home while artillery shells exploded all around them was not simply a courageous or obstinate act. It was affirmation of an economic and social reality: the indigenous valley natives had nowhere else to go.

The population of the Jordan Valley was long settled in its ways – cultivating the land, raising animals, trading a bit with merchants from the hills on both sides of the valley, and fearing only God. For Fahd Mreiwid Khaled to leave the ancestral *tell* and the adjacent village, both of which carried the family name, would have been an act of atavistic profanity and despair. Quite simply, Fahd Mreiwid Khaled, his three wives and a score of children *were* the Jordan Valley. They would find it hard to live anywhere else and make a living away from the land, even though in recent years they have had to earn some non-farm wage income to make ends meet. They lived in mud brick homes without electricity or running water, but could only endure one month in a rented house in the relative opulence of Salt. They were attached to the land in a way that few other people were in the rest of the country, anchored by a combination of profitable farming and a profound family legacy. They would remain in their home atop Tell Khaled, just as Mreiwid, Fare', Mheiwish, Sadr, Mohammad, Abdullah, Mohammad and Khaled had done before them.

Chapter Seven
Integrated Development: the bold experiment

The June 1967 war would prove to be another historic turning point, just as the 1948 Arab-Israeli war had been. Ironically, it was usually in the wake of a war that people in the area and beyond focussed their attention on developing the valley. There were a flurry of Anglo-French survey plans for the valley after World War I, and a series of major irrigation and power projects came forward after the 1948 war in Palestine. History, embodied in the human instinct for reconstruction and rehabilitation, would repeat itself in the Jordan Valley after the June war. The Jordanian government was soon to turn its attention once again to fully exploiting the valley's land, water and human resources to achieve maximum agricultural production. The planning process would be reactivated, but with one significant difference from past attempts: a comprehensive and integrated development plan would be implemented this time around, with the twin aims of increasing food production *and* providing a complete social service infrastructure to make the farming life in the valley an attractive proposition.

The 1967 war and its aftermath were a catastrophe for the Jordan Valley. Most of the pre-war population of 60,000 abandoned their homes, farms and businesses for the safety of the nearby eastern hills, or the cities of Salt, Amman and Irbid. No reliable statistics on damage to property and farmlands are available for the 1967-71 period, nor are there accurate studies about the number of people who fled the area, so it is difficult to draw a precise picture of how badly the valley suffered. Government officials and valley residents say that only about 4,000-5,000 people remained in the valley, braving the crossfire between Israel on the one hand and Jordanian army and Palestinian resistance forces on the other. Citrus farmers, who had the most to lose from neglecting their valuable plantations, dauntlessly returned to the valley from their hill sanctuaries every few days to water and care for their trees. Khalil Khayyat, Operations and Maintenance Manager of the East Ghor Canal, remained in the valley with his seven hundred employees throughout those chaotic years,

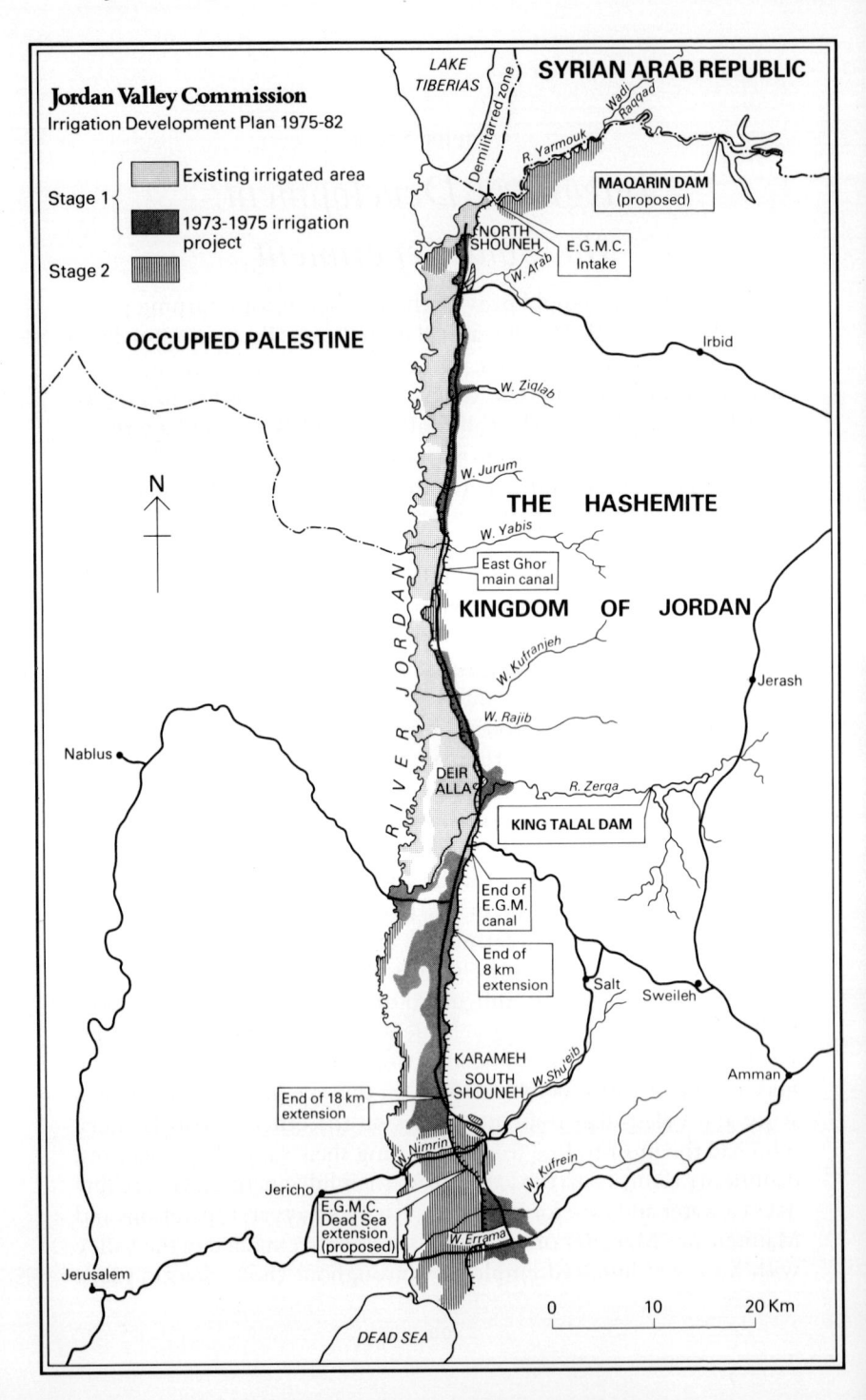

The Jordan Valley

Integrated Development: the bold experiment

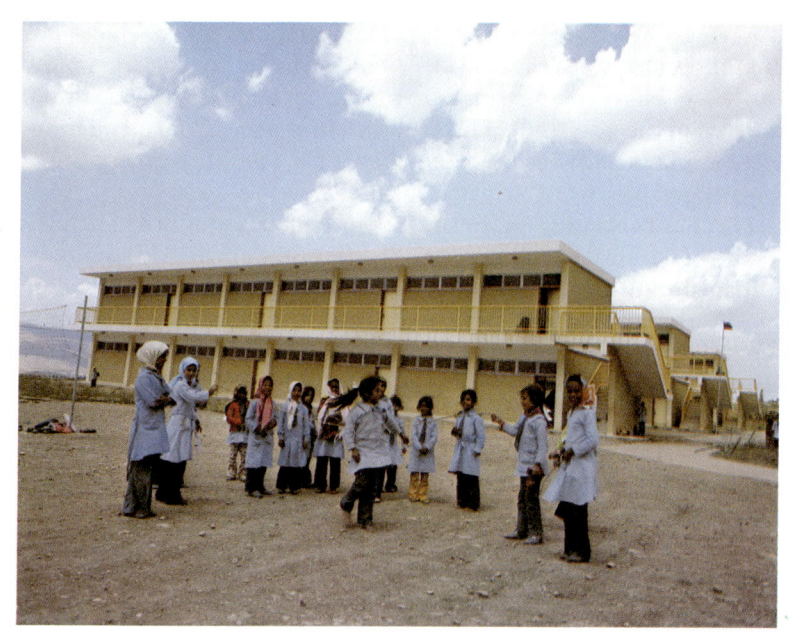

Girls' primary and secondary school at Kreimeh

keeping the canal in operation in the most difficult and dangerous of circumstances. Israeli units routinely bombed or mined the main canal and its many sub-structures. In the northern end of the valley, Khayyat recalls, the Israelis were quick to bomb the Jordanian side of the river to protect the Jewish colonies that had sprung up in northern Israel since 1948. The main canal was hit and knocked out of service on four separate occassions between June 1967 and August 1971. The twin-pipe inlet to the canal from the Yarmouk-Addasiyyeh diversion tunnel was damaged by shelling in 1969. One pipe was closed, while the second remained just 10 cm open, enough only to allow 1.3 cubic metres of water/second to flow into the canal. With the additional side wadi flows, the canal operated for a full month on 2 cubic metres/second, one-tenth of its normal capacity of 20 cubic metres/second. Crops were threatened with death from thirst. The Natural Resources Authority (NRA), which had been established in 1965 by amalgamating the East Ghor Canal Authority, the Central Water Authority and the minerals section of the Economy Ministry, and which operated the canal, had to decide quickly how to apportion the little amount of water that was flowing.

It gave priority to citrus and banana plantations (17,000 and 3,800 dunums respectively), whose loss would have been a shattering blow to the willingness of farmers to invest in long-term agricultural projects in the *ghor*. In practice, all the citrus and banana plantations were irrigated and saved, while only ten per cent of the area planted with vegetables was cultivated in the 1969–70 season.

For four frustrating years, the Jordan Valley languished, a helpless victim of regional hostilities. At the battle of Karameh in March 1968, Jordanian army and Palestinian resistance units jointly repulsed an Israeli armoured attack, inflicting heavy casualties on the invasion force. The victory was a major psychological boost to the entire Arab World, whose morale had hit a low point after the humiliating defeat in June 1967. But for the valley, Karameh was a catastrophe. It demolished buildings and homes throughout the south, while Israeli aerial napalm and phosphorus attacks ravaged thousands of dunums of prime land.

The NRA personnel kept the canal operating as best they could, despite its being knocked out by Israeli artillery and the repair crews themselves being shelled while carrying out repair work. As even

JVA engineer inspects drip irrigation wire inside a large plastic hothouse

routine maintenance became more hazardous, the canal started silting up. Providing farmers with irrigation water became a daily struggle. As if the Arab-Israeli conflict was not enough, internal clashes between Jordanian and Palestinian forces in 1970–71 extended the period of turmoil in the valley. It was only in the early autumn of 1971 that a semblance of calm returned to the area, and people started drifting back down to assess the damage. Individual farmers usually returned first to see if they still had a home, and if they could start planting for the 1971–72 season. Their families followed soon after, and then labourers returned to the market towns of North Shouneh, Wadi Yabis, Sawalha and South Shouneh, to pick up whatever work was available. Just as had happened in the aftermath of the 1948 war in Palestine, the 1967 war resulted in another mass influx of Palestinian refugees into the East Bank. At least 300,000 crossed the bridges over the Jordan River, with about half remaining in emergency camps first set up throughout the valley. During the post-war border clashes, most of the Palestinians also fled to the hills, but some came back down in late 1971 looking for jobs. Most of them, like their 1948 predecessors, were from agricultural villages in Palestine, and they instinctively looked to the valley as a source of work and income. Immense pressures were felt by the government in Amman to alleviate the social and economic burdens caused by the dislocation of so many people. National production plummeted, investment was frozen and basic infrastructural services were woefully overburdened. The West Bank had accounted for forty-five per cent of Jordan's GNP in 1966, and one-quarter of the country's cultivated area, even though it made up only six per cent of its total area. In the agricultural sector, it had accounted for sixty-five per cent of all vegetable output, sixty per cent of fruits, thirty per cent of cereals and eighty per cent of olives.

The efforts to revitalize the national economy immediately after the war started showing results in 1969; GNP increased by fifteen per cent that year compared with each of the two previous years, while gross capital formation — the measure of productive investments — rose to JD 39.3 million ($130 million) compared with JD 26.5 million ($88 million) in 1967. Total exports regained their 1966 level, and imports rose sharply, reflecting the need to feed the suddenly expanded population. Production in all sectors of the economy surpassed pre-war levels. Even in agriculture, thanks to good rainfall, the 1969 harvest was worth JD 41.5 million ($137 million). Once again Jordan seemed to be bouncing back from a severe shock that had paralysed its development momentum. But there was one exception to the rule: the Jordan Valley. The country's plateau-based cereals production in 1969 had increased by about sixty-five per cent over pre-war levels; but the fruits and vegetables output in the Jordan Valley that year decreased, as the destructive after-effects of the June War continued to be felt. When calm was restored in late 1971, government planners immediately looked to the valley as a priority area for rehabilitation and development. Here was Jordan's only hope for increased food production, large-scale employment and a quick increase in exports, with the resulting favourable effect on the national balance of trade and payments.

The 1965 agricultural census had shown a total of 440,000 irrigable dunums of farmland in all of Jordan; 300,000 dunums were in the Jordan Valley, on both banks of the river. According to a report presented to the government by the Dutch-Lebanese consortium of Netherlands Engineering Consultants (NEDECO) and Dar al Handasah Consulting Engineers, in the 1965-66 season vegetables accounted for fifty-three per cent of the total cropped area in the valley, while cereals had dropped to second place (forty-four per cent) and fruit trees took up only three per cent of the land. The NEDECO-Dar al Handasah study, commissioned one year before the June War, on 26 June, 1966, was handed in in April 1969. It recommended setting up an all-powerful institution to be called the Jordan Valley Authority, to irrigate 481,000 dunums on both sides of the river, using all the 720 million cubic metres of water a year it estimated as the average net water available (excluding groundwater) for irrigation in the valley. It also recommended maintaining farm sizes of 30-40 dunums, which ideally would be owned and operated by a single family. Thus when the post-war planning effort had gotten under way once again, officials had the NEDECO-Dar al Handasah study available as a starting point for discussion.

In the late summer of 1971, several meetings were held at the National Planning Council (NPC) to formulate a tentative plan for the valley, by identifying only the most general requirements of rehabilitation in such areas as manpower, projects and equipment. No effort was made to estimate financial costs, which would have to wait for a more detailed plan of action. The NPC committee could only list the order of priorities of the immense task at hand. NPC Secretary General Dr Hanna Odeh, a member of the team who was later to become President of the NPC, notes that pre-1967 work in the valley had always been done by individual ministries, working indepen-

Integrated Development: the bold experiment

Sharecropper and daughter in greenhouse in Masri Intersection area in Central Valley
Library at boys' secondary school in North Shouneh

dently of one another. The NPC itself had no direct role in the area before the June War beyond lining up finance for large, expensive projects. Whatever development had taken place in the valley had a very narrow focus. The Ministry of Education built a few schools; the Ministry of Health opened some clinics; the Ministry of Public Works paved parts of the main road; the NRA operated the canal. But nowhere did the isolated efforts of government ministries and departments converge into a meaningful whole, either to anticipate or assess the impact of their work on the standard of living of the itinerant population of nomadic bedouin farmers, seasonal labourers, directionless Palestinian refugees and the handful of large landed families.

The preliminary planning committee, like its many foreign predecessors, drew up a plan in late 1971 that was purely technical, covering engineering works for water, land rehabilitation, housing and infrastructural projects. The committee realized its own narrow focus, Dr Odeh says, and asked itself a few major questions about where the valley was heading, and the purpose of formulating a development plan.

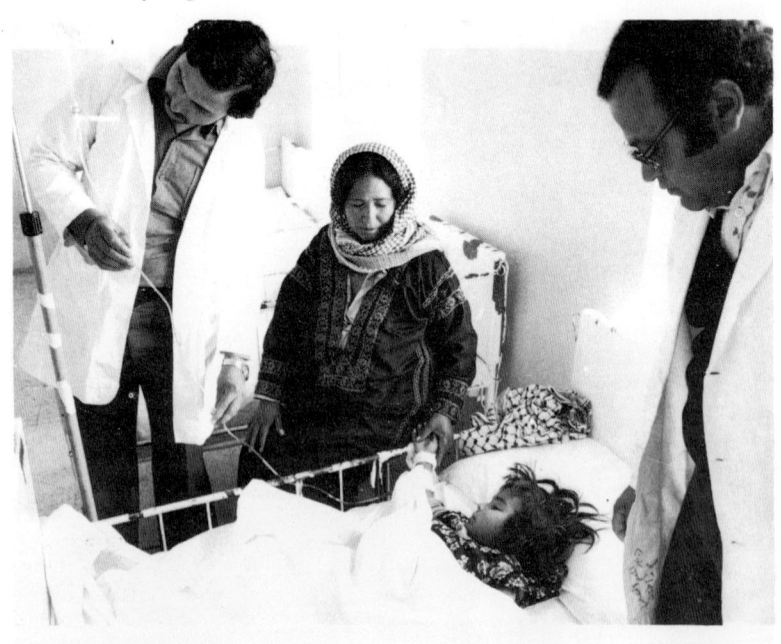

Doctors with young burn-victim and her mother at Wadi Yabis Hospital

"We came up with a first draft that was geared to engineering and technical work, and only then did we ask where all of this work was supposed to lead us. We had reviewed all the previous plans of foreign consultants, and realized that there had never been any balance in those plans. All had assumed that everything else would follow the technical work, that if you built a canal or a road or an irrigation network, the standard of living of the area would increase by itself. We thought this assumption was not valid, based on the experience of the early 1960s; the East Ghor canal then had raised agricultural production and income, but little else happened afterwards to raise the social standards of the area's inhabitants."

The Prime Minister reviewed the preliminary plan outlines and appointed a committee in late 1971 to formulate a detailed and definitive plan for the Jordan Valley. The six-man committee was chaired by Dr Hanna Odeh, and included representatives of the NRA, the ministries of agriculture and municipal and rural affairs, the Jordan River and Tributaries Regional Corporation and the Royal Scientific Society. Its mandate was to formulate a plan that would restore activity in the valley to its pre-war level, while laying the groundwork for more long-term developments, as had been envisaged when work started in the early and mid-1960s on the Khaled Ibn al Walid dam and raising the main canal.

It was about this time that the young Crown Prince Hassan, twenty-three year-old Oxford University graduate, took a direct interest in the valley's planning effort. Since returning to Jordan on the first plane into the country after the June War (a June 18, 1967, flight that had to land at the small northern airport at Mafraq, because Amman airport was still out of service), the Crown Prince had been at the centre of the hectic post-war development effort. It could hardly even be called a reconstruction effort, because the continuing destruction caused by the border clashes with Israel, the demographic pressures of hundreds of thousands of refugees from Palestine and the chaos of mass internal displacements hardly allowed the government to do anything but try to meet day-to-day basic needs. Prince Hassan had been appointed Crown Prince by his elder brother, King Hussein, in 1965, and that year made a tour of every major town and village in the country. The first development project he inaugurated as Crown Prince was the Ziglab dam, which he visited with the king in 1966. As a child, he and his brothers and sister used to spend much of each winter with their parents at the family farm at South Shouneh. The smell and contrast of the valley were sensations that remained vivid in his mind throughout his adolescence. When he was mandated by the king three weeks after the June War to take responsibility for the social and economic development of the country, his mind immediately turned to the Jordan Valley.

According to both Dr Hanna Odeh and Omar Abdullah Dokhgan, who were at the focal point of the valley planning drive then, Crown Prince Hassan provided both the conceptual ideas for an integrated plan and the top-level political support to sustain it through its various levels of formation, adoption and implementation. Six years later, he would once again provide the crucial backing to transform the Jordan Valley Commission into the all-powerful Jordan Valley Authority, despite the narrow vested interests of individual ministries and departments. Crown Prince Hassan recalls today:

"It was crucial to our credibility to get the valley back into productive shape. I remember visiting the World Bank in 1971 and trying to raise support for Jordan on the basis of our past track record, and effectively the comment of Mr Robert McNamara (the World Bank President) was that we had to restore credibility before becoming eligible for loans. I remember distinctly that the World

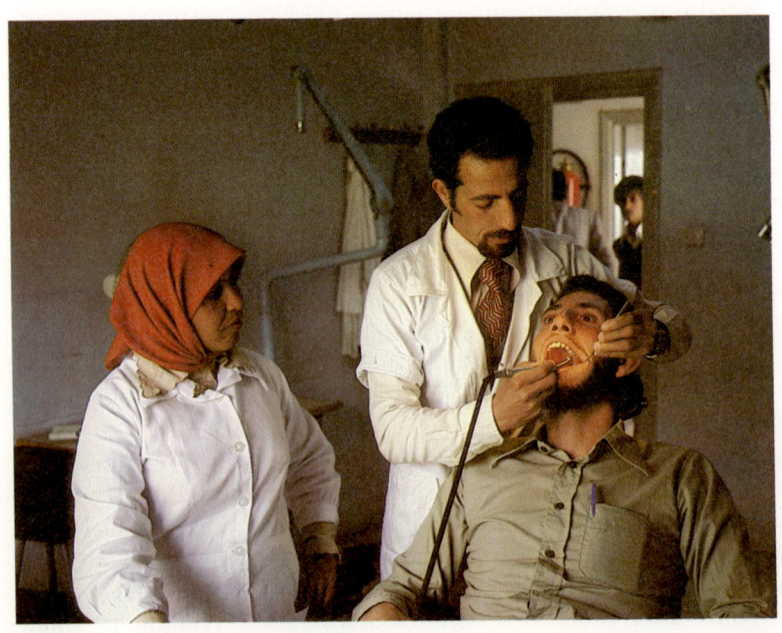

Dental clinic at North Shouneh

Bank had just provided Israel with a considerable loan, something like $30–$40 million, for its flower exports, and yet Jordan's previous credibility was not considered as significant. In addition there was the threat, as verbalized by members of parliament in Western Europe and the United States, that assistance to refugees should be terminated because the refugee camps had been the breeding grounds of unrest in the 1967–71 period. The reality was that after 1967 over 300,000 people had been sent over the bridges, and I recall being actively involved in the building of illogically sited, spontaneously chosen refugee camps throughout the country. But always at the back of one's mind there was the need for an alternative, especially after one saw a deliberate attempt by the Israelis to depopulate the valley. That was not only in the north and centre, but also in the southern sector, as evidenced by an Israeli incursion into Ghor Al Safi. Our challenge was to repeat earlier examples of well planned agriculture in the valley while proving to the world that we were not interested in dole for its own sake, and to prove to ourselves that despite the tremendous psychological trauma of the 1967 period – when really it was impossible to get people to think constructively again – that we were able to take physical control of our own destinies. One of the things that irritated me tremendously was to stumble across a plan developed by the International Labour Organization, a ten-year development plan for Jordan that made particular reference to the valley. I felt to a certain extent that this kind of approach was overlooking the ability of the country to plan for itself, because our growth from 1967 to 1970 had obviously come down to zero and because we were living hand-to-mouth. That an international organization should make such an effort was obviously a clear indication that our own ability to plan was in question. It was a combination of these factors that started what I would call our parallel approach to chaos. While one couldn't do very much other than firefight, I was coming back on many evenings from visits outside Amman and talking to our planners, most of whom didn't have anything to do other than just worry about the future. From those worries about the future came the seeds of the three-year development plan (1973–75), the Jordan Valley Commission concept, the development of the Royal Scientific Society, and others. Given the restoration of stability after 1971, these things were ready to go, and much faster than we had expected. In the period from 1971 to 1975, we were able to raise something in the neighbourhood of JD 600 million ($2 billion) in development investment, from both private and public sector sources, while in 1971 the World Bank was not prepared to give us assistance of any kind because of our lack of credibility."

The agricultural potential of the valley took top priority in reactivating the national economy. But in 1971, the country's planners were also looking at the valley as a prototype of what could later take place in other parts of the country. Crown Prince Hassan says today:

"The entire rift valley, from the Yarmouk River through the potash project site and down to Aqaba as an outlet to the sea, was considered as the main productive trunk of the country in terms of planning. To achieve a demographic presence there, to thwart the attempts of Israelis to depopulate that area leading to direct military intervention across the river, to achieve a level of parity in economic development in what was obviously the most self-generating of projects in the long run, to give hope to the people there that there was an alternative to hand-to-mouth existence, these were all part of the challenge. We regarded the valley as not only rewarding to its own inhabitants, but also as the focal point on which our entire indigenous planning concepts could succeed. As a model of pulling together an inter-disciplinary Jordanian team, the valley provides us with possibly the only live, open-air classroom of our own, to inspire regional planners working in the other three or four regions of the country where the planning initiatives today are not being taken by us so much as they are by the foreign counterparts we've called in. In terms of administrative concepts of local governments and regional approaches, whereby fulltime participation by civil servants and technicians with the people in changing their patterns and modes of thinking is invited, in addition to the organization of the people themselves — to meet with 120 valley university graduates and to feel that they are interested in changing modes of thinking is a very healthy sign — all of these elements make of the valley a major qualitative breakthrough."

"The second half of 1971 was the turning point in the development strategy for the Jordan Valley," Dr Odeh says. This was when the concept of integrated development first took root. It was conceived in the minds of Crown Prince Hassan and the NPC's preliminary planning committee in 1971 as an antidote to the narrow irrigation-only focus of previous programmes. It would be born less than one year later, formally embodied in the 135-page report submitted to the cabinet in June 1972, entitled *A Plan for Rehabilitation and Development of the Jordan Valley.*

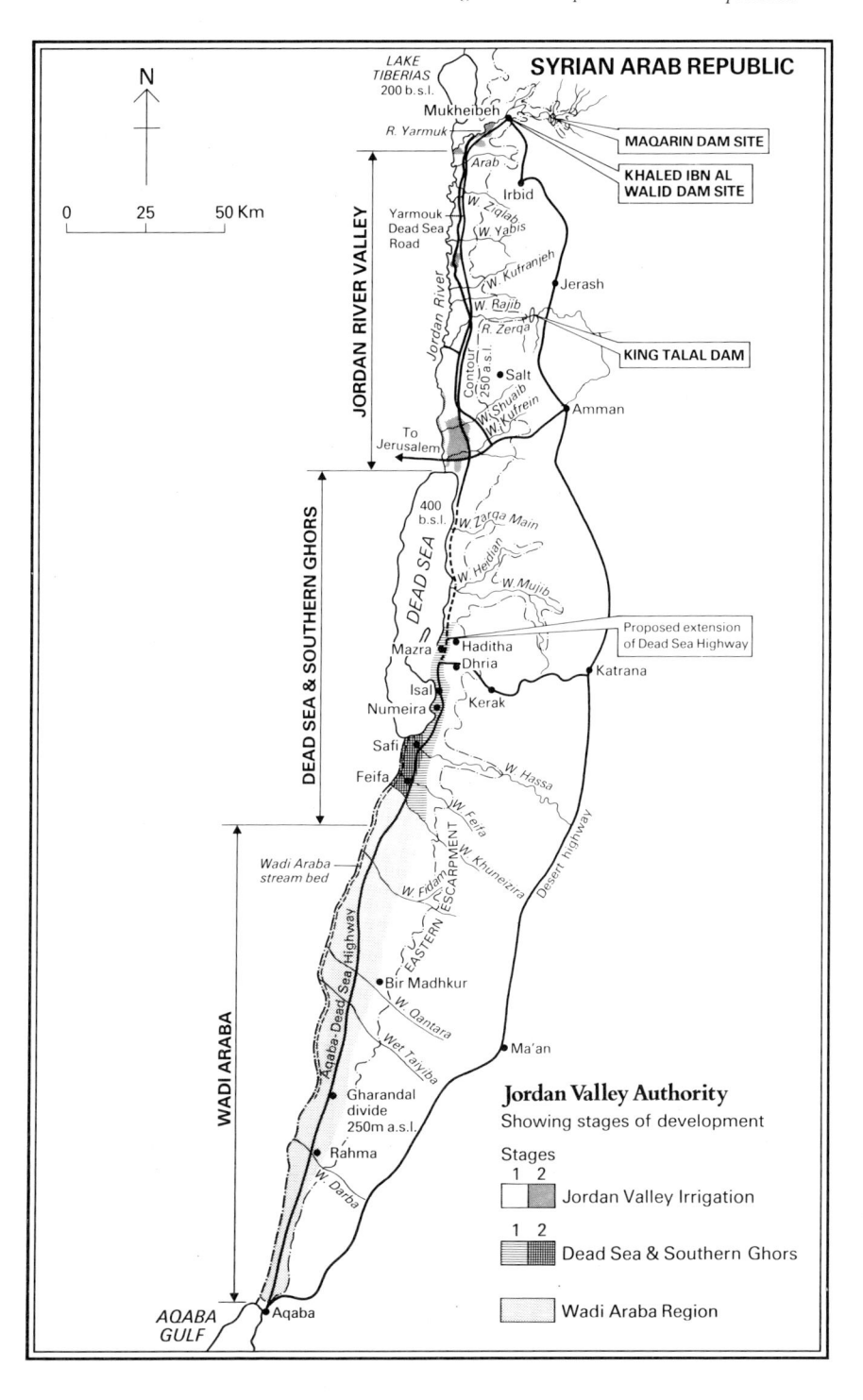

Integrated Development: the bold experiment

Wadi Jurum weir

The six-man committee estimated, discussed and finalized anticipated requirements in the three sectors of land resources and irrigation, agricultural development and social development. Within three months, it completed the draft report of a three-year plan. Its priorities were already dictated by circumstances. Suspension of the Yarmouk project (Khalid Ibn Al Walid dam) shifted attention to harnessing other water resources wholly in Jordanian territory; this meant using the Zerqa River and side wadis to irrigate lands below the eight-kilometre extension of the East Ghor Canal that had been initiated in 1968, and other farms above the main canal. The plan envisaged spending JD 25 million ($83 million) over three years, of which JD 14 million ($46 million) was to rehabilitate existing irrigation works and expand irrigated farming areas by another 76,000 dunums; 48,000 dunums of these would be irrigated by the new King Talal Dam on the Zerqa River. Planning for the dam had started in 1968; final designs were completed in 1970 by Energoprojekt, and Planum Zemun contractors of Yugoslavia began construction in January 1972. The Kuwait Fund for Arab Economic Development had provided a JD 5.1 million ($17 million) loan for the dam and allied irrigation works.

Besides irrigation schemes, the committee's plan called for social services to meet the projected expansion of the valley's population from 40,000 in early 1972 to 120,000 in 1975, and to 156,000 upon full development of the Yarmouk project. It proposed five "regional centres" (type A villages) of 10,000–15,000 population each, at North Shouneh, Wadi Yabis, Arda, Karameh and South Shouneh. These would have full social services, including schools, water supply, electricity, health centres, roads, community centres, government office complexes and slaughter houses. Smaller farm communities (types B and C villages) would spring up throughout the valley, but would look to these five centres for their basic needs. The social services projects would cost JD 5.4 million ($18 million).

The third component of the plan, agricultural services, envisaged spending JD 5.49 million ($18.2 million) for research and extension services, land improvement, equipment servicing, marketing, afforestation, agricultural credit, farm management and feasibility studies for future projects.

The integrated approach had never been attempted before in the country, and quickly confronted the planners with the problem of how to implement such a broad scope programme. Hanna Odeh recalls: "We had many concepts that were new and had never been tried in Jordan. We knew we had to establish some kind of new organization to administer the plan, but we had no previous experience in integrated development to fall back on. The EGCA had a narrow focus of running the canal and redistributing land. The NRA was also sectoral in its approach. We had to create something new."

The NPC's report noted innocently that "it is expected that the requisite organizational structure will be drawn up in the very near future," but in fact nobody had any clear idea of what that would be.

"We looked on the first plan as the cornerstone for a development strategy that would be detailed later on," Dr Odeh says, "but we still were not sure if what we were coming up with was realistic, if we were on the right track." Therefore in early 1972 the NPC had asked the US AID office in Amman to send a team of specialists to review the plan with the Jordanians who were still formulating it. The four-man mission arrived in February 1972, stayed for five weeks, and participated actively in formulating the plan's guidelines and reviewing its basic tenets. The final plan document was presented to the cabinet in June 1972.

The cabinet reviewed the NPC plan and decided in principle to go ahead with it. But detailed studies were needed to validate its basic assumptions and to come up with more accurate technical designs and cost estimates. The government appointed a three-man Jordan Valley Committee to complete this task, and to formulate a definitive Jordan Valley development plan that would be presented to the king for his approval. The committee included Budget Director Farhi Obeid and the NPC's Dr Hanna Odeh; it was chaired by the minister of agriculture, a veteran of Jordanian water and agricultural affairs named Omar Abdullah Dokhgan. He had been with the irrigation department in the mid-50s, which was amalgamated into the Central Water Authority (CWA) in 1960. The CWA was headed by an American engineer, with Omar Abdullah Dokhgan as his deputy. In 1965, when the CWA and the East Ghor Canal Authority merged to form the Natural Resources Authority (NRA), he was named Director-General, and effectively ran the NRA because formally its president was the prime minister. In 1970 he became agriculture minister, and already had considerable personal knowledge of the Jordan Valley by the time he was picked to head the Jordan Valley Committee in 1972.

The task before the committee required a seemingly incongruous combination of applying common sense and navigating uncharted territory. Omar Abdullah Dokhgan recalls today: "The integrated development concept was being advocated all over the world in the early seventies, and we'd discussed the idea of self-contained regional plans in Jordan with United Nations experts in the mid-sixties. The technical studies for water works, irrigation, cropping patterns, agricultural services and increasing yields were available. This had all been studied and restudied many times during the previous two decades. But never had anybody made a thorough study of the social services needs of the Jordan Valley, and certainly nobody had ever tried simultaneously to formulate and implement large-scale projects in both fields. There was no precedent for organized rural development in the valley. Before 1967, some foreign aid and government funds went to individual projects, but there was always a functional division of responsibility among different government agencies."

The plan, largely based on the NPC rehabilitation programme, was finalized in October 1972, and presented to King Hussein for his approval in the same month. Though nominally the result of eighteen months of urgent work, it was in fact the culmination of over half a century of separate, intermittent attempts to marshal the total resources of the Jordan Valley for maximum food production, economic benefits and human development. It went a significant step further than all previous plans in its integration of social services with irrigation and agricultural projects – and therefore it would prove more complicated to implement than other plans that had preceded it.

The thick, telephone-book-like plan document of three hundred pages was entitled *Rehabilitation and Development Plan of the Jordan Valley (East Bank): 1973–1975*. Like its NPC predecessor, it was divided into three sections: irrigation, agriculture and social services. The preface stated that the task of formulating the plan "consisted of preparation of sub-projects in various disciplines, to the preliminary design stages, and the co-ordination of their implementation programme so that harmonious and synchronized results could be obtained."

To rehabilitate the valley to its pre-1967 status and also set in motion future developments, the plan envisaged spending JD 31.179 million ($103 million) over three years. Over half (JD 16.16 million, or $53 million) was earmarked for new irrigation works for 80,471 dunums of land, and repairing existing irrigation systems for 124,397 dunums. The biggest scheme was the Zerqa River Project, which included the King Talal Dam and an irrigation network covering 48,171 dunums south of the river. Smaller projects on six of the major side wadis in the north (Arab, Ziglab, Jurum, Kufranjeh, Rajib and the northern side of Wadi Zerqa) would irrigate 24,410 dunums. In the south, the flows of wadis Shu'eib, Kufrein and Hisban would be controlled to irrigate 7,890 dunums. Other projects included rehabilitating the East Ghor Canal, drainage facilities for 14,665 dunums, flood protection works for thirty kilometres of river banks, land grading, groundwater exploration, and a feasibility study for a dam on Wadi Arab.

Agricultural sector projects estimated to cost JD 2.9 million ($9.6 million) were divided into six areas:

1 *Research and extension:* a comprehensive socio-economic census of the valley, production economics studies, marketing studies, analysing the feasibility of agro-industries, farm management extension, research into soils, irrigation, field and industrial crops, vegetables and fruit trees, plant protection and livestock, and development of the agriculture ministry extension services by increasing the number of extension agents from six to thirty-eight and locating them in three offices spanning the length of the valley.

2 *Development of veterinary services:* five veterinary centres to be

established in the valley and staffed by a total of thirty-eight people. The facilities proposed were to be operated by the private sector and supported by the government.

3 *Agricultural marketing development:* three agricultural grading and packing centres to be set up, where produce also would be auctioned to wholesalers.

4 *Agricultural credit:* the Agricultural Credit Corporation would expand its activities in the valley by opening new offices, adding staff and increasing its lending, which had almost come to a halt between 1967 and 1971.

5 *Co-operative development:* the Jordan Co-operative Organization (JCO) would establish five large multi-purpose co-operatives and their branches providing members with credit, marketing, procurement and agricultural processing facilities. A co-operative association would be set up in the valley to provide marketing, importing and co-ordinating activities for the separate co-ops. Other co-ops were contemplated for consumers, loans and savings, traders, women's handicrafts and schools.

6 *Erosion, soil conservation and afforestation:* 60,000 dunums in the catchment area of King Talal Dam to be afforested to protect the dam against too much sedimentation. The government would build nurseries to provide seedlings for private tree plantings.

The social services sector takes up half the plan document, and JD 12 million ($40 million), or thirty-nine per cent of total expenditures. Its rationale was that the influx of people returning to the valley and new residents who would be attracted there by the prospects of a decent farming life would require properly organized communities to meet their basic needs. The plan projected the valley's population would increase from 65,000 before 1967 to 130,000 in 1975 and to 150,000 in 1980; these estimates proved to be wildly over-optimistic, but in the hopeful days of mid-1972, when Jordan was starting to get back on its feet after five years of warfare and domestic chaos, they were thought to be realistic. One of the problems in planning for social services was, in the words of Dr Odeh, "a very small information base, to put it very mildly." He says the plan team scoured all corners of the government bureaucracy to come up with accurate statistics about the scope and condition of existing services in the Jordan Valley, an area which Amman-based government bureaucrats had visited rarely, if at all, during the previous five years.

What the planners could gather painted a depressing picture. More than sixty per cent of the houses in the valley were destroyed during

Integrated Development: the bold experiment

and after the 1967 war, and partially damaged structures deteriorated due to a lack of maintenance or repair. Even before June 1967, existing social services were minimal. These included thirty elementary and intermediate schools with a total enrolment of 4,838 students: three secondary schools with 844 students; twelve primitive clinics visited periodically by government doctors; locally generated electricity and drinking water only in North and South Shouneh and Karameh refugee camp. The rest of the valley's residents drank from ill-maintained wells or the irrigation canals, both of which were a health menace, causing intestinal disorder in more than half the population. There was not a single hospital in the entire valley.

The plan assumed that it was reasonable for farmers to walk or ride a maximum of three kilometres between home and farm. By grouping together in one village the families of 140–200 30-dunum farm units, (between 1,500 and 3,000 persons) the government could provide them with basic social services in a planned community near their land.

Crafts class in girls' secondary school in Kreimeh

The Jordan Valley

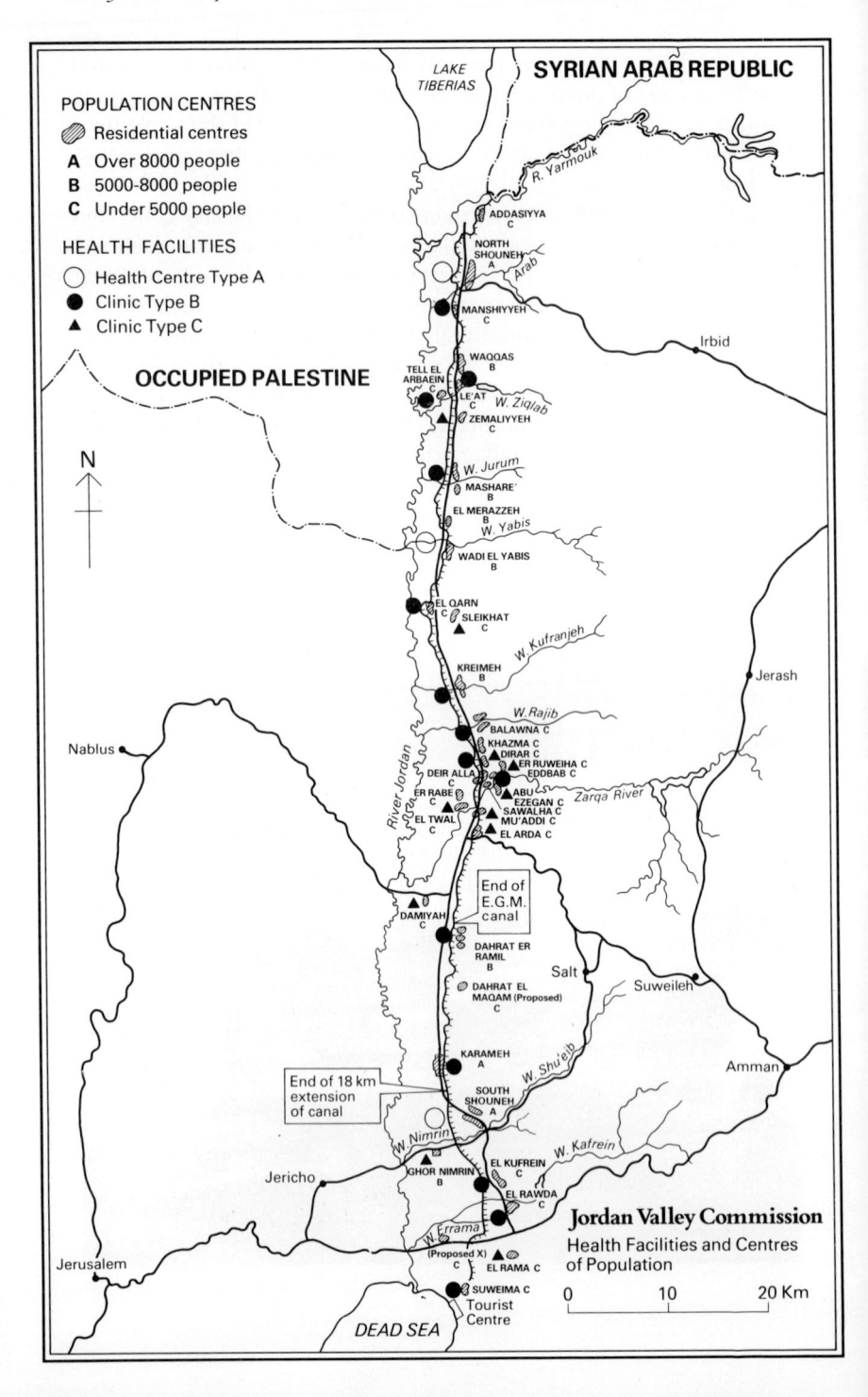

On this basis, and siting villages on non-cultivable land, the plan outlined the following social services:

1 **Regional villages and town planning** – Five type A villages would be established at North Shouneh, Wadi Yabis, Arda Intersection, Karameh and South Shouneh, each accommodating 10,000–15,000 people. They would have schools, health centres, commercial centres, government office complexes, transport and communications facilities, parks and places of worship. Six type B villages would be established, each with a population of 5,000–7,000. They would act as centres serving clusters of an unspecified number of smaller type C villages, and would have services higher than type C but lower than type A. Whenever possible, existing villages would be chosen for new town developments, except if they were located on agricultural land.

2 **Roads** – Road transport is the primary means of transport into and within the valley, for both people and produce. To handle the anticipated increase in traffic, the plan proposed rehabilitating the main Addasiyyeh-Dead Sea road by a combination of reconstruction, widening and resurfacing. The dirt service road running adjacent to the East Ghor Canal would be graded, gravelled and asphalted. Ninety kilometres of farm roads running along the canal laterals would be gravelled and asphalted, and another 250 kilometres would only be regravelled. The 2.5 km road to Ziglab Dam would be asphalted.

3 **Electricity** – Anticipating widespread new demand for power for domestic, institutional and irrigation (pumping) requirements, the plan called for three 33-KV power lines entering the valley at North Shouneh, Kreimeh and South Shouneh, from where spur lines would reach all villages. Some power would also be produced at South Shouneh, by expanding the existing diesel generator from 216 KW to 3966 KW.

4 **Domestic water supply** – The projected population of 130,000 people in 1975 would require 13,000 cubic metres of drinking water per day. The plan anticipated meeting this need by constructing five projects delivering well and spring water to all villages. The projects would be at 'Ain Zahar springs and Tabaqat Fahl (Wadi Jurum) springs in the north, Wadi Subeira and Wadi Rajib wells in the centre of the valley, and Wadi Jarei'a wells in the south, serving a total of forty villages.

5 **Telecommunications** – The existing telephone network in the valley consisted of single overhead copper lines connecting North Shouneh with Irbid, Deir Alla with Salt, and South Shouneh with Salt; an open-wire two-channel rural carrier system connecting South Shouneh with Amman; and an independent single overhead line system run by the NRA exclusively for operation and maintenance of the canal. The rudimentary network was of poor quality, unreliable and totally inadequate. A call from North to South Shouneh had to pass through Irbid and Amman. The Plan proposed a 100 kilometre-long main underground cable connecting North and South Shouneh, with separate exchanges in all villages ultimately providing automatic telephoning facilities within reach of all residents. The intra-valley network would connect with the national telephone system via two suspended cables between North Shouneh and Irbid and between South Shouneh and Salt.

6 **Schools** – The plan calculated new school requirements on the basis of 25,300 students in 1975. The total area of new school facilities to be built was 36,850 square metres, with 4,100 square metres of existing facilities still suitable for use.

7 **Health centres** – Three separate types of health centres were designed, corresponding to types A, B and C villages. Type A centres, covering 588 square metres included a pharmacy, dental clinic, maternity and child care centre, store, outpatient clinic, registry, laboratory, administration rooms, minor operating unit and 8–12 beds for emergency cases. Type B centres, 290 square metres each, included an outpatient clinic, maternity unit, pharmacy and stores, while the 70-square-metre C centres were simple first aid units.

8 **Administrative centres** – These also corresponded to the three village sizes. Type A centres (1,300 square metres) housed the local government seat offices of the national ministries and government departments and a judicial court. Type B and C centres, each 250 square metres, included the local governor's office, an agricultural extension office, a post office and a library.

9 **Commercial centres** – They were intended to house private shops and businesses. Only preliminary designs were made for cost estimates. Ten centres of 200 square metres each would be located in type A villages. Type B villages would have five centres of 200 square metres each, and type C villages would have four centres of 160 square metres each.

10 **Streets and parking areas** – The plan excluded parking areas and kept village roads to a minimum during the 1973–75 construction period. It assumed that home-building burdens would preclude residents being able to finance street and parking area construction, while paved streets would not be needed initially because the major type of traffic expected during the three-year construction phase would be heavy machinery. Therefore the plan included only gravelled main streets, graded ring roads for type A and B settlements, and road bed grading for feeder and local streets in all villages.

11 **Slaughter houses** – These were provided only for type A and B villages. The plan included 11 slaughter houses of 120 square metres each, of which three already existed.

12 **Agricultural school** – One agricultural school was proposed covering a 300-dunum plot in the East Ghor Canal project area.

13 **Housing** – The plan anticipated a total of 20,096 families living in the valley by 1975; but it decided against a large-scale, crash programme to build houses for them all in the three-year plan period, preferring a gradual housing build-up over many years. The village plans allocated 300 square metres for each family, of which 100 square metres would be taken up by a house. Several house designs were prepared and studied. The design chosen consisted of four rooms, a kitchen and bathroom, covering 95 square metres. Various building materials were also considered, including the traditional mud bricks made from clay and straw. Roofing materials considered included mud-covered bamboo and timber, asbestos corrugated sheets and mud-covered galvanized sheets. The final design used hollow concrete bricks for load-bearing walls, solid thin concrete bricks for partitions and a thin reinforced concrete roof. The reasons for this combination of materials, the plan explained, were that aggregate and other construction materials were locally available; the farmers themselves could easily handle concrete bricks to build the walls; bricks are less subject to damage; maintenance requirements are minimal; and the farmers themselves indicated a strong preference for brick construction. The plan was based on constructing a simple house with two rooms, kitchen and bathroom, light steel doors and windows, but without plumbing, electrical wiring or outside or inside plastering, at a total cost of JD 568 ($1,875) per house. The owner, typically a farmer, would finish it at his own pace and cost, choosing his own materials. The additional finishing cost was

The Jordan Valley

Graduation ceremony for secondary schoolgirls at Deir Alla
Aerial view of new housing scheme at Karameh village

estimated at JD 220 ($725). He would also decide himself on whether or not to add on the two other rooms.

Houses for government employees, to be totally finished before being turned over to their occupants, would include electrical and plumbing fixtures. This 95 square-metre house would cost JD 1,900 ($6,270).

The plan proposed an initial self-help programme, whereby the farmers would be given the construction materials free but would provide labour and build the houses themselves. If the farmer wanted a larger house, he could borrow money from the government and repay it on soft-loan terms over a long period of time, which the plan did not specify. Initial plans called for 5,000 houses built on a self-help basis, and 500 houses for government employees.

Compiling the three-year plan and having it approved by the government started a bold new phase in the 10,000 year-old human history of the Jordan Valley. Twenty years earlier, the East Ghor Canal had already induced a sharp break with the past, by providing the base for large-scale, intensive, year-round irrigation of fruits and vegetables to be marketed outside the valley. In 1972, the elusive process of "development" was being taken forward another large, qualitative step. The object and measure of planning became the human being, where it had once only been dunums of land, tons of tomatoes or millions of dinars in exports. But as all the planners of the past had already discovered, implementing a plan was considerably more difficult than preparing it. It would be the same in 1972. Unbeknown to the young team of Jordanian officials who had put in more than a year of work on it, the Jordan Valley plan would remain ink on paper for another two frustrating years.

The immediate problem, foreshadowed in the preliminary NPC plan, was how to devise and establish an administrative structure to implement all the projects. The previous NPC plan had evaded this task, and so did the new plan. During subsequent meetings at the end of 1972, the NPC, Prime Minister Ahmad Lawzi and Crown Prince Hassan, among other senior government officials, agreed that something new was required. The existing government machinery had neither the experience nor the time to pay adequate attention to the ambitious programme that had just been formulated for the Jordan Valley. Every government ministry and department was busy enough with its own sector's rehabilitation work after the 1970–71 fighting in the country. The 1973–75 national plan for socio-economic development – the first since the early 60s – was on the verge of being launched. The time and talent of the country's most efficient civil servants were already overtaxed. Throwing the valley projects on their shoulders would have been an act of irresponsible naiveté. By the end of 1972, the idea of an all-embracing Jordan Valley Commission (JVC) had been discussed and accepted as the most feasible solution. Once again, Omar Abdullah Dokhgan was tapped to head the new body. He resigned as Minister of Agriculture and immediately started work on writing the JVC law. He says, in retrospect: "Though we had to write the Jordan Valley Commission law from scratch, the idea of a single organization to co-ordinate all activity in the Jordan Valley had been proposed and discussed informally as early as 1959, when we were first working on the East Ghor Canal. In 1972, we thought the JVC would be a temporary institution that would dissolve itself after its work was finished. From the start, its duties were only to construct projects and turn them over to other government agencies to operate and maintain. The JVC would only have a small full-time staff of specialists who would be supported by technical personnel seconded from existing ministries and government departments. We thought we could get a few engineers from the health ministry, for example, design the health centres in the plan, award and supervise implementation of the construction and equipping contracts, and then turn over the completed projects to the health ministry to operate."

Cucumbers are loaded for transport to Sawalha market

The JVC law would have to break new ground, establishing a "super-ministry" with more authority than individual ministries. The JVC required full authority over all aspects of life in the valley, and therefore had to usurp powers from existing government agencies, while staying in their good graces to maintain a healthy working relationship.

"It was no simple thing to take power from another ministry," Omar Abdullah Dokhgan says. "We had to be tactful and patient; we had to put up with and overcome their objections."

The JVC law was as comprehensive as it was clear: "The Jordan Valley Commission shall be responsible for the economic and social development of the Jordan Valley, and may construct and carry out to achieve the said goal, including the repair and supply of materials to public and private construction, study, design and execution of irrigation, agriculture and domestic water projects, town planning, housing, roads, communications, electricity networks, processing and marketing of agricultural products, establishment of public services, health, social, educational and touristic services centres and others."

It also prohibited any private construction that was not licensed by the JVC, effectively giving it total authority over every aspect of life in the valley.

The law was completed and immediately approved by the government in January 1973. With the publication of its law in the Official Gazette, the Jordan Valley Commission was formally established on 1 February, 1973, and quickly got off to an inauspicious start. In its first days, it proved to be an institution built more on hope and high ideals than on a practical understanding of what was required to bring to life the last fifty years of grandiose development plans for the Jordan Valley. The JVC, which consisted of Omar Abdullah Dokhgan, used the offices and underworked staff of the JRTRC, in its building near Third Circle, Jabal Amman. In September 1973, the JVC moved into its own premises, in the present JVA headquarters in Jabal Amman. Its aim to implement the 1973–75 plan in the proposed three years quickly fell victim to over-ambitious scheduling and a series of unanticipated, simultaneous regional and international developments.

The valley's rehabilitation and development plan was purely a Jordanian effort, whose only foreign input was the US AID mission of advisers that helped review the NPC's preliminary plan in February 1972. One year later, the JVC started work on the assumption that seventy-five per cent of the plan's cost of JD 31 million ($103 million) would come from foreign donors, in the form of grants and soft loans. The donors required far more detailed feasibility and design studies than were included in the plan document, and therefore the JVC had to undertake a new series of studies to justify its projects to prospective foreign donors. This delayed most projects by a year or more. Even where the JVC did its own feasibility and design studies, such as for the main highway, the Zerqa Triangle Project, and the eighteen-kilometre extension of the canal, lining up foreign financing set back the work at least one year.

Almost all the technical help the JVC had counted on from other government agencies failed to materialize. The Water Supply Corporation was unable to take charge of the domestic water project. The Public Works Ministry did not have the spare capacity to design and build all the roads and schools. The Ministry of Municipal and Rural Affairs lacked the expertise to come up with masterplans for the new villages. Those ministries that had the expertise to help did not have the spare capacity to free several engineers to work exclusively on the development of the Jordan Valley. The demand on their services from other parts of the country had already stretched their resources thin. Revitalizing Jordan's main cities, industries, transport and communications networks and social services was the task of the day in 1972–73. The JVC realized very quickly that it would have to do most of the work itself, or contract it out to foreign and local consultants. This meant quickly increasing its own small staff, and lining up financing to pay for consultancy work. By the end of 1975, JVC had a staff of sixty people, which reached 1,200 when it became the JVA in May 1977.

"We looked around to see what other ministries could help us with, and saw that they all had their hands full," recalls Dr Munther Haddadin, JVA Senior Vice-President who had joined the JVC in May 1973. Not only did the JVC have to add to its own technical personnel, but it had to master project implementation techniques that were beyond the normal responsibilities of engineers. The first day after Dr Haddadin joined the JVC from his previous post at the Royal Scientific Society's computer department, Omar Abdullah Dokhgan piled a handful of thick documents on his desk and asked him to study them. They were manuals outlining the conditions that had to be met by recipients of German Capital Aid funds.

"We needed people with managerial skills, knowledge of donors' rules and an ability to handle the complexities of the integrated

Laden trucks leave from open market at Sawalha heading for export markets in neighbouring Arab countries

approach, which required co-ordinating many different aspects of several projects at one time," says Dr Haddadin. "Our engineers needed more than just technical expertise, and the only way that we could obtain this was on the job. We threw ourselves into the work and learned as we went along."

Some government agencies did play their assigned roles. JVC delegated the Jordan Electricity Authority from the start to design the electrification project jointly with the West German consultants Lahmeyer International, and to handle tendering and construction supervision work on behalf of the JVC, whose only role was to provide the money. The Public Works Ministry designed the improvement of the main highway and supervised construction, with some assistance from the American consultants DeLeuw Cather International. Ministries that did not extend design and contracting assistance still had to provide the JVC with specifications for equipment, layout and facilities. The Education Ministry, delighted to have someone else design, pay for and build fifty-five new schools, eagerly co-operated from the very beginning. Some other ministries were less forthcoming. One took much longer than anticipated to give JVC specifications for some vital equipment and furnishings, and after one cabinet change the new minister complained about the designs approved by his predecessor. JVC officials often had to resort to personal contacts, asking their friends in different ministries to speed up the work that normal bureaucratic channels had held up. One person in each ministry involved in the valley plan was appointed to a permanent co-ordinating team that sought to keep all the projects moving together. One of the attractions of the integrated approach, in the minds of JVC officials, was that it would prevent any one or two sectors from lagging behind. But the other side of the coin prevailed; a delay in one project set off a chain reaction that held back several others. If electrification work was behind schedule, power would not be available on time to run the pumps that had to be in place for some irrigation schemes that were vital to attract families who wanted to live in the new villages. An error in one project invariably set back the entire plan, and taught the JVC to move more cautiously and to think in terms of a more reasonable time frame. The three-year target, by now seen as hopelessly beyond reach, was made even more so by a sharp increase in international prices. The plan was based on 1972 prices and included provisions for reasonable price escalation of five to ten per cent a year. But the eighteen-month delay that hit the JVC pushed it into the thick of the global inflationary spiral that followed OPEC's oil price increases of 1973–74. The cumulative increase in the costs of construction materials, labour, transport and machinery, coupled with the need for more detailed studies by the JVC's own staff, doubled and tripled initial price estimates. This forced a new search for international financing, which in turn required the hiring of more consultants to do the feasibility studies required by foreign donors. The man who lead the search for foreign aid was NPC President Dr Hanna Odeh: "In the 60s and early 70s, we usually got international financing based on very preliminary studies that we had done ourselves. When we were raising finance for the valley projects, our preliminary work was not enough. We had to go back and do more studies, and in that time the cost of a project went up very much. We ended up adopting a new approach in 1974 that has since applied to all projects in Jordan. We identify a project and complete a detailed feasibility study *before* approaching potential donors. This way, the time needed to line up the financing is drastically reduced, and the actual cost of the work is very close to what would have been projected in the feasibility study."

The JVC also ran into unexpected problems in awarding contracts.

The first village development tenders for schools, health clinics and government administration buildings were too small to attract bids from big international contractors. Only a few local contractors submitted bids, which were fifty per cent costlier than anticipated. Construction bids, for example, came in at JD 96 ($317) per square metre of covered area, whilst the JVC had anticipated bids of JD 45 ($148) per square metre. The JVC then repackaged its work, grouping several small contracts into one larger project, which attracted bids from South Korean contractors. After several tenders were floated, Shin Seung Corporation of South Korea won the $16 million contract for Phase I village development in early 1977 at a cost of JD 62 ($205) per metre of roofed construction, compared to the initial local bids of JD 95 ($314) per metre.

Another delaying factor was the inability to conduct thorough ground surveys for the proposed village development works. By November 1973, the JVC had received the final report on village planning and housing from the American consultants Planning and Development Collaborative International (Padco), which included detailed designs for three villages (Damiyah, Dahrat Al Raml and Arda). The basic concept of how thirty to forty villages in the valley would be developed was clear by this time. The JVC eventually selected thirty-six villages to accommodate the population at full development, and were eager to press on with work inside the village boundaries. Before the proposed municipal areas could be divided into housing plots to be sold to farmers, a thorough ground and air survey was required of every village site. The Lands and Surveys Department had its hands full throughout the rest of the country, while the status of the valley as a military zone required time-consuming security audit and censorship of all photographs for aerial surveys. The JVC had given top priority to the village development programme and was anxious to get a credible housing programme under way, after the failure of self-help housing schemes in Damiyah. The lack of surveys meant the JVC could neither build houses itself nor sell plots to farmers to build their own. Within two years, continued delays in the village development programme would prod the JVC to build over 2,000 houses itself to get the village housing schemes moving.

The fact that the JVC had to assume responsibility for projects in which it had no previous expertise also caused delays which, in the inflationary years of 1974–76, meant large cost increases. The initial plan had projected the cost of each agricultural grading, packing and

Aerial view of Arda grading, packing and marketing centre

marketing centre at JD 60,000 ($198,000). The Arda centre, which entered service in 1980, ended up costing JD 1.4 million ($4.6 million), or twenty-three times the original estimate. When the JVC started to design the centre, Dr Haddadin says, "we realized that we had no idea of what such a centre required to function properly. We had to send people abroad to visit other such centres, to find out what they were all about and how they operated. When we finally learned, we saw that we had badly underestimated what was needed to build and operate such centres."

Crown Prince Hassan recalls: "The main difficulty was that the government in Amman, given the financial constraints of the time, found it difficult to give support to valley projects. Consequently, a valley project had to be self-indicating. Provided the technical credibility of projects presented to foreign donors was clear, then the government did not ask too many questions, and basically regarded the criteria set by foreign donors as satisfactory."

"The second problem is one that relates to long-term planning as against band-aid solutions. When destruction was rife in the valley, requests always came for an immediate show of resolve in re-

Tomato grading and packing at Arda centre

constructing what had been destroyed. An example of that was Karameh. An Arab committee was formed to reconstruct Karameh; unfortunately, emotions didn't go very far and the new Karameh never emerged. It was the reconstruction of Dahrat Al Raml and other such logically sited villages that appears to have gained ground."

The most significant result of the lessons of 1973–75 was the transformation of the Jordan Valley Commission from a planning, financing, co-ordination and supervision body into a design, construction, operation and maintenance agency. It found itself responsible for all phases of a project, from initial identification, to pre- and final feasibility studies, design work, arranging financing, prequalifying contractors, tendering and awarding construction contracts, supervising construction, commissioning, and, finally, taking on operation and maintenance.

The end of the planning stage in Amman coincided with the start of a process of consultation and discussion to exchange ideas with, and explain the development plans to, the valley's residents. Omar Abdullah Dokhgan thought then that little formal consultation was

The Jordan Valley

Housing at Kreimeh village
Science class in boys' secondary school in North Shouneh

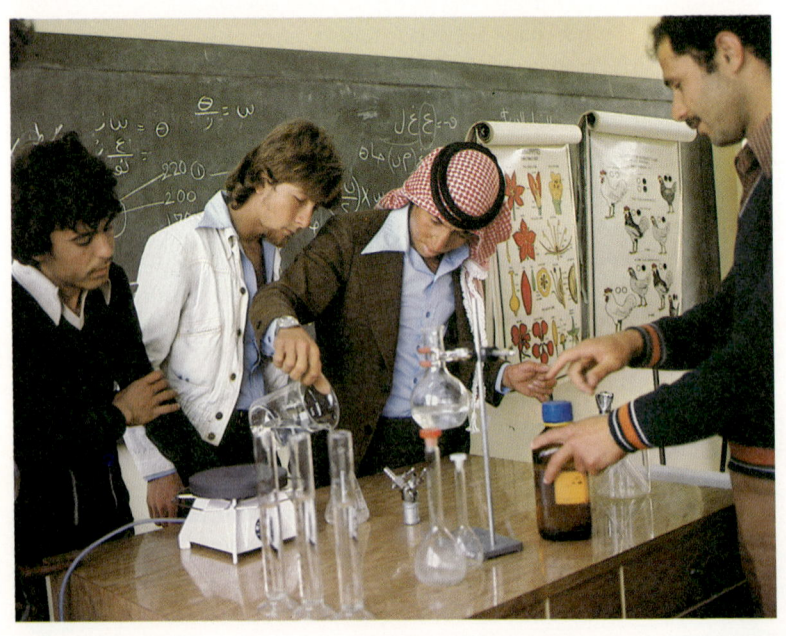

necessary because the required work was obvious. Basic human needs had to be met, which meant providing 'housing, schools, health services, water, power and roads. There was nothing complex about assessing the people's needs. "We had worked in the valley for several decades," he says, "we knew each other very well, we had been in constant contact and we knew their needs."

In early 1973, he and Dr Munther Haddadin, sometimes joined by Crown Prince Hassan, made several trips a week to consult with the farmers in the valley. The JVC plans were posted in public places for all to see and discuss. Open meetings were arranged with the *mukhtars*, or village leaders, often taking place in the few schools that existed to allow the greatest number of people to participate.

"They nodded their heads a lot and told us they'd heard the same thing before many times," Dr Haddadin recalls. "We wanted feedback from them about the specific facilities that we were going to provide. They were beneficiaries of these social services, and they had to comment about them. We were faced with great scepticism; they'd all heard government promises before, but saw little follow-up. They were used to running after the government in Amman to get the most rudimentary social services, and here we were telling them we were going to build them schools, houses, roads, clinics, and water and electricity systems. They didn't believe us."

Crown Prince Hassan adds: "The idea of dialogue and give-and-take was not fully developed at that time. Meetings that took place in the valley were basically with local *mukhtars* and village councils. Their requests were piecemeal, naturally enough, rather than being part of an overall concept, which was being developed by the planners and took into consideration immediate needs of the various communities."

Outside the valley, the JVC adopted a low-key approach, generating little publicity so as not to raise expectations too quickly. The give-and-take sessions with the valley residents resulted in several changes. Four villages were added to the plan (Maisara, Twal, Dayyat and Rama), and the locations of some secondary schools were shifted to suit villagers' convenience. More generally, the JVC formulated an order of priorities for its projects, though this depended on who was consulted. A mother wants a school in the village so her children will not have to walk along the main road to the next village. A farmer wants a new irrigation system. A young school graduate contemplating marriage wants a new house to live in. In the social services sector, it became clear that electricity and water were the people's two top priorities, followed by schools and health clinics, and improved roads. Social services were so bad in 1972 that anything new would be an improvement over the *status quo*. The JVC assumed – wrongly, it turned out – that housing was the immediate concern of most residents. In early 1973, it initiated a self-help housing scheme at Damiyah village, which had been totally destroyed in the aftermath of the 1967 war. Farmers were offered free building materials if they built their own homes, using a simple design of precast concrete panels developed by Padco and JVC, but few people took up the offer. They were too busy farming and earning money to support their families to give precious time and energy to building cement block houses. In a few cases, well-off farmers accepted the free materials and hired contractors to build a house for them. The JVC itself put up the bare skeletons of some two-bedroom houses, with kitchen and bathroom, which cost the buyer JD 165 ($545). The owner would finish the house himself, installing doors and windows, plastering and painting and surrounding it with a low wall. This scheme was hardly any more successful than the self-help attempt. Several dozen units were built. Abu Lina, a bedouin farmer who has lived in Damiyah most of his forty-five years, built a unit in 1974 and spent another JD 200 ($660) to finish it. He lives there now with his wife and eight daughters, but complains that the house is too hot in the summer. Abu Adnan, who thinks he was born in Damiyah in 1910, also built a unit in 1963 and spent JD 175 ($578) to finish it. He complains the house is too small. "We are Arabs. When a man comes to me and says 'salam alaykum', I have to reply 'wa alaykum al salaam', open my house for him, offer him coffee and tea, feed him and invite him to stay. But where do I put my guests? There is not enough room."

Abu Adnan says his ancestors came to the Jordan Valley during the Islamic conquests in the seventh century and fought in the battle of Yarmouk. He was born and raised in Damiyah in his father's goat's hair tent, which had four sections, four centre support poles, and sixteen ropes, and lasted twenty years. After Abu Adnan's first wife died he married again and lived in his own tent home until the 1967 war forced him to leave the destroyed village, evading Israeli aerial bombardments as he and his family headed for Arda village with all their belongings on the backs of a team of donkeys. He wanted to build his own large house with a big guest room after the war, but could not afford it. When the JVC offered its semi-finished two-room units, he took one and moved in with his wife and six daughters, his seven sons having married and already left home. He complains about his house, but has accepted it as the most feasible arrangement given the circumstances after 1967. He has expanded the usable area of the house by building a sturdy, vine-covered canopy of tree branches, which overhangs the open porch in front of the house and provides a cool, shaded place where the family spends most of the year. "But where do I put my guests," Abu Adnan asks with concern, "in the same room as the women and girls?"

After the semi-finished housing scheme fizzled out, the JVC thought to offer farmers long-term, low-interest loans and let them build their own homes. Once again, only several dozen people took advantage of this scheme, and the JVC finally acknowledged that the farmers were too busy getting their land back into productive shape to bother about building homes. Dr Haddadin suggests one reason for the early failure of JVC housing plans may have been the farmers' hope or expectation that the government would end up giving them free houses, and therefore they did not take advantage of the JVC's several home-owning options. A total of just eighty houses were built as a result of the Damiyah self-help schemes.

Chapter Eight

The New Realism

The only major new project that was under way by mid-1973 was the King Talal Dam, whose designs had been done in 1970 and construction begun in early 1972, before the JVC was even born. The NRA had resumed normal maintenance and repair work on the main canal, and those ministries that had the capacity to do so started to revive their services in the valley. The JVC itself, having produced a broad-ranging development plan and discussed it with the inhabitants of the valley, was busy preparing detailed project designs for almost two years during which it did not start construction work on a single project. Its credibility in the eyes of the people, like that of any government agency, was low to begin with. After two years of work with nothing to show for it in concrete terms, the JVC faced almost a total loss of credibility. Its complex explanation for the delays elicited little sympathy or understanding. It sounded like just another bureaucratic government ministry making excuses for its inefficiency.

"Our plans were seen as just promises," Omar Abdullah Dokhgan remembers. "It took a long time for the people in the valley to feel any impact from our work."

One key task that was completed early on was the comprehensive socio-economic survey of the *ghor* that was called for in the plan. In the first four months of 1973, the Jordan Department of Statistics designed and conducted a census-like survey that interviewed each household head in the valley, between the Yarmouk River and the Dead Sea. Its findings would be crucial for the JVC, which could henceforth base its work on accurate data that was not available when the 1972 plans were formulated.

The survey confirmed most of the assumptions that officials had made about the poor state of social services in the area. It showed a population of 64,012 people divided into 11,213 households, a relatively low average household size, compared with the rest of the country, of 5.7 people. This probably reflected the tens of thousands of inhabitants who had still not returned from their post-war refuge in the hills. Children under fifteen years of age accounted for 53.2 per cent of the population, indicating both a high demand for schools and small possibility of increasing the labour force from the valley's indigenous population. The labour force totalled 19,495 people, or 30.5 per cent of the population (this excludes day workers who did not live in the valley). Women accounted for a very high 28.1 per cent of the workforce, compared to 11 per cent in the rest of the country.

Almost four-fifths (79.4 per cent) of the population had less than an elementary school education. Only 2.4 per cent of the people had completed secondary school or higher, compared to 5 per cent for the rest of the country. The 2.4 per cent figure for the valley is probably distorted by the presence of many educated government employees with the NRA, JVC and ministries of education and agriculture. It is more likely that less than 2 per cent of the valley's indigenous population had completed secondary school.

Only 33.2 per cent of people over twelve years old could read and write, though the younger generations were becoming progressively more literate than their parents. Illiteracy among the over-fifty age group was 90 per cent, but only 40.5 per cent among fifteen to nineteen-year-olds.

The people of the Jordan Valley lived in forty-eight settlements, most of which were haphazard groupings of scattered houses, mud brick rooms and tents. The largest village was North Shouneh, with 7,662 people, followed by Karameh with 6,678 people. Only four villages had more than 3,000 people; seven villages had 2,000–3,000 inhabitants each, and nine villages had 500–1,000 people. The other eighteen villages had less than 500 people each.

The survey listed 11,312 households living in homes that covered a total area of 399,999 square metres, or 35.6 square metres per family on average. The average number of people per bedroom was 4.3, while the average housing area per person in the valley was 6.2 square metres. More than two-thirds of all the houses covered less than 36 square metres each. More than 58 per cent of the homes lacked a separate kitchen; over 90 per cent lacked a separate bathroom, even though a full 78 per cent of the families owned their own homes. Small mudbrick units of one or two rooms accounted for three-quarters of all the houses in the valley; six per cent were made of cement bricks, and nine per cent were goat's hair tents, mostly used by nomadic, livestocking bedouins. The survey staff were appalled by the destruction they saw: "The impressions of the survey general manager [Mr Wasef Azar] and the field supervisors were that more than 99 per cent of all unoccupied housing units in the eastern Jordan Valley are unsuitable for immediate occupation for living purposes."

The total number of agricultural holdings was 4,425, covering 181,533 dunums, for an average holding of 40.5 dunums. The survey found that 34 per cent of holdings were owner-operated, and 59.3 per cent were rented or sharecropped. The last 6.7 per cent included a combination of both forms of tenure. Irrigated land totalled 174,979 dunums, of which 65.5 per cent (114,609 dunums) were in the East Ghor Canal project area. Side wadis and springs irrigated 16.2 per cent of the land (28,373 dunums), and underground wells irrigated 8.2 per cent (14,420 dunums). Water pumped from the Jordan River only irrigated 0.9 per cent (1,509 dunums), while the last 9.2 per cent (16,068 dunums) was rainfed land.

By the summer of 1974, it was obvious that none of the plan's projects would be completed within the original three-year period. Although work moved ahead on all the projects simultaneously, it covered feasibility studies, designs and raising finance. Project implementation required a much longer time-scale, which the JVC provided in the form of a new 1975–1980 five-year plan, packaged to coincide with the national five-year plan for social and economic development. In November 1974, the JVC combined its 1973–75 and 1975–80 plans and published a 1975–1982 seven-year Jordan Valley development plan. It took into account the lessons of the previous two years in extending implementation periods and setting more realistic cost estimates. Its most important new feature was the proposed development of the Yarmouk River to exploit all the surface water resources in the valley. The three-year plan projects had aimed to irrigate 200,000 dunums, or 61 per cent of potentially irrigable land in the valley. The 1975–80 projects would irrigate the remaining 39 per cent, or another 125,000 dunums, while converting the existing surface gravity irrigation systems of the East Ghor Canal project area to overhead sprinklers.

Every project in the original three-year plan was still in the study, design or tendering phase. Only the King Talal Dam was actually under construction, but only because it had predated the establishment of JVC. Of the JD 33 million ($109 million) total cost of the three-year plan, JD 23.5 million ($77.5 million) was already secured, of which JD 14.87 ($49 million) were foreign loans from the Kuwaiti and Abu Dhabi funds, the International Development Association (World Bank) and US AID. Negotiations were well under way to secure another JD 6.4 million ($21 million) in loans from US AID and the Federal Republic of Germany, working through its Kreditanstalt fuer Wiederaufbau (KFW).

The new projects in the 1975–80 plan, estimated to cost JD 147.34 million ($486 million), included:

A 150 million cubic metre-capacity earthfill dam at Maqarin that could be raised later to a capacity of 350 million cubic metres;

Two power plants at Maqarin to generate an average annual output of 46 million KWH;

A carrier canal 24 kilometres long to deliver the water from the second power-house at Maqarin to the East Ghor Canal;

Irrigation systems for 5,000 dunums in the Yarmouk Gorge;

Construction of an earthfill dam on Wadi Arab and converting its irrigation lands from surface to sprinkler systems;

Converting 114,000 dunums of surface irrigated land in the East Ghor Canal project area to sprinkler irrigation;

Building two power houses downstream from the King Talal Dam to generate 45 million KWH of electricity a year;

Extending the East Ghor Canal to use Maqarin dam waters to irrigate 125,000 dunums of land in the southern part of the valley, and installing a sprinkler irrigation and drainage network;

Raising the level of Kufrein dam to irrigate all the lands above the canal by sprinklers;

Investigating ground water resources above the canal;

Expanding the village development projects (electricity, domestic water, telecommunications, schools, health clinics, housing, government office complexes, business centres and village streets) to meet the needs of the entire expected population of 150,000 in 1980;

Building new roads linking Deir Alla with the King Talal Dam, Kreimeh with Ajlun and Addasiyyeh with Mukheibeh;

Establishing a vocational training centre to train personnel in such jobs as repair and maintenance of agricultural equipment, vehicles and electrical works, carpentry, plumbing and metalworking;

Designing touristic schemes at Mukheibeh hot springs, the Dead Sea, Mashare' and North Shouneh.

The extended seven-year plan envisaged 1975 as the overlap year during which the three-year plan projects would get under way while negotiations would be held to raise the financing for the 1975–80 projects, and to complete feasibility studies, designs and tender documents. In less than three years, the Jordan Valley Commission had grown from an idea in the minds of the country's planning team to a burgeoning agency handling over $600 million worth of

Sprinkler system available to farmers from the JVA

contracts. Its fast growth, however, was commensurate with a still exaggerated idea of how quickly it could implement its varied projects. By the end of 1974, design and prequalification work was completed on several irrigation and transport projects, and in early 1975 the JVC signed its first contracts for construction work.

The first to be awarded in January 1975 was the $6.4 million main highway project which was partly financed by a $3.9 million US AID loan. Shahin Engineering Company of Amman completed the work in eighteen months, widening forty-four kilometres of the existing road, building a 7.8 kilometre section in the south linking the village of Joufa to the Amman-Jerusalem highway, asphalting the entire 7.2 metre-wide, 105 kilometre road and adding a two-metre shoulder on each side.

Irrigation works got under way a few months later. In March 1975, Cho Suk Construction Company of South Korea was awarded the $5.8 million contract for the Zerqa Triangle project, largely financed by a $4.5 million US AID loan. It irrigated 15,000 dunums of land above the East Ghor Canal via a pressure-pipe network fed by the King Talal Dam.

The eighteen-kilometre extension of the East Ghor Canal was started in March 1975, and completed in June 1978. Also designed by Dar Al Handasah and executed by Cho Suk Construction Company at a cost of $15 million (with a $10 million US AID loan), the project consisted of an eighteen-kilometre extension of the main canal, from the end of the previous eight-kilometre extension to a point two kilometres south of Karameh. It irrigated 36,500 dunums of land divided into 944 farm units of 30–40 dunums each.

By mid-1975, the momentum of work was finally picking up. If the residents of the valley still had a few years' wait to use the new irrigation and transport projects, they benefited immediately from new employment opportunities created by the JVC contracts. In the second half of 1975, the JVC once again looked ahead and realized that its time scale was still unrealistically tight. In November 1975, it reassessed its 1973–80 plan and came up with another extended programme of work spanning the period 1975–1982.

The new seven-year programme acknowledged that the initial three-year plan "had been conceived without reference to the long-range perspective of a master plan. . . . Preparing a master plan for the water and land resources (of the valley) requires intensive ground-work in developing design criteria, a time-consuming process. It also needs a longer time horizon than three years. It was, therefore, considered proper to view the three-year plan in a long-term perspective so that the first three years of plan implementation constitute its initial phase in laying the foundation for achieving the desired results in later years."

It also introduced the concept of "rolling plans", whereby new projects are added to the plan as others are completed, and "the process of plan implementation is thus carried on until such time as a state of full development is reached." The year 1982 was chosen as the end of the plan because that was the anticipated completion date for what had become known as Stage II projects: the Maqarin Dam and allied irrigation works.

The seven-year plan aimed to irrigate 360,000 dunums of land by pressure-pipe systems designed for sprinklers but also adaptable to drip or surface irrigation methods. This included converting the existing 127,000 dunums of surface-irrigated farms to sprinklers, and bringing another 230,000 dunums of unirrigated land under sprinkler irrigation. Specific production and income targets were set on the basis of raising irrigation efficiency from fifty-five to eighty per cent and cropping intensity from 106 to 131.6 per cent. When all 360,000 dunums were under irrigation, the valley would produce 460,000 tons of vegetables a year (compared with 129,000 in 1975), 31,800 tons of cereals (3,750 in 1975), 150,400 tons of fruits (46,800) and 850,000 tons of fodder (1,710). Crop cultivation would be worth JD 32.5 million ($107 million), compared with JD 7.3 million ($24 million) in 1975, while the total gross domestic product of the valley (including trade, transport, construction, housing, services and livestocking) would rise from JD 10.7 million ($35.3 million) in 1975 to JD 47.7 million ($157 million) in 1982. The population of the valley would have increased from 70,000 to 140,000, making for a *per capita* GDP increase of 123 per cent, from JD 153 ($505) in 1975 to JD 341 ($1,125) in 1982.

All the ongoing irrigation projects from the original three-year plan would be completed, including the Zerqa River Project (King Talal Dam, Zerqa Triangle, eighteen-kilometre canal extension), the Wadi Arab complex, and Kufrein-Hisban. New irrigation works, henceforth known as Stage II, centred around the 200 million cubic metre-capacity earthfill Maqarin Dam, extending the East Ghor Canal sixteen kilometres to the Dead Sea, sprinkler and drainage systems for 150,000 dunums, a network of farm roads, and converting the existing surface irrigation network of 117,000 dunums to overhead sprinklers.

The only transport project, upgrading and extending the Addasiyyeh–Dead Sea road, was a carry-over from the previous plan, and was already in progress.

The JVC assumed that about 8,000 people a year would be attracted into the valley starting in 1976, to meet its full manpower needs by the time all Stage II works were completed. The sixty-odd settlements in the valley would be consolidated into thirty-six villages provided with all basic services outlined in the previous 1973–1980 plan, including schools, houses, health centres, commercial and government complexes, streets, electricity, water, telecommunications and community centres. Thirty-one villages already existed, and five others would be established from scratch. Four would be type A villages with more than 10,000 people each; nine would be type B with 5,000–10,000 people, and 23 would be type C with less than 5,000. The JVC had already floated a tender to build twenty-one schools, ten health centres, eight government complexes and one community centre to serve twenty-three villages, as the initial phase of the village development programme. In November 1975, the JVC had anticipated starting construction work on this contract in

Bore sample of Maqarin Dam site

October 1976 and finishing in late 1977. As it turned out, the work would start in February 1977 and be completed by the end of 1979, 18–24 months behind schedule.

On the troubled housing front, the JVC expected to construct 18,000 units during the plan period, mostly by lending up to JD 2,000 ($6,600) to each farming family to choose its own design, materials and contractor. The total cost of all ongoing and new projects in the 1975–82 plan was estimated at JD 173.8 million ($574 million).

By the end of 1975, the JVC started to have second thoughts about its original self-concept as a planning, co-ordination and funding agency without operation and maintenance responsibilities. It felt this most acutely in the irrigation sector, where the Jordan River and Tributaries Regional Corporation (JRTRC) was in charge of new dam and irrigation works in the side wadis, and the Natural Resources Authority operated and maintained the East Ghor Canal. The new projects being implemented in both the irrigation and social services sectors heralded complex operating procedures that could not be efficiently handled by three agencies with their separate technical and administrative staffs. The canal itself was the biggest challenge. With its extension and the entry into service of the King Talal Dam and smaller side wadi water harnessing schemes, the East Ghor Canal would be fed by multiple sources of dams and unregulated stream flows, powered by both gravity and pumps. Therefore it was decided that the work of the JRTRC and the NRA in the valley should be turned over to the JVC, which would assume full operational and maintenance responsibilities for all water and irrigation works in the valley. This was the decisive precedent that launched the JVC on an expansionist path that would transform it within eighteen months into the Jordan Valley Authority (JVA), in May 1977, giving it full control of all water works previously handled by JRTRC, NRA and the Domestic Water Corporation. The functional scope of JVA would continue to broaden, in such fields as housing, irrigation technology, and agricultural packing and grading; its territorial responsibilities would also encroach on other government agencies in the late 1970s, as it took charge of the north Jordan domestic water project and the Southern Ghors and Wadi Araba.

Two factors prompted the upgrading of the JVC to the JVA. In 1975, the government had returned to the idea of building the Maqarin Dam on the Yarmouk River, to irrigate the full 360,000 dunums of cultivable land in the eastern half of the valley and fulfil the ambitions of the early 1950s. In March 1976, Harza Engineering Company won the contract to conduct an economic and technical feasibility study for the dam and its allied irrigation systems. The government in Amman was certain that it could raise the required funds. When the Maqarin Dam scheme went ahead, Omar Abdullah Dokhgan says, the JVC had to be changed to a more permanent organization to implement a project that was far bigger than anything attempted before. Without the Maqarin project, he says, the JVC eventually would have dissolved itself.

The second factor was the revised nature of the JVC's work. It could not, as originally envisaged, only build projects and turn them over to existing government agencies to operate. It had to operate and maintain, as well as plan and build. Dr Munther Haddadin explains: "We needed an authority to make sure that benefits were delivered by the same group that predicted them in the plan. There is far more challenge in operating a project than in building it, and we had to have the additional authority to carry a new project through to the operation and maintenance stage."

In the five years between January 1975 and January 1980, the valley passed through an unprecedented period of construction and growth. Almost all Stage I projects of the original 1973-75 plan would be completed, after being refined by further feasibility and design studies. Stage II projects would pass through the rigorous and time-consuming process of being appraised, approved and financially supported by a score of international and regional funding agencies. By June 1978, Stage I irrigation projects were completed, as were most social services, with the exception of a few that had been deliberately phased over a longer time period. Nine years after they had been conceived in the minds of the National Planning Council, eight years after being formally identified and approved in the 1972 Jordan Valley rehabilitation and development plan, and five years after the original 1975 target completion date, the following projects were completed and operating by the summer of 1980:

1 **Irrigation Sector**

(a) Zerqa River Complex: This project regulates the flow of the Zerqa River, to feed a new sprinkler irrigation system for 50,760 dunums and 13,000 dunums served by the eight-kilometre extension of the main canal. Main components are:

The King Talal Dam, a 92.5 metre-high earthfill dam on the Zerqa River with a live storage capacity of 48 million cubic metres, constructed between 1972 and 1978 at a cost of $46 million, with a $16.8 million loan from the Kuwait Fund for Arab Economic Development and a $5.6 million loan from the Abu Dhabi Fund. Energoprojekt of Yugoslavia were consultants, and Planum of Yugoslavia the contractors.

The East Ghor Canal 18 kilometre extension, including four pumping stations, a diversion weir on the Zerqa River and a 2 kilometre-long carrier canal discharging water into the main canal, a 350 kilometre network of pressure-pipes and a network of farm roads, irrigating 36,500 dunums divided into 944 farm units. The project cost $15 million, of which $10 million was a loan from US AID. Construction started in March 1975 and finished in June 1978. Dar Al Handasah of Lebanon were consultants, and Cho Suk Construction Company of South Korea the contractors.

(b) Zerqa Triangle irrigation project, including a diversion weir on the Zerqa River and an adjacent desilting basin, 27.5 kilometres of 400-900 millimetre-diameter carrier pipes, 150 kilometres of pressure pipes and a network of farm roads, irrigating 15,000 dunums above the main canal divided into 411 farm units. The project cost $6 million, of which a US AID loan provided $4.5 million. Dar Al

Handasah and Cho Suk were consultants and contractors respectively.

(c) North-east Ghor Complex: This includes two separate projects to irrigate 40,100 dunums of land:

The North-east Ghor irrigation project, using the unregulated flows of wadis Arab and Jurum and the regulated flow of Wadi Ziglab, irrigates 27,600 dunums via a pressure-pipe network (17,600 dunums are new lands above the main canal, while 10,000 dunums are converted from the main canal's surface irrigation network). It includes a diversion facility on Wadi Jurum and a one kilometre-long, 600 millimetre carrier pipe, a 30 kilometre-long distributary pipe ranging in diameter from 200 to 900 millimetres, a carrier pipe connecting the distributary pipe to Ziglab reservoir, a 278 kilometre network of pressure pipes, one pumping station and a network of farm roads. Work started in August 1976 and was completed in March 1979, at a total cost of $13 million, partly financed by a $6 million loan from the International Development Association (World Bank) and a $1.65 million loan from the OPEC Special Fund. Dar Al Handasah and Cho Suk were consultants and contractors.

The Wadi Arab dam and irrigation project, estimated to cost $52 million, will regulate the flow of Wadi Arab and irrigate by sprinklers 4,500 dunums of new land and 8,000 dunums of converted land. It consists of a 63.5 metre-high, 411 metre-wide earthfill dam with a live storage capacity of 6 million cubic metres, a 3.2 km-long, 1,350 mm-diameter carrier pipe connecting with the distributary pipe of the North-East Ghor project and the Wadi Arab project area, an 11.5 km-long distributary pipe ranging between 250 and 700 millimetres in diameter, and a 136 kilometre pressure-pipe network ranging in diameter from 100 to 200 millimetres. The Japan International Co-operation Agency funded a feasibility study completed in September 1976, and Japan's Nippon Koei in association with Nagai Engineering Company completed designs and tender documents in April 1980. The Overseas Economic Corporation Fund of Japan has pledged a $33 million loan towards the estimated project cost of $52 million. Fifteen shortlisted contractors were given the tender documents in June 1980, with contract awarding scheduled for 1981. Construction of the dam will take almost four years.

(d) Hisban-Kufrein irrigation project provides sprinkler irrigation for 15,500 dunums divided into 560 farm units. It consists of the 4.8 million

cubic metre-capacity Kufrein dam, built in 1967 with aid from the United Kingdom, a diversion weir and carrier pipe to channel the flood of Wadi Hisban into Kufrein reservoir, a pumping station and seepage collection pond to return seepage water from Kufrein reservoir back to the reservoir, a 63 kilometre network of pressure pipes and a network of farm roads. Work started in August 1976 and finished in December 1980 at a total cost of $9.6 million, of which $7.2 million was a loan from West Germany's KFW. Sir M. MacDonald and Partners of the United Kingdom were consultants, and Cho Suk the contractors.

(e) Portable pipes and sprinklers to install aluminium irrigation systems on 2,785 farm units in new project areas were bought by the JVA in 1979, and are stored in three locations in the valley. The materials are sold to farmers on a long-term credit basis (ten years, six per cent interest). The equipment cost $5.5 million, of which a US AID loan covered $4.5 million.

(f) A sub-surface drainage project estimated to cost $3 million got under way in early 1980 to install perforated PVC drainage pipes under 32,000 dunums in the East Ghor Canal project area at the rate of 8,000 dunums a year. Harza Overseas Engineering Co. are consultants, with the JVA's own crews doing the work.

Jordanian engineers have known about the drainage problem for many years, but are only now starting to tackle it. "We first had drainage problems in 1958, in the northern part of the valley," JVA Vice-President for Irrigation Dr Fahed Natour recalls, "but we didn't have the money to do anything about it." The drainage problems are caused by an impervious, two to three-metre-thick underground layer of marl, a clay and calcium carbonate mixture that was deposited hundreds of thousands of years ago when the valley was covered in water. The marl traps irrigation water under the soil, and eventually salt accumulates in the plant's root zone area or the accumulated water itself kills the roots. By 1966, about 15,000 dunums were affected, and by the mid-1970s this had risen to 20,000 dunums. The JVA tried to deal with the problem in 1976, but found it lacked the experience to design a drainage system itself. In 1979, with the aid of a consultant from Harza, four JVA engineers started designing the comprehensive drainage system that entered the implementation phase in 1980.

The system lays perforated plastic or concrete pipes about two metres beneath the soil. Water seeps into the pipes and is carried off to

Routine cleaning of the main canal

the Jordan River. The drained water is being monitored for quality; if it is not salty, it will be recycled and used for irrigation.

2 Public Utilities Sector

(a) Electrification works are designed to supply power to thirty-six villages and to several pumping stations in the irrigation and domestic water supply projects. The first phase, completed in July 1978, includes three high-tension 33-KV feeder lines bringing power into the valley at North Shouneh, Arda Intersection and South Shouneh, connected with a 110-kilometre-long intra-valley 33-KV line parallel to the main road between North and South Shouneh, low voltage networks and fifty-four transformers serving eight pumping stations and twenty-six villages, and 8,500 house connections. The second phase, now under construction, will build a fourth 33-KV feeder line bringing power from Ajlun to Kreimeh, and low voltage networks and transformers to supply electricity to the University of Jordan's agricultural research station and to five villages. The $12.2 million works are financed in part by a $8.3 million loan from KFW.

Turn-off on main canal at Sawalha village, feeding secondary canals

Consultants are Lahmeyer International of West Germany, and contractors are Elektrim of Poland (high tension), Kabelmetal of West Germany (low voltage) and Jordan Electricity Authority (poles).

(b) Domestic Water Supply project, being implemented in two phases, will provide potable water to all villages from five springs and wells. Phase one covers installation of pumping stations, chlorinating units, main pipelines and reinforced concrete reservoirs; it has been completed for sixteen villages in the centre of the valley, five villages in the south and ten villages in the north. Phase two, which got under way in January 1980, covers the supply and installation of smaller diameter pipelines (75 millimetre or less) and the supply and installation of house connections and water meters. The entire system was scheduled to enter service by March 1981. The $8.3 million project is assisted by a $3.4 million loan from West Germany's KFW. VBB of Sweden are consultants, and General Contracting Company of Jordan and Cho Suk Construction Company of South Korea the contractors.

The Jordan Valley

Main road and housing scheme in northern part of Valley

3 Transportation Sector

(a) Yarmouk–Dead Sea road has been widened along forty-four kilometres, extended by 7.8 kilometres in the south and asphalted throughout to provide a 105 kilometre-long, 7.2 metre-wide main road with two-metre shoulders on both sides. Work started in January 1975 and finished in August 1977. DeLeuw Cather International, of the USA, were consultants, with Shahin Engineering Company of Amman and the Jordanian Ministry of Public Works as contractors. The $6.4 million cost of the work was assisted by a $3.9 million US AID loan.

(b) Operation, Maintenance and Farm Roads are being rehabilitated and upgraded to provide a uniform network reaching every farm unit in the valley. These roads are five-metre carriageways with one-metre shoulders on both sides, with a base course, a prime coat and a bituminous seal coat providing an all-weather surface. The first and second phases of the work covering the East Ghor Canal project area

began in September 1977 and finished in May 1979, at a cost of $1.2 million partly financed by a US AID loan of $605,000. This covered one hundred kilometres of roads. Dar Al Handasah were consultants, with Cho Suk and Amer Building and Contracting Office (Amman) the contractors.

4 **Agricultural Grading, Packing and Marketing Centres**
Three new centres for processing and marketing fresh produce are being built throughout the valley to join an existing citrus centre at North Shouneh.

(a) Arda centre, the first to be completed, entered service in May 1980 after thirty months of construction, equipping and testing. Its cost of $3.6 million was assisted by a $2.1 million grant from the Netherlands. Jordan Engineering Consortium were consultants, with Jordan Development Company the contractors. The centre covers an area of 40,000 square metres.

(b) Wadi Yabis centre, covering 22,000 square metres, was designed by Covell Matthews Partnership of Great Britain based on a feasibility study by the Tropical Products Institute of Great Britain. Construction started in March 1980 and was expected to take eighteen months. The $5.6 million cost of the project is assisted by a $2.9 million loan from Great Britain's Overseas Development Administration.

(c) South Shouneh Centre, also designed by Covell Matthews Partnership, was scheduled to enter construction in mid-1981, and to be ready after fourteen months at a cost of $2.65 million. It is aided by a KFW loan.

5 **Social Services Sector (Village Development)**
The work has been divided into two phases to provide basic needs for an ultimate population at full development of 150,000 people grouped in thirty-six villages.

(a) Schools: Twenty-six schools of various sizes have been built, furnished and equipped, and all entered service in the 1979–80 academic year. They contain 274 classrooms, accommodate 9,864 students, and include twenty-five libraries, twenty-six chemistry laboratories, nine physics laboratories, twelve home economics rooms, fourteen handicrafts halls, stores, athletic uniforms and equipment, twenty-six school administration buildings, refrigerators, televisions and stereo equipment. Phase Two covers thirty-five more schools that are under construction and will be operational in the 1981–82 academic year.

(b) Health centres: Ten health centres have been built, furnished, equipped and turned over to the Ministry of Health. They include three type A centres, four type B and three type C, all of which entered service in 1980. Phase Two covers the construction, equipping and furnishing of four more centres, one type A and three type B; they are under construction and are expected to enter service by the end of 1981.

(c) Local administration complexes: Seven complexes completed in Phase One include one type A and six type B, all of which entered service in 1980. Phase Two includes six more complexes, one type A and five type B, all of which are scheduled to enter service in early 1982.

(d) Community and social development centres: One centre at Kreimeh, covering 1,500 square metres, has been completed and entered service in 1980, providing literacy training, sewing and typing lessons and a nursery. Plans for nine other centres to be built during Phase Two have been suspended to give priority to other projects.

(e) Housing for government employees: Three hundred housing units for government employees in five villages have been completed; each 93 square-metre house consists of two bedrooms, living room, kitchen, bathroom and porch. They have been built to provide adequate housing for employees who will operate the new schools, health centres and local administration complexes, and were fully occupied in early 1981.

The total work in Phase One village development projects cost $16 million, of which $11.55 million was a US AID loan. Phase Two projects will cost $17.2 million, assisted by a $6 million US AID loan.

(f) Housing programme: The JVA's housing programme was launched in 1977 to overcome previous delays in providing decent housing for the valley's farmers and to expedite village development plans. Farmers have two options. They can borrow money from the JVA to build their own home, or expand or improve an existing home, providing the applicant has a title to the plot of land where the house is or will be built, has obtained a building permit from the JVA to ensure that the house is in a village development area and will benefit from water, power and telecommunications facilities, and the house will include a bathroom and kitchen. Since its inception in 1978, the programme has only approved 110 loan applications, which average JD 1500–2500, repayable in twenty years at 4.5–7 per cent interest, depending on the repayment period.

The second option is for a valley resident to buy a house already built by the JVA. The JVA decided in 1977 to build 2,100 houses in twenty villages after farmers responded slowly to the home loan scheme, mainly because loan fund applicants either rarely had legal title to the land or because plots of land in the village boundaries were often jointly owned. This required land parcellation, which in turn needed time-consuming surveying and often lengthy legal procedures. Because the JVA and the Lands and Surveys Department are concentrating on farmland redistribution and surveying pipeline routes for Stage II irrigation works, the municipal land redistribution effort sanctioned by the 1977 Jordan Valley Development Law Number 18 has been further delayed. Therefore the JVA initiated its own home-building programme to meet a small part of the valley's need for new housing, on the assumption that this would provide an impetus for residents to undertake their own housing projects in the village areas. There was also some polite pressure from the West German and American donors, who hinted they would retract their housing loans if the programme remained stalled. Over ninety per cent of the 2,100 homes were completed by the end of 1980. Each house of 62 square metres includes two bedrooms, kitchen and bathroom, and is designed to be expandable to four bedrooms. Four hundred houses are on 288 square-metre plots of land, and the remaining 1,700 are on bigger, 586 square-metre plots more in tune with a farmer's desire for some open space around the house, either for use by the family or to keep a few farm animals, such as chickens, rabbits, goats, sheep or even cows. Over 4,000 people submitted applications by mid-1980 to buy the houses, which sell for JD 3,100 ($10,230) each. Typically, a farmer pays a JD 600 ($1,980) down payment, and the balance in instalments of JD 10 ($33) per month for twenty years if his income is less than JD 60 ($198) a month, or JD 19 ($63) if his income is above JD 60 a month. The mortgages are handled by the semi-state Housing Bank, which charges an interest rate of 4.5 to 7 per cent, depending on how quickly the loan is repaid.

The housing project has cost $22 million, of which $4 million mortgage loan financing was provided by a loan from US AID and a $5.34 million loan from German Capital Aid. Consultants for the mortgage loan programme are the National Savings and Loan League of the USA. Construction consultants are Jordan Engineering Consortium, and contractors are Trans-Orient Engineering Company of Amman and Shin Seung Corporation of South Korea.

The housing programme has been the most controversial part of the social services sector, rivalling only farmland redistribution in arousing the passions of valley residents. At first, few people showed any interest in the JVA houses, blue, green and pink pastel units which appeared almost overnight in neat rows and clusters throughout the valley. The houses were too small, farmers complained, or too drab, or too close to one another, or too expensive, or too hot in summer. Many farmers did not like the idea of living away from their farms and having to commute back and forth from their village homes. More cynical people never bothered to apply for a home, assuming the new units would be sold only to influential people in Amman, Salt or Irbid who wanted a winter cottage in the valley.

The JVA-built houses were standardized in the interest of speed of construction and cost efficiency, but it seems that the JVA was more in a hurry to build houses than the farmers themselves, who did well enough in their existing mud brick, tent and cement block homes. Few farmers applied to buy the houses at first when they were being built in 1978 and 1979. Priority to buy the units goes first to school teachers and to farmers (owners, sharecroppers or renters) who already live in the valley; and second, to landowners who live outside the valley and typically rent their land or assign it to sharecroppers. When farmers did not rush forward to buy its houses, the JVA opened sales to non-valley residents who had nothing to do with the area. The prospect of buying a small, relatively inexpensive house in the valley appealed to many residents of the Jordanian plateau, who imagined themselves spending winter weekends in the warmth of the lowest spot on earth. Orders for homes rushed in, and the word spread among farmers that the JVA's units were being sold to "rich people" in Amman, Irbid and Salt. Valley residents themselves then started applying for the houses; by the summer of 1980, 4,000 applications had been submitted and were being processed by the JVA, the Housing Bank and the foreign aid donors. Over 1,400 of the 2,100 houses were sold by the end of 1980, with the rest expected to follow in early 1981. The rush of orders from non-valley residents has prompted the JVA to consider building more housing schemes specifically for those who would put up cash in advance, thereby eliminating the need for foreign loans and keeping most of the original houses for farmers. Omar Abdullah Dokhgan acknowledges: "We thought the houses would sell like hotcakes; but when this didn't happen, we decided to allow sales to people in other parts of the country." He maintains that the JVA's policy from the start was to sell some houses to non-valley residents, "to get some doctors and lawyers and businessmen from Amman to spend time in the valley, to mix up the population there and to introduce new attitudes to help raise the general standard of living." By the end of 1980, it appeared that twenty per cent of the houses, or some 400 units, would be sold to non-valley residents.

Many farmers or salaried employees in the valley refrained from applying for new homes because they were told there were none available in the village they specified. Offered a house in a different village, they often turned it down.

Mohammad Abdullah Salem Maher has worked in the Jordan Valley for twenty-four years, but he is angry and frustrated – because his stomach hurts and he cannot buy a house where he wants. One of the 500,000 Palestinian refugees who were driven from their homes in the 1948 war, Mohammad Maher and his family left their village of Sakieh, ten kilometres from Jaffa, in 1948 to end up at Deir Abu Mash'al, west of Ramallah. He came to Amman in 1950 looking for work, lived in the Jabal Hussein refugee camp and eventually built a four-by-four-metre cement room there, where his wife and ten children still live (two other boys married and set up their own

Children in new housing scheme for farmers and government employees in North Shouneh

homes). He found work with the public works ministry, and came to the valley in 1958. Soon after, he worked on building the East Ghor Canal, and lived for four years in a tent that he kept moving southwards with the progress of the canal, then for another two years in a *barrakiyyeh*, a room made of zinc sheets that was also taken apart and reassembled further down the road as work on the canal progressed. For the past decade, he has been a maintenance supervisor for the central portion of the canal, between Kreimeh and Karameh, living with three other JVA employees in a small house in Sawalha. Abu Abdullah, as he is better known, would like his wife and family to join him in the valley, now that better services are available for their medical and health needs. Living alone in the valley for twenty-four years has done strange things to his stomach. He complains of pains, which he attributes to so many years of preparing his own food and being away from the family. "If my wife were here with me, I could eat a proper meal every day; and if I had my children with me, I'd feel like a young man again. How long can I continue like this?" he asks.

Abu Abdullah applied to buy a house in Arda or Ma'addi villages, where most of his friends are in the area he prefers, but he was turned down because those units were all sold. He was offered a house in Ruweiha village, just east of Deir Alla, but does not want to live there. He says Ruweiha is directly in the path of the hot east winds that come in off the Iraqi and Arabian deserts, has a muddy soil and catches winter floods from the Wadi Zerqa region to the east. If he cannot get a new house in Arda or Ma'addi, he doesn't know what he will do. He is adamantly against Ruweiha, but also wants to bring his family to live with him, which he cannot do until he secures a house. "I built the canal with my own hands," he says, his large, dark body swinging in a 180° arc, following his outstretched arm as it points first to the northern and then to the southern end of the canal. "Am I not entitled now to a house, so I can live a normal life with my family?"

Abu Radwan, a Ruweiha bedouin farmer, does not want a JVA house because he finds them too small and too expensive. He has spent his entire forty-five years of life in the Ruweiha area, first with his parents when they lived as sheep herders, spending the summers in Ajlun and the rest of the year in the valley, and then on his own as a sharecropper for the last twenty years. He had always cultivated some state-owned land on an informal basis, and sharecropped one and a half farm units, or about 50 dunums, combining rainfed cereals with irrigated vegetables. In 1980, when the JVA redistributed the land in the Zerqa Triangle project area, he bought 27 dunums of sprinkler-irrigated farmland. Owning his own land, Abu Radwan proceeded to build his house, a four-room concrete dwelling with a separate well and a large veranda that cost him JD 4,000 ($13,200). He built it on state-owned land near his new farm, and after it was finished the state sold him the land for a nominal fee, as happens with most owner-built homes on non-agricultural land along the foothills of the valley. He discounts the stories about Ruweiha's bad weather, admitting only that it might get an occasional blast of hot eastern wind. After forty-five years, he has gotten used to it. What bothers him more is the rising cost of farming. He used to hire labourers for 250 fils per day, but now pays 500 fils an hour, or JD 3–4 per day. The rising cost of labour, fertilizers and seeds is reducing his income. He cannot complain, though, he says, now that he owns his own home and farm, sends his five children to a nearby school, and gets domestic and irrigation water delivered to his doorstep and farm by the JVA. "I'm entitled to it," he insists. "I paid at least JD 1,000 in taxes to the government when I worked the state's land for twenty years."

Neither is Sweileh Al'Abed Al Omeirat much interested in buying a new house from the JVA. He is perfectly content living in his one-room mud brick house with its separate kitchen. The two rooms provide no more than 30 square metres of indoor space, but Sweileh and his family are satisfied for the moment. In 1978 his house was connected with the JVA-built electricity network. He gets drinking water from a faucet twenty-five metres away, which is part of the JVA's new domestic water system. Sweileh Al 'Abed Al Omeirat is also a son of the *ghor* who has lived in the area around the Zerqa River and Deir Alla all his life. According to the guess of the official in Amman who filled out his application for a passport a few years ago, Sweileh was born in 1931, making him some fifty years old. He thinks he is older, but it would not make much difference because whatever his age he would still be a sharecropper in the Zerqa Triangle, as he has been all his life. He was born and raised in the goat's hair tent of his father, a hard-working sheep herder who married five successive wives during his life. Sweileh remembers the *khatib* coming to their home to teach the children reading and writing from his Koran. Sometimes, the children would dress in white robes, carry their books and pencils in small slings under their arms and march off to the local sheikh's tent, where the *khatib* would hold class for all the village children. Sweileh missed out on an education; he was always off with the family herds as a young child in the 1930s and '40s, learning the task he had expected to perform for the rest of his life.

He started farming in the late 1940s on the same plot of land he works today. It was owned by Issam Kamal but was later handed down to his son Nabil. Sweileh works both as a sharecropper, cultivating 50 dunums, and as a local farm manager, overseeing twenty-five other sharecroppers who work Nabil Kamal's 600 dunums of land.

"The first time we grew potatoes in the late 1930s, everybody laughed at us," Sweileh says, fondly remembering long-gone decades, "because they saw no fruits growing above ground and thought our crop had failed. There was very little vegetable farming then, only a few dunums here and there irrigated from the Zerqa River."

The produce was mostly consumed in the valley, with any surplus marketed in the nearby towns of Palestine and Transjordan.

"If we had extra tomatoes, cucumbers or beans, we would load them in bags and take them to Salt or Jerash on the back of a donkey. The trip to Salt took about eight hours, with the donkey fully loaded with 200 kilograms and the farmer walking alongside. We picked the vegetables early in the morning, loaded the donkey and left early in the afternoon, reached Salt at night, and sold the produce in the market early the next morning. It cost us 250 fils to rent the donkey; to make it worthwhile, we loaded him up with coffee, tea and other supplies for the return trip to the valley."

Wheat and barley were sold mostly in the valley, often to Palestinian merchants from Nablus who sent trucks to pick up their purchases. Road traffic to Salt was less frequent; a dirt road connecting it with the valley was only built in 1935, when Salt Governor Abdul Mehdi Shamayli ordered the local sheikhs each to send a contingent of their men to work on a section of the road. In twenty-eight days the bedouin tribes had cleared a simple dirt pathway with their own hands; it could hardly be called a road, until it was paved by the government in the mid-1940s.

When someone fell ill, Sweileh recalls, he would be treated with local cures based on traditional herbal recipes. A very sick person needing the attention of a doctor was taken to Salt laid flat on the back of a horse, held in position by two large sacks of grass on either side. A good horse reached Salt in about five hours and the patient was then taken to see the venerable "Dr Tannous" (Tannous Kawar, a malaria specialist).

"If we got the patient to Salt, Dr Tannous could usually keep him alive. But if the patient died on the way, well, we'd go back home and bury him."

It was only in the mid-1950s that doctors and clinics made their first appearance in the valley.

Sweileh built his one-room mud brick home in 1960, at a total cost of JD 40 ($132). A year later, after a good harvest, he added on the kitchen, which cost him another JD 20 ($66). The house is on state-owned land. Like almost all the other simple homes in the area, it was built without a permit or a land title deed. But because it is against the foothills, on non-cultivable land, the government turns a blind eye.

Sweileh paid JD 20 ($66) in 1978 to connect his house with the new electricity system. Since then, he has bought a refrigerator, a fan and a radio-cassette that broke down and has never been repaired. He is paying about JD 4 ($13) a month in electricity bills. The refrigerator cost him JD 160 ($530). He made a JD 60 ($198) down payment, and pays the rest whenever he has extra cash.

Now Sweileh wants to build a bigger concrete house, but does not have the money. He figures it would cost him JD 2,000 ($6,600) to build a simple three-room house. His brother recently built a three-bedroom house with kitchen and veranda for JD 2,500 ($8,250). Sweileh looked at the JVA houses, but does not think they are right for his family, which includes his wife and three children (a fourth child, the eldest daughter, was recently married). "I think the new houses are good for a small family, but they are too small for big families that need room around the house for their animals."

He also thinks they are too expensive. "How am I supposed to make monthly payments? I'm not a salaried employee working in an office and getting a regular paycheck every month. I'm a farmer. I have money at the end of every season. If it's a bad harvest, I don't have any money. I can't make regular payments for my refrigerator. How am I supposed to pay monthly for a house?"

He will wait a few years and hope to save some money to build his own. "I want a new concrete house for my family. I want good quality. I don't want to be left behind while there is progress all around me."

His two youngest children, Tayseer and Abeer, attend the nearby secondary school at Deir Alla, built in 1979 under Phase One of the JVA's village development works. His oldest son, Sa'ed, studied until the seventh grade, then quit to help him run the farm.

The family rarely uses the government's health clinic at Deir Alla, preferring to see a private doctor who charges them JD 1 ($3.30) per visit, compared with the clinic's 300 fils ($1).

If Sweileh is not impressed by the JVA houses or the health ministry's clinic, he is full of praise for the pressure irrigation system installed in the Zerqa Triangle. He had always irrigated his land from dirt canals built in the 1930s and lined with concrete in the 1950s, bringing water from the Zerqa River. The pressure system now delivers even and regular water supplies that he controls by walking a hundred metres in front of his house and turning a valve on the farm turnout. Sweileh directs the water gushing from the risers into his surface furrow irrigation system. "It's easy," he says, demonstrating the system to a visitor, "and beautiful".

Besides building his own house, his other ambition is to own his own farm. But like most of the sharecroppers in the valley, he senses that only rich and well connected people can buy land. "Do you think a little guy like me has a chance to buy a farm? Don't believe it. Only the important people and the bigshots get land."

Sweileh's attitude, typical of many sharecroppers and small farmers, aptly reflects the communication gap between government agencies and the man-in-the-street that the JVA has been unable to narrow in its own sphere. The fact is that he might well be eligible to buy a farm unit under the land redistribution programme, as other sharecroppers in his area have already done. But he has such fixed perceptions of his place in the prevailing social structure that he simply assumes buying land is beyond his good fortune. Therefore he sets his targets a bit lower, content to build a new home for himself and his family.

The JVA's senior officials recognize in this typical attitude the symptoms of perhaps their biggest disappointment – their inability to develop a two-way communications system with the residents of the valley to help eliminate the attitude reflected in Sweileh's thoughts. In a "self-criticism" session held with senior government officials, headed by Crown Prince Hassan, in October 1980, Dr Munther Haddadin summed up the JVA's disappointment: "We admit that we were unable to find the necessary means to get to know the people in the valley well, we could not find the right channels to tell them about our projects and fully understand their social and economic situation. It's a shortcoming we could not resolve."

The arguments over the JVA's houses are symptomatic of a larger struggle that is magnified in the Jordan Valley because of the compressed time and space in which the development programme is being implemented. The struggle is between the discipline and uniformity demanded by a large-scale development effort, and the

Wadi Shu'eib Dam

free-wheeling, obstinate individuality of the farmer. When the government was only concerned with providing better irrigation works, the farmers' living arrangements were of no concern. But when the JVC and then the JVA took charge of every aspect of life in the valley, including where people lived and built new homes and what facilities these included, the farmers felt threatened by a loss of their formerly unchallenged decision-making powers. Not only did the JVA strike a psychological soft-spot in dictating to them new rules about how and where they could live; it also encroached on the sensitive political infrastructure that revolved around the big tribes and families in the valley, such as the Adwan, Abbad, Nu'eimat, Balawni, Wahadni, Zinati and Ghzawi. The JVA's policy from the start was to respect the existing socio-political power structure, and to employ as many qualified valley natives as possible, but not to favour the biggest tribes at the expense of smaller families.

The JVA studied different options on how best to provide basic social services to an anticipated population of 150,000 people. "We debated whether we should encourage life on the farms or in villages," Omar Abdullah Dokhgan says, "and decided that the best option was to develop village-based services to preserve agricultural lands in the long run. Therefore our laws encourage people to move into the villages, though it's possible that in the future this policy could change."

Dr Haddadin recalls early JVC discussions that weighed the benefits of both village and farm life: "Is it easier for a farmer to travel from the village to his farm every day, or for his entire family to travel to the village from the farm to make use of social services? We studied both options, and quickly agreed that it would be incredibly complicated and expensive to try to provide electricity, water, telecommunications, schools and health clinics to a population dispersed on thousands of farms. The objective of the development of the Jordan Valley is both economic and social; we aim to provide the greatest benefits to the largest number of people. The adoption of a 30–40 dunum farm owned and operated by a single family is one way to try and achieve this. The provision of integrated social services in village communities is another. This is the essential social objective of our work, which would be virtually impossible to achieve if every person lived wherever he or she wanted to."

He argues that allowing people indiscriminately to build homes on their farms would mean an eventual loss of nearly 25,000 dunums of prime agricultural land, assuming that each of the 8,000 farm houses at full development, with an access road, parking area, garden, storage sheds and other facilities, takes up an average of three dunums.

In practice, the JVA has been flexible, but on two conditions: it allows some houses to be built on farms as long as they do not impede the right of way of irrigation pipelines, farm roads and public utilities, and the value of a house is not calculated if the JVA should ever buy the farm in the future for resale to others. One prominent Jordanian's luxurious JD 30,000 ($100,000) mansion, sitting in the middle of his farm in the southern part of the valley, is officially licensed by the JVA as a storage shed, and would be valued as such if he ever decides to sell the land. Because land can only be sold to the JVA, this policy effectively rules out new construction on farms except by those people committed to living and investing money in the valley. In such a case, the JVA rationalizes, there is a reasonable trade-off between the loss of a few dunums and the long-term commitment of the farmer to a substantial investment in agriculture. A farmer who builds a house and asks for electricity on his farm has to pay the full, nearly prohibitive, cost of extending lines. A transformer alone costs JD 8,000 ($26,400), and laying the power lines costs JD 4 ($13) per metre outside the village development areas. After considerable pressure from farmers throughout the valley, the JVA decided in 1980 to permit construction of homes and sheds on a maximum of one dunum of farmland, acknowledging a reality that it had tried to discourage.

Weak communications channels sometimes prevent the widespread dissemination of relevant laws to all valley residents. The JVA uses radio and newspapers to announce new regulations, but finds it still misses many illiterate farmers, who remain oblivious to construction restrictions and build houses or shops in unauthorized places. In several cases, the JVA had to stop people who were digging foundations for their houses in the middle of what was to become a village street. In other cases, it rerouted streets to avoid new homes that had already been completed. In a recent case in Dthirar village, the JVA went to court to demolish an unauthorized shop that had been built on top of an existing pipeline, with a paved parking area blocking several irrigation risers. The court ruled in favour of the JVA and ordered the shop to be demolished, which was summarily accomplished by a JVA bulldozer the next day. While such forceful displays of its authority are rare, the JVA occasionally takes severe action to assert itself – in an area where a person's effectiveness is largely a function of his power.

By 1978–79, Phase One projects started to have an impact on people's lives. The effect of irrigation systems, land redistribution and integrated social services on the lives of farming families already in the valley was relatively easy to gauge. The residents of the valley, traditionally the most backward segment of the Jordanian population, suddenly faced new opportunities. A skilful farmer could increase production and income, given a more reliable water delivery system. An ambitious young student could finish secondary schooling without leaving home. An enterprising merchant could open a business to cater to the needs of the fast rising population.

But the most significant impact of the JVA's projects was not to be measured only in improved living standards and economic opportunities for people already resident in the valley. It was, also, the impact on non-valley residents that was the dynamic new element in the developmental pattern of the Jordan Valley, because the JVA's work ultimately would have to be assessed on the basis of its twin objectives: the maximization of agricultural production *and* spreading the benefits of development to the greatest possible number of people. The latter meant nearly tripling the pre-1967 population of the valley, which could only be done by enticing an itinerant class of people to live there. The Jordan Valley – the wild and sometimes dangerous last frontier of the country only a few decades previously – emerged as a pole of socio-economic opportunities that attracted residents of the highlands to settle and work there permanently, raise their children, invest their money and build their future. For a change, many Jordanians were suddenly offered an option, perhaps the first meaningful alternative they had ever had to existing jobs, place of residence and access to essential services. In many cases, the valley's need for people coincided with the enterprising instincts of individuals who had hovered on the periphery of the area for many years. Jobs, housing, medical services, schooling, money – all these were held out as the tangible, immediately deliverable promise of life

At the open tomato market at Karameh

at 300–400 metres below sea level. The theoretical models of economic planners of the past three decades were becoming reality. Harnessing the water of the Yarmouk River and the side wadis promoted new farming activity, which meant new jobs, which in turn lead to a growing population in need of more social services, once again creating more employment and inviting new people to move into the valley, or former residents to move back there. In case after case, the income from wage labour or self-employment was the main, though not the only, attraction for those who made the decision to go and live in the Jordan Valley.

Some young people, like Saleh Abu Sheikh, support their families by providing farm services. A Palestinian who came to Jordan from Gaza as a penniless refugee in 1967, Saleh is now married, operates a pickup truck hauling vegetables, and owns a small house in the valley where he lives with his wife and four children.

He came to Jordan with his family on 2 November, 1967, five months after his home in Gaza had been occupied by the Israelis. The family went immediately to Amman, in search of work and income. For two years Saleh operated a small bakery. Then he moved to Mahes, a small village about fifteen kilometres north-west of Amman near Fuheis, where he worked in a bakery at night and operated a small café-restaurant in the day. In 1972, he heard from his younger brother that he could find work in the Jordan Valley, where life was slowly getting back to normal after the fighting and turbulence of the 1967–71 years. Saleh found a job in a small grocery store at Arda Intersection in early 1972, and lasted six months before his entrepreneurial instincts pushed him to open his own roadside restaurant and café in the nearby Masri Intersection area. One year later, a big local farmer needed someone reliable to help manage his farm. Saleh took the farm manager's job at a salary of JD 25 ($80) a month, and lived in a tent for the first two years. In January 1975, he married his first cousin from Gaza. He stayed in the job for six years, and earned JD 65 ($200) a month when he left it in 1979, by which time he had been living in a room provided by the farm owner. In early 1979, Saleh's compulsive business mind again propelled him to set out on his own. He sold his family's small collection of gold jewellery for JD 500 ($1,600), gathered together some savings, borrowed a bit, and bought a used one-ton Toyota pickup truck for JD 1,600 ($5,300). He transports fruits and vegetables to the market at Sawalha, from farms ten to twelve kilometres away, for 70 fils (23¢) per box, and to the Amman wholesale market for 120 fils (40¢) per box. On a good day, he can make two trips to Amman, and perhaps one extra journey to Sawalha. He averages a monthly income of around JD 100 ($330), and owns a small house in the valley, with two rooms, kitchen and bathroom, that he built in June 1979 at a cost of JD 2,600 ($8,600). In 1980, the oldest of his four children, a girl, Samar, entered a new primary school built by the JVA as part of Phase One. He and his family use the nearby JVA-built clinic when the need arises, but also visit a private doctor at Sawalha if the clinic is closed. When there is little work hauling agricultural produce, before and after harvest seasons, Saleh puts his truck to other uses, moving commercial goods, agricultural inputs such as fertilizers, seeds or chemical, or even household belongings.

Other young men, unlike Saleh, have returned to the Jordan Valley after previously leaving their homes there. They have been lured back not only by the attraction of new jobs, but also by the chance to live and work in one's ancestral village, among family, friends and old colleagues. In a world where the trend is for rural families to migrate to the city in search of jobs and services, the Jordan Valley is proving to be an exception. It is a rural area that attracts back its emigrant sons.

The availability of government jobs has been a strong factor drawing people into the valley. Even for the sons and daughters of native valley bedouins, whose lives take them in and out of the valley every year, the permanence of a civil service job often brings with it a stronger awareness of the valley's economic opportunities. Abdul Hamid Al 'Imad, one of these native sons, is face-to-face with an important decision: should he leave his job as a school teacher and become a full-time farmer? Or should he secure a small farm for himself and work it in the summer, when school is out? The choice would not appear to be a difficult one. But it represents a major commitment for a thirty year-old, newly married young man to establish himself and his family on a small farm in the Jordan Valley. There is an element of risk that does not exist with his teaching job. Yet he weighs the pros and cons.

Abdul Hamid Al 'Imad was born in a bedouin tent in the Damiyah area in 1951, the son of a livestocking family that wintered in the valley and spent the summers in its home at the village of Arda, in the cool, green hills near Salt. He graduated from secondary school and continued studying to obtain his English language teacher's diploma from the teachers' institute at Salt. He has been teaching at the Deir Alla secondary school for girls since the JVA turned it over to the ministry of education in 1978. Seven of the fifteen teachers at the school are, like him, Jordan Valley natives who were educated in the highlands but returned to live and work in the valley. He likes teaching English; yet he is also attracted to the farming life, owning land, building a small house for his family and settling down in one place he could call home. His family owns land at Arda village, half an hour away, and he has thought of building his house there. But he also feels that he belongs in the valley.

"My uncles and cousins all own land and have built homes in the valley. I'd like to do the same myself," he says. But he is torn between two conflicting opinions.

"When I sit in the café in the evening," he says, "and I tell my friends that I'm thinking of establishing a small farm, I get different advice. The old timers who have farmed in the valley for many years discourage me. It's too risky, they say; there's too much uncertainty. But the younger farmers encourage me. They suggest that I join a co-operative, work my farm in the summer to start with and then manage it all year round. I'm not sure what I'll do. Sometimes I'm worried about borrowing a great deal of money to get started if there is a chance that I might fail and have to spend years working to pay off my debts. But this is where I belong, this is where my family lives. This is where my future is."

Abdul Hamid Al 'Imad is in a quandary that is something of a luxury for a thirty year-old citizen of a small developing country with a *per capita* income of some $1,000. He has a choice – an option – of how to earn a living and where to raise his family. To choose a farming career involves risking time, money and effort. Yet there are potentially big financial returns from properly running a small farm in the Jordan Valley. There is also the attraction of building his own house. He estimates this would require JD 3,000 ($10,000). He now rents a small mud brick house from a friend for an unspecified rent. When he has extra money, he pays some of it as rent. If he has no spare cash, he pays nothing. A similar arrangement governs payments for the refrigerator he recently bought. He pays it off whenever he can. Like the sharecroppers who only come into cash seasonally, during the harvests, Abdul Hamid pays his bills on a casual basis, when he has some spare money. The merchants know him and trust him. He is part of the culture of the Jordan Valley; but he has been in and out of it so often in his three decades of life that he feels pulled between two worlds – the valley and the hills.

The influx of people (there were 85,000 residents in the valley in

November 1979, according to the first national census in 20 years) has brought with it the first wave of professionals. University educated agricultural engineers are in constant demand, as are teachers, school directors, health personnel and commercial staff such as accountants and bank managers. Many of the professionals who started working in the valley in the past five years are not natives of the area. Typical of this mobile young breed is Dr Mustafa Shneikat, a doctor who graduated in 1974 after completing six years of medical studies at Basra University, in southern Iraq. He returned to Salt, eight kilometres from his village of Yarga, and worked for a year in the government hospital there before deciding to start his own practice. Looking around in 1976 for a good place to open a clinic, Dr Shneikat decided on South Shouneh, one of the biggest villages in the valley. He stayed there for one year before moving to Sawalha, where he has a two-room clinic at the entrance of the village, where the road and the canal meet. There was only one other doctor in Sawalha in 1976; now there are three, and a fourth, a young pediatrician, plans to open shop soon. There are twelve private doctors and one dentist in the valley, says Dr Shneikat, who is also head of the Doctors' Association branch in Balqa Governorate, which includes the central part of the valley.

"I'm a young doctor at the start of my career," he says. "I have to start working in the villages before I can open a clinic in a bigger city." He is uncertain about whether his professional future lies in the valley, or in Salt, or another city in the Jordanian plateau. For now, he lives in Salt and drives his car to Sawalha every day. He doesn't anticipate living in the valley, but he sees promising professional opportunities there.

Dr Shneikat sees an average of fifteen to twenty patients a day, charging JD 1 ($3) per consultation. All his patients are local farmers, mostly sharecroppers who often do not have enough cash to pay his fee. He ends up seeing six or eight patients a day for no payment. If they come into cash at harvest time, they will pay him something. He also makes house calls in emergency cases. "Private doctors have more of an incentive to give a better service than the government hospitals and clinics," he claims, "and that's why so many farmers prefer coming to a doctor rather than visiting a government clinic. We probably offer similar services, but the farmers perceive us differently."

Only two of the valley's twelve doctors, including Dr Shneikat, have full-time nurses, who are trained on the job. His nurse is a young woman from Sawalha who completed ninth grade before leaving school, and has learned basic nursing skills during her first year on the job.

A local pharmacy has all basic medicines which he prescribes for the most frequent ailments. In a hot agricultural area like the valley, the most common problems he treats are stomach ailments, poisoning from chemicals and fainting from the heat and sun (sunstroke).

"It's hard to raise the health standards of people who live ten in a room and still drink dirty canal water," Dr Shneikat says. "It's hard to teach good health habits to poor people. Fortunately, the valley is probably the fastest developing area in all of rural Jordan, and is open to outside influences. But poor municipal services and insufficient checking by the health ministry are also to blame. Nobody checks on the food being sold in the markets and the restaurants."

He treats many food poisoning cases in summer, which he says could be prevented with better inspection of shops and restaurants.

Most of the Egyptian workers Dr Shneikat sees suffer from bilharzia and weak blood, and many have kidney ailments resulting from poor diets. Because they are in Jordan to earn money to send back to their families, the Egyptians skimp on food, and live on a few staple items such as bread and beans, along with whatever fresh vegetables they consume on the farm. "I always tell them to eat more protein and iron, in foods such as lentils, eggs, meat and chicken. Most of the Egyptians I see are in very bad health. About eighty per cent of them have bilharzia."

He says the Pakistani workers are better off, because they usually bring their families with them and spend more of their income on themselves, including food.

When he opened his clinic in 1976, Dr Shneikat took electricity from his pharmacist neighbour's diesel generator. In May 1979, he was hooked into the new power network installed by the JVA, and since then has been able to run his medicines refrigerator all day, along with the ubiquitous fans. He thinks the general level of health will rise slowly in the Jordan Valley, but remains worried that the influx of cheaper foreign labour will drive out Jordanians. He warns: "It's a real danger. The skilled Jordanian farmer may be driven off the land if the landowners prefer to hire cheaper foreign workers to reduce their costs and make more money."

For Dr Mustafa Shneikat, the Jordan Valley is a professional opportunity, a stepping stone in his young medical career. He may still be in Sawalha in ten years, or he may be back in Salt, or somewhere else in Jordan. He doesn't know. "For the foreseeable future, my professional interests are right here in the valley. I can't say where I will settle permanently. There are good things here, but there are also good things in the cities. We'll just have to wait and see." In the meantime, he remains a telling example of inter-Arab and global dynamics: a Jordanian trained to become a doctor in Iraq treating Egyptian labourers attracted to the Jordan Valley by a $1.5 billion development project funded by fifteen national and international agencies.

The availability of education in the valley through the secondary school cycle may prove to be the single most decisive factor in transforming people's attitudes, aspirations and values in the long term. As it is in all other rural areas of the country, schooling is a big attraction for the nomadic population, and is often a key factor in a family's decision to settle down permanently in one village. The JVA's school-building programme barely keeps up with the demand for new places in primary and secondary schools. The increased enrollment is due to three factors: the children of new families moving into the valley, and indigenous families sending their children to school at an earlier age than they had previously done, or schooling them instead of keeping them at home to work on the farm.

Between 1972 and 1978, the number of schoolchildren in the Jordan Valley increased from 12,028 to 19,345. In the 1979/80 academic year, when the JVA's Stage 1 schools entered service, total enrollment increased by nearly 20 per cent, reaching over 23,000 students. In the five years after 1973, the number of school-age boys enrolled in schools increased from 78 per cent to 87 per cent, while the percentage of girls in school increased even faster, from 50 to 65 per cent. The fastest growing segment of the school-age population is the six to nine-year-olds. Between 1973 and 1978, their numbers increased from 5,393 to 7,950, with the fastest increase among the six to nine year-old girls.

In many parts of the valley, secondary students used to have to travel 20 or 30 kilometres a day to attend classes, thereby discouraging all but the most determined from completing their basic education. Girls in the Karameh area who wanted to complete secondary school before 1967 had to travel to Jericho or even to Salt. Some boys commuted daily to Nablus. In 1967, the Ministry of Education opened a series of new secondary schools for boys and girls, laying the foundation for the brisk expansion in education that would follow a decade later with the implementation of the JVA programme.

Crafts class of girls' secondary school in Kreimeh village

Mrs Baheeji Khayyat, a former English teacher in the main secondary school in Nablus, came to the valley in 1967 as headmistress of a new girls' school at Karameh. Classes began in September 1967 with twenty-four girls, in two classrooms and a nearby tent to house the administrative staff. By the end of 1967, Mrs Khayyat transferred to take charge of the new primary school for girls at Ma'addi, which never formally closed during the 1968–71 war years but more often than not held classes with one or two students, instead of the customary fifteen. By 1972, enrollments inched back up to their pre-war level. Mrs Khayyat had twelve girls in her twelfth grade class that year, and twenty-five in 1973, as girls from nearby villages started enrolling. The same year, the ninth grade class swelled to thirty girls, compelling the education ministry to open a girls' school at nearby Deir Alla, to relieve the pressure on the facilities at Ma'addi. Mrs Khayyat took charge of the new school, which opened with a tenth grade class of twenty-four girls from twenty villages around Deir Alla. The JVA completed the new Deir Alla school for girls and turned it over to Mrs Khayyat in 1978. Its enrollment has increased to 262 preparatory and secondary students (grade 6–12), with an average annual graduating class of thirty to thirty-five students. In the 1980–81 academic year, students in grades 9–12 increased from 140 to 197, for a forty per cent increase that is higher than the average for the entire valley. Mrs Khayyat estimates that many schools are increasing their enrollments by twenty-five per cent every year, and some have had to institute two shifts, from 7 to 11 a.m. and from 11 a.m. to 4 p.m., to accommodate all the students. This very high rate of increase will taper off to a more normal pace as the bulk of children in the valley are enrolled in the sixty-one new schools being established by the JVA. The rush to education, however, mirrors a new attitude among the valley's parents.

"School enrolments are increasing as new families come to live permanently in the valley," Mrs Khayyat says. "Now that there is electricity and housing, people working here will bring entire families with them, where only the man would live before. There are also changes taking place in the farmers who have been here for decades. They used to be lax about sending their children to school, often waiting until the child was nine or ten years old, whereas the law says that children have to start school at the age of six. Now the parents are more anxious to enroll their children in schools as early as possible. We also see more interest in the higher classes. Because only the first years of schooling are compulsory, with the last three years optional, many families used to pull their children out of school after the ninth grade, perhaps because they needed them to help on the farm or they wanted to save the money spent on the child's transport and school expenses. Or maybe they just didn't think it was important to finish secondary school. Now things are changing. More families are keeping their children in school for the full twelve grades."

One reason for the change is the availability of well paying jobs in the valley for secondary school graduates. Ten or twenty years ago, a secondary school certificate was worth very little in the Jordan Valley in terms of better work or higher pay. Besides farming, little work existed outside a handful of government jobs. Today, the fast expansion of social services and the influx of private businesses, such as banks or doctors' clinics, has opened up new work opportunities for school graduates.

Miss Afaf Ameed Ibrahim is one valley native who has taken advantage of such opportunities, but still feels the forces pulling at others like her who want to be educated and take up non-farming work. She was born and raised in the central part of the valley, and enrolled in Mrs Khayyat's two-rooms-and-a-tent secondary school at Karameh when it opened in 1967. The battle of Karameh in March 1968 forced her to suspend studies for eighteen months. In early 1970, she finally enrolled in a secondary school in Salt, and commuted daily from her family home near Deir Alla. In 1973, she returned to the *ghor* in search of work, and took a job as administrative manager of the new Deir Alla girls' school.

"Most parents are too busy farming to pay attention to their children's education," she says, "so they rely heavily on the schools for many aspects of their children's upbringing. There is a new awareness among the schoolgirls in the valley. Many want to go on to the teachers' training institute in Salt, so they can come back here and teach. In three or four years, all the school-teachers in the valley will be local men and women who earned their teaching diplomas in Salt or Amman."

She sees the need for more educational institutions in the valley, such as a post-secondary institute for secretarial and commercial training. The new businesses springing up – tailors, metalworking shops, banks, agricultural services companies, retail shops, medical services and government complexes such as the Arda packing and grading centre – offer new work opportunities that require a basic education and some specialised training.

"As new jobs become available," Afaf predicts, "they will go to those young people from the valley who have an education and are willing to try new kinds of work; but I think teaching will remain the favourite option for girls for many years to come."

She believes many girls want to complete their secondary and post-secondary studies but are prevented from doing so by their families, who cannot afford the expenses, or are afraid that an educated daughter will leave the valley. After finishing secondary school, some girls have to make the difficult choice of getting married or continuing to study. "I even know cases where the boys in the family defend the right of their sisters to study," she says.

Schools are also slowly expanding the non-academic activities open to young people in the valley. Sports is one fast growing sector, with many schools already fielding teams in football, volleyball, handball, table tennis and badminton. Students are taken on at least four day-long field trips every year, usually to the country's main archaeological, educational or technological sites, such as Jerash and Petra, the Royal Scientific Society, the Dead Sea or Yarmouk and Jordan universities.

The Jordan Valley

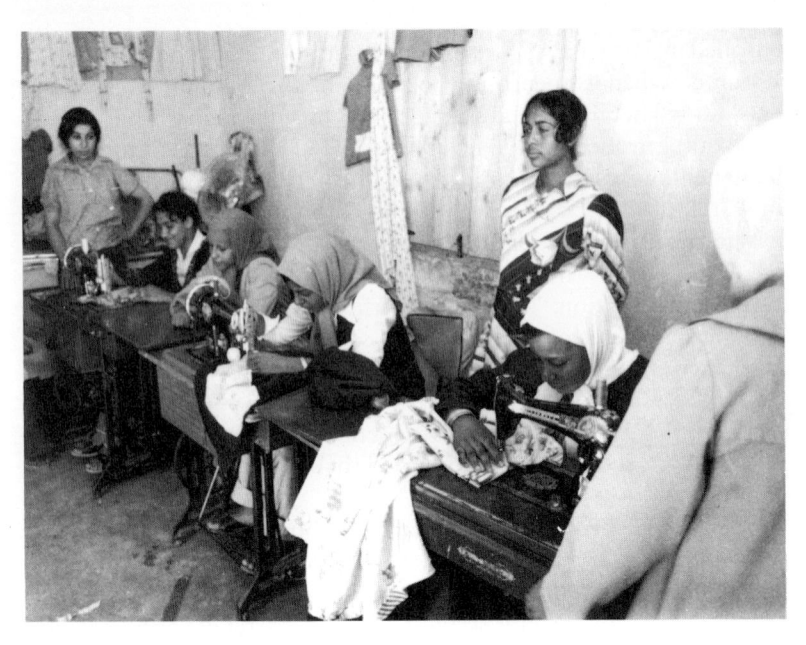

Sewing centre at Deir Alla operated by the Central Ghor University Graduates' Club

The enthusiasm of the valley's school graduates generates its own momentum, leading to the establishment of institutions such as the Central Ghor University Graduates' Club, which, contrary to its name, is open to graduates of secondary schools, post-secondary training institutes and universities. It was set up in 1978 in rented rooms in one of the co-operative buildings in Ma'addi. It provides a meeting place where young graduates gather in the afternoon or after dinner, as most of the valley's population does, to drink tea, chat, play chess or cards, listen to radio or watch television. The club's volleyball team, after only one year of competition, moved up to the first division in the national volleyball league in 1979, causing considerable excitement among local sports enthusiasts who previously had little to cheer about.

The club's biggest and most successful project is a three-year-old sewing centre at Deir Alla, occupying three small rented rooms in a complex that also houses a mother and child care centre run by the Ministry of Health. The club established the centre to offer practical training in a skill that could be applied locally to earn money. The centre offers a nine-month course in all aspects of hand embroidery and machine sewing, and grants a diploma to those who successfully complete the course. The diploma is approved by the Ministry of Social Development. In the first two years, the centre graduated two classes of sixteen girls each, most of whom had never completed secondary school. The sixteen to twenty year-old graduates typically work at home, sewing clothes for friends and relatives for a fee that ranges between JD 2–5 ($6.50–$16.50) per dress, which requires between one and two days of work. The course itself costs JD 2 ($6.50) per month, and requires students to attend classes from 8 a.m. to 1 p.m., every day except Friday. The director of the centre is a Jordan Valley native, Miss Khadeeja Hweirim, who herself completed a sewing course at Salt run by the Ministry of Social Development. Modest as it may seem by any other standard, the sewing centre operated by the Central Ghor University Graduates' Club represents a new attitude among the younger generations in the valley. Unlike their more fatalistic parents or older brothers and sisters, they take matters into their own hands and initiate projects themselves, instead of passively asking the government or the local sheikh to do everything for them. The sewing centre plans to move to bigger quarters near Damiyah in 1981, and there is serious discussion about forming a co-operative sewing society for the graduates, organizing them into a more effective, business-like operation that would increase their earnings and provide the nucleus for yet more sewing enterprises in other parts of the valley. There is also serious discussion about the club opening a typing centre. There is a ring of permanence in this effort, an activist commitment to improving one's standard and quality of life. This is a new phenomenon, a sign of the 1970s that there is more to life in the Jordan Valley than just farming and livestocking. The widening of human concerns reflects both the number and kind of young people moving or returning to the valley in the wake of the government's provision of essential services. Sa'id Jamil, thirty-eight year-old Ma'addi farmer and businessman and one of the founders of the Graduates' Club, gave up a legal career in Amman in 1979 to devote all his time to his 600-dunum farm and his new business of selling and erecting plastic greenhouses. Ambitious from youth, he completed primary school in Ma'addi, where he was born, and travelled to Salt and then to Nablus to complete secondary school in 1964. After six more years of study, he received his law degree from Beirut, trained for two years and opened his own legal office in Amman. For seven years, he worked as a successful lawyer, sleeping in Ma'addi but

Open field and plasticulture cultivation near Rabee' village in central valley, with eastern hills in background

travelling 120 kilometres every day to make the round-trip from his home to office and back. He had never seriously thought of leaving the valley altogether, but professional interests drew him to work and spend most of his time in Amman, leaving the family farm in the hands of eighteen sharecroppers.

"There are new commercial opportunities in the valley today, that didn't exist a few years ago," he says. "As a landowner, I'm reluctant to leave the valley to live somewhere else, but as a lawyer I also cannot practise here because there are no courts in the valley yet."

In 1974, he was a member of the preparatory committee to set up the Jordan Valley Farmers Association (JVFA), but failed to get elected to its board in the 1976 elections. In 1980, he tried again and succeeded, winning election for a four-year term.

"The JVFA is still getting on its feet, and has not yet offered farmers much beyond low-cost seeds, fertilizers and chemicals. In the long run, though, it has to assume responsibility for key operations, such as grading, packing and marketing. It should also replace the commission agents and the middlemen, and help farmers achieve maximum earnings. The nature of farming in the Jordan Valley is changing. Plastic houses and tunnels are the wave of the future; in a few more years, most farming will be intensive cultivation under plastic houses and in controlled environments. This also brings with it a whole new set of problems and challenges. If plasticulture continues spreading as it is today, in a few years we will have a surplus of cucumbers and tomatoes that will drop the price and ruin many farmers. It may be time to look into production planning systems and marketing arrangements to avoid this, and to study the potential for local agro-industries to take up excess production and process it into canned goods."

The Jamil farm includes seventy-five dunums under plastic houses, representing a capital investment of some JD 175,000 ($575,000). It costs another JD 45,000 ($148,000) per season to operate the plastic houses, and almost JD 80,000 ($260,000) to cultivate the 525 dunums of open field farmland. Such an investment is not made lightly, Sa'id Jamil says; it is a natural consequence of the momentum of the 1970s. "The valley is changing quickly. The population is increasing, new government services are available, and new private shops are opening. Before 1972, we didn't have carpentry or steel-working shops here. You couldn't change your car's oil or grease, or find a qualified auto mechanic. We had to generate electricity from small diesel motors. The way of life has changed today. Women are working in agricultural and non-agricultural jobs. New farming techniques are applied. Many private services are available; but essential social services, such as electricity and drinking water, are the key to people's decision to live in the valley instead of somewhere else in the country."

Chapter Nine

The Business of Farming

Traditionally, the farmers of the Jordan Valley had been slow to pick up technical advances in agriculture developed in other countries. Even by the mid-70s, when the JVC was well into its rehabilitation work and the valley's population had returned to its pre-war level, cultivation techniques were the same ones that had been used by valley farmers for the past forty years. The East Ghor Canal had expanded the area under intensive cultivation and introduced double cropping (by which a farmer grows two successive crops on the same piece of land) thanks to a reliable, year-round source of water. But it did not change established habits. Cereals were flooded three or four times in winter and early spring. Vegetables and fruit trees were irrigated by zig-zag and meandering furrows, called *dawaleeb*. Tractors for ploughing were the only commonly used farm machines, while the choice and use of inputs, such as seeds, fertilizers, and chemicals, were determined more by the marketing skills of commercial agents and retailers than by the technical requirements of the farmers themselves. Wastage was prevalent. Water was inefficiently used because the land was not always properly levelled. Seeds, fertilizers and chemicals were casually applied by hand, with as much going to waste or flying off with the wind as entered the soil and performed their job. Yet nature, eternally forgiving, compensated for man's inefficiency.

Lying as it does between 200 and 400 metres below sea level, the valley is hotter than the rest of the country in spring and summer, but milder in autumn and winter. A clever farmer can plant three crops a year, using the earth from September through to July, with only the month of August to let the soil rest and then prepare it for the new season. The unique advantage of the valley is its winter season. Vegetables planted in October and November can be harvested and shipped to markets in January, February and March, at least two months before fresh produce is available from plateau and coastal farmers throughout the rest of the Middle East or Europe.

The autumn season, called *tishriniyyeh* (the October one), runs from September through to January. The normal spring-summer season runs from March-April to June-July. In between, the farmers plant a third crop called *muhayyarah*, an Arabic word denoting uncertainty or indecision – because this crop falls between the two outer seasons and does not know to which it belongs. *Muhayyarah* crops are planted in November and harvested in April-May. The *tishriniyyeh* and *muhayyarah* harvests are the most valuable, bringing high export prices in the markets of the Arabian Gulf, only a forty-eight-hour truck drive away from Amman. Using refrigerated trucks, Jordanian exporters and wholesalers can transport fresh valley produce and have it in retail shops in Kuwait, Saudi Arabia and Iraq two to three days after it was picked off the plant. The demand from these high-paying, and seemingly insatiable, markets had always covered up deficiencies in production and marketing in the Jordan Valley.

After 1976, the technical proficiency of farmers started to rise quickly. Two factors were responsible: the competition for market shares in the wealthy Gulf states, where indigenous intensive

Strawberry unit of farm in southern Valley

agriculture picked up and fresh produce was even being flown in from European or Asian suppliers; and production competition among the Jordan Valley farmers themselves, after a few of them introduced new technology such as drip irrigation, plastic houses, row tunnels and mulch cover systems.

Plasticulture cultivation systems have dominated investment and production trends since the late 1970s, fuelling a fast and extensive transformation of an agricultural area that had remained virtually unchanged in the previous several hundred years, excepting a shift into irrigated fruit and vegetable cultivation in the early 1960s. The first plastic hothouses were introduced into the Jordan Valley as far back as 1968, as part of experimental work by the Ministry of Agriculture's research stations at Deir Alla and Wadi Yabis. Both had been set up in 1951, and by the end of that decade concentrated on research in industrial crops and cereals, such as wheat, barley, corn, rice, cotton, flax, sugar beets, soya beans and ground nuts. A similar station at Wadi Far'a, in the West Bank, had focussed on irrigated fruit and vegetable production since 1952. Research into industrial crops was quickly dropped, because Jordan lacked the industrial plants to transform agricultural produce into finished products. The two research stations east of the river concentrated on breeding a better variety of wheat with shorter stalks that would not bend over with every rainfall. Crossbreeding different foreign varieties eventually produced a suitable new strain in 1965 dubbed Deir Alla I, a cross of Pakistani and Australian wheats that had shorter, stiffer stalks and held up well under the valley's climatic conditions. Several other wheat and barley varieties were also produced in the 1960s and '70s, when researchers were paying more attention to vegetable production techniques. Dr Jamil Qheiwi, Director of the Ministry of Agriculture's research and extension division, was a young ministry employee in the valley in the mid-'60s: "We started looking at plastic houses in the 1967–68 season. The first house actually to be built was set up at the Wadi Yabis station in 1968. We took some steel pipes, bent them into shape and covered them with plastic sheeting. Everybody thought we were crazy, but our initial experiments with tomatoes and cucumbers were encouraging. In 1969, we tried to interest some farmers in using plastic houses on their land, but only two of them agreed to try them out."

The experiments were short-lived. The aftermath of the 1967 war brought research work to a halt. By 1972, however, it was resumed. Steel bars that had been destined for the Khaled Ibn Al Walid dam and were stored in Irbid were taken to the Wadi Yabis station, bent into shape, erected on the ground and covered with plastic sheeting. When the plastic ran out, ordinary white bed sheets were used to complete the job. By the 1973-74 season, a few of the wealthier farmers who could afford the expense started importing their own plasticulture systems from commercial retailers abroad, seeing as none were yet available on the market in Amman. One of the first to use plastic houses on a large scale was Farid Kamal, who returned to run the family farm in the Jordan Valley in 1971 after thirteen years of racing and selling cars in the United States. He first made four large plastic houses in 1972, using steel arches and simple plastic sheeting, and instantly doubled his yields of cucumbers, watermelons and cantaloupes. The next year, he ordered a shipment of complete greenhouse sets from a French company, but had difficulty getting them out from the Amman customs post. "The customs official had never heard of a greenhouse," he explains. "He thought it was a house painted green that I would live in, and wanted to charge me tax. I explained that it was to grow crops in, and as agricultural material it should not be taxed. Finally, I asked him to let me set one up so he could see it, but he was still suspicious that I might use it to house employees, or that the plastic sheeting would be sold for car seat covers." After several months of fruitless effort, Farid Kamal finally asked Crown Prince Hassan to intervene; he did, and the plastic houses were imported without duty payment, erected, and went into service on the Kamal farm in the 1973-74 season. Yields doubled, and tripled. The plasticulture systems protected the winter crops from the occasional frost, speeded up growth by intensifying daytime heat and humidity, and reduced the incidence of many diseases because the closed environment could be kept clean by spraying insecticides, herbicides and fungicides. According to a farm-by-farm survey conducted by Dr Akram M. Steitieh and Abdul Hameed Musa of the University of Jordan's Faculty of Agriculture, by 1977 there were 285 dunums under plastic houses and 3,795 dunums under the smaller row tunnels. By 1978-79 row tunnels more than doubled to cover 6,015 dunums, while the area under plastic houses grew by 160 per cent, to reach 741 dunums. Since then the growth of row tunnels has slowed down, in favour of the more expensive but more profitable plastic houses. In the 1979-80 season, row tunnels covered 7,227 dunums, while plastic houses covered 1,366 dunums (compared to 285 dunums in 1977-78).

Yields have increased sharply with the use of plasticulture, in part

The Jordan Valley

Seedling machine at vegetable nursery
Farmer in his houseplants unit in southern Valley near Karameh

due to more efficient drip irrigation systems that have been introduced into the valley in tandem with plastic houses and tunnels. The many commercial drip systems all work on the same principle: plastic pipes running the length of a planted row have emitters located at each plant, and release water by drops at a slow rate that is set by the farmer. Its advantage is that it wastes little water by runoff or evaporation, because the water released by the emitters goes directly down into the plant's roots. It also makes more efficient use of fertilizers, which can be mixed into the main water supply and therefore also reach the root zone without much wastage.

The first drip systems were installed in the valley in 1976, and quickly caught on with profit-conscious farmers. By 1978–79, according to Dr Steitieh's surveys, open field farms using drip irrigation (for both vegetables and fruit trees) totalled 10,283 dunums; one year later, they increased to 18,321 dunums. Another 1,919 dunums under plastic covers were irrigated with drip systems in 1979.

The plastic houses are all imported and come in several standard sizes, depending on the manufacturer. They range from 7–8 metres wide, 2.75–3 metres high and 25–50 metres long. The most popular size covers half a dunum, or 500 square metres. Their main constraint had been the relatively high initial cost that is beyond the means of most sharecroppers and many small farm owners, though in the past few years the widespread availability of both medium-term and seasonal credit has put plasticulture within reach of all but the most destitute farmers. Plastic housing to cover one dunum costs JD 2000–2400 ($6,600–$7,900), with another JD 150 ($500) per dunum required for the drip irrigation system. It costs an average of JD 600 ($2,000) to operate a dunum of plastic covered land per season, including the cost of labour, seeds, water and chemicals. A farmer who wants to set up plastic houses for the first time needs JD 3,000 ($10,000) per dunum to get through the first year.

The smaller plastic row tunnels are 50–70 centimetres wide and half a metre high, and can be as long as the farmer wishes. They are made of simple semi-circular steel wires that are anchored in the ground, arched, and covered with plastic sheeting. They serve the same purpose as the larger plastic houses, but their disadvantage is that the plastic has to be opened every time the farmer needs to spray, weed, ventilate or harvest. They cost JD 400 ($1,300) per dunum.

The third system, plastic sheeting laid directly on the surface of the ground with its edges either tucked into the soil or held flat by rocks, is called plastic mulch; it is only the latest form of ground-level plant covering, having been preceded by half-rotten vegetable matter, hay and even foam. Black plastic mulch is favoured in the valley. It is laid on the ploughed land and punctured with an old tin can every half metre, where the farmer inserts a seed (new kinds of plastic come with the holes already cut out). It not only retains heat and humidity, like the plastic houses and tunnels, but also blocks out light everywhere except at the seed holes, and therefore prevents weeds from growing around the plants. It costs JD 20 ($66) per dunum.

Since its initial decision in 1975 to develop the valley by using sprinkler irrigation systems, the JVA has modified its plans in the face of widespread adoption by farmers of plasticulture and drip irrigation. Its policy now is to leave the decision about irrigation methods to the farmer. At ultimate development, the valley is likely to include a combination of surface, sprinkler and drip irrigation systems. The sprinkler-drip combination is logical because it offers farmers great flexibility in choosing their crop patterns. Sprinklers are well suited for field crops, which can be alternated with drip-irrigated vegetables. Sprinklers will also be the most efficient means to leach soil that has been irrigated by drip systems for three or four consecutive years, and therefore built up salt concentrations that have to be flushed away. Because of the ease with which the sprinkler aluminium-pipe lines can be assembled and moved, co-operatively bought and operated sprinkler systems loom as one of the most practical options for farmers who might alternate between sprinkler and drip irrigation systems from one crop season to the next, or even from year to year.

The sprinkler method was adopted originally for the following reasons:
1 Shallow soils can be irrigated without being graded.
2 Sprinklers can be operated by natural pressure heads.
3 Water application efficiency is estimated at seventy-five per cent, compared with about fifty per cent for surface furrow irrigation ("efficiency" is the amount of water that reaches the plant after losses in the field due to evaporation, deep percolation and surface run-off).
4 Conveyance efficiency (measuring losses of water from source of supply to point of use) is projected at ninety-four per cent, compared with eighty-six per cent for surface irrigation.
5 The irrigation efficiency (combining water application and conveyance efficiency) using sprinklers can be increased from forty-seven per cent to around seventy per cent.

The Business of Farming

Mulch system and drip irrigation under plastic hothouse with farm manager in foreground
Miniature sprinklers in operation

6 Less complex and expensive drainage networks will be required with sprinkler irrigation, given the smaller amounts of water that are applied to the land compared with surface irrigation.
7 Higher crop yields are anticipated because of more flexibility in timing and quantities of water to be applied to the land.
8 The relative costs of sprinkler irrigation, including both capital expenditure and labour, are lower in the long run than surface irrigation, and farmers' net returns are correspondingly higher.

The JVA's pressure-pipe system in Stage I lands can be used for various kinds of irrigation, including surface furrows, gated pipes, hose and hose-basin, trickle and drip, and sprinklers. The conveyance system delivers the water to farms via pipe networks that end in small risers that jut out from the earth. How the farmer takes the water from the risers to his crops is his own business. So far, farmers have tried drip, sprinkler and furrow systems, and results vary with the skill and efficiency of each farmer.

The JVA bought 3.3 million feet of two-inch and three-inch aluminium pipes, cut into six-metre lengths, to provide sprinkler irrigation systems for some 3,000 farms covering 93,000 dunums. Most of the equipment, including one-metre-high risers, valve elbows, pressure gauges, end plugs, filters, couplers and stabilizing battens, is stored in three JVA storage areas in the valley. Very little of it has been sold so far, given the current preference for drip-and-plastic cultivation. Farmers can buy the sprinkler equipment via an eight-year, seven per cent interest loan from the Agricultural Credit Corporation.

One reason for the slow adoption of sprinkler systems has been farmers' fears that sprinkling tomatoes, cucumbers and squash would promote fungus and disease problems, or cracking of tomato skins, such as happens after heavy rainfalls. Farmers are not going to adopt sprinklers on a large scale until they can see them successfully used in the valley, as they have seen drip and plastic cultivation succeed.

The relative advantage of each system is being studied by a joint JVA-US AID research project headed by Dr George Marlowe. In the northern (Wadi Yabis) and southern (Kufrein) parts of the valley, they set up research plots to grow tomatoes under drip, sprinkler and surface furrow irrigation, using different combinations of insecticides and fungicides, with or without stakes and with or without mulch. While the first year's results are not sufficient to make definitive judgments, they do provide an initial idea of the large scope that exists for increasing vegetable production by better cultivation techniques.

The research is also testing fifty varieties of tomatoes to see which of the highest yielding ones suit local taste buds.

Dr Marlowe suggests that the farmers of the Jordan Valley, who are already spending an average of JD 360 ($1,200) per dunum on open field cultivation of tomatoes, or about the same investment as tomato farmers in Florida, should be getting far higher yields from their plots. Valley farmers are now averaging twenty-five to thirty fruits per plant, compared with eighty-five to ninety fruits in Florida. "The farmers of the Jordan Valley have shown they are willing to spend money and take risks," Dr Marlowe comments. "They are innovative, and often ahead of the government in trying new techniques." Based on his experience in the United States and the results of the tests completed to date in the valley, he estimates that output of tomatoes could be increased five-fold simply by adopting more efficient cultivation methods. Of the fifty tomato varieties tested in the valley, some produced 105 fruits per plant. The highest producing varieties yielded 6.6 kilograms of fruit per plant, or 6.6 tons per dunum, compared to the current average of two tons per dunum achieved by open field cultivation. Dr Marlowe and JVA officials all stress, however, that three full years of testing are required before firm conclusions can be drawn about the most appropriate seed varieties and cultivation methods for the valley.

The director of the US AID Water Management Technology Project, Mr Charles Jenkins, who has also overseen the tomato tests, says that some clear results are already in hand. Half the twenty-four demonstration plots set up on farms in the valley, using a "full bed mulch" system, have produced an average yield of four tons per dunum, double the valley's existing average of two tons per dunum. The full bed mulch system in some cases has produced as much as eight tons per dunum. The technique involves forming a six-inch high raised bed of earth; methol bromide gas fumigation to control fungus diseases, nematodes and weeds; tightly tucked-in plastic mulch cover for efficient moisture conservation; stringing the plants on wooden stakes for better spraying and picking, less rotting from moisture, fewer attacks by insects and diseases, and less cracking of plant skins from differences in temperature between the ground and the air; and pruning (cutting off the first three leaves) to increase the maturity and size of the season's first tomatoes, which bring the best price because of high demand in the winter season. With drip irrigation, and choosing the most appropriate varieties in terms of consumer tastes and highest yields, Mr Jenkins predicts valley farmers should be able to produce eighty to one hundred tomatoes per plant, or five times their present average. Specially designed small machines can form the raised beds, inject the gaseous fungicide and lay down and firmly tuck in the plastic mulch. Two weeks later, the farmer punches holes in the plastic mulch, plants the seeds, applies drip irrigation and then stakes the plants as they start growing. The first such machines entered service in the valley in the 1980–81 season, on a trial basis to adapt the full bed mulch system to valley conditions.

One of the most important potential advantages of improving open field cultivation would be to restrict the growth of plastic houses. Ironically, the widespread adoption of plasticulture has brought with it some increased pest problems. By providing a mild environment (high humidity and temperature) for plants in plastic houses during the winter season, farmers have also created a propitious breeding place for insects and viruses that attack the vegetation. The plastic houses provide an "over-wintering" environment that does not exist naturally, and that allows pests to flourish that would otherwise have died off during the colder winter weather. The most destructive of these is the yellow leaf curl virus, which is spread via the tiny tobacco white fly. The fly, as small as one-fifth of a millimetre at one point in its cycle, injects an enzyme into a plant's skin and sucks out vital juices. The enzyme aborts the plant's blossoming cycle, ultimately retarding or even totally inhibiting the production of fruit. The tomato plant's leaves start to curl and turn yellow, its flowers drop off and its stem elongates, leaving a spindly plant instead of a foliating one. The height of the tobacco white fly's life cycle is during September and October – or just when the early *tishriniyyeh* crop is planted. Because tomatoes account for about forty per cent of the total crop value in the valley, the spread of the yellow leaf curl virus is potentially catastrophic for tomato production, and it is compounded by the brisk spread of plasticulture. Raji Kamal, an American University of Beirut and University of California at Davis agriculture graduate, and the youngest of the four generations of Kamals who have farmed in the valley for the past fifty years, notes that "the same conditions that make the Jordan Valley an optimum environment for plants also apply to insect pests and viruses." Dr Marlowe adds: "The yellow leaf curl virus problem is getting so bad that there might not be a tomato grown in the valley in a decade if corrective measures are not adopted soon."

Plasticulture has extended the tobacco white fly's annual presence in the valley, and there have been recent ominous signs of the yellow leaf curl virus in the highlands as well. The problem first hit the valley in 1974–75, and has grown ever since. Because the virus is peculiar to the Fertile Crescent (it is also found in the West Bank, Israel and Egypt) it is relatively new, and resistant varieties of tomatoes have not been developed elsewhere in the world. A 1979 survey of 200 valley farmers named it as one of their three main problems (the other two were the regular availability of water and the powerful role of the middlemen, or commission agents, both of which are being addressed by the JVA and other government agencies).

There are several possible solutions to the problem; but the traditional weakness of the Ministry of Agriculture's extension services in the valley, coupled with the lack of continuity inherent in regular changes at the top of the ministry, have hindered the emergence of an applied research programme in this area. A further inhibiting factor has been the division of responsibility in the valley among the JVA, the ministry and the University of Jordan's

Bags of onions

agricultural research station, all of whose resources and experience could probably solve the problem rather quickly if they could be pooled into one decisive effort.

Commonly used pesticides have not been successful, while spraying insecticides is ineffective if some farmers spray and others do not. Better crop rotation would slow down the growth of the virus, but this is inhibited by the farmers' market-oriented cropping patterns. Research to breed resistant varieties of tomatoes is also a long-term possibility, but work in this field is moving slowly, due to the absence of intensive co-operation programmes by the three main agricultural agencies in the valley. One joint effort already under way by the JVA and US AID involves growing virus-free seedlings in a tightly controlled and protected environment, typically mesh-covered plastic houses that keep out the tobacco white fly vector. Some kinds of oil have proved effective in repelling the fly when they are mixed with water and sprayed on plants or seedlings. The non-infected seedlings produce healthier tomato plants, even if they are later attacked by the virus, because they grow faster and have a stronger, healthier root system that was pruned in the seed bed.

Farmers have experimented with all different combinations of plastic houses, tunnels and mulch, traditional open field cultivation and drip, sprinkler or surface furrow irrigation. The 1978–79 agricultural survey showed farmers using open field farming with drip (for both fruit trees and vegetables), plastic mulch with drip or surface irrigation, plastic tunnels with drip and surface irrigation, plastic houses with drip, surface and sprinkler irrigation, and even some plastic mulch underneath plastic tunnels and houses, using drip irrigation.

The increased yields (and income) from plasticulture cultivation have been startling, and explain the rapid spread of these systems throughout the valley. Dr Yousef M. Rushdi, of the University of Jordan's Faculty of Agriculture, did some early surveys of plasticulture use in the valley in 1978 and recorded average yields at least triple those obtained in open field cultivation. Tomato farmers who had harvested two tons per dunum in open fields were picking between six and nine tons per dunum under plastic. Cucumbers, which were only grown in open fields during the autumn or spring seasons, produced ten to twelve tons per dunum under plastic in the middle of winter. During its first few years of use in Jordan, plasticulture was almost totally devoted to cucumbers, which brought the best prices because they had never been available before in winter. Cucumbers still dominate the plasticulture sector, but in the last five years a wide variety of other vegetables has also been grown successfully under plastic. In the 1978-79 season, cucumbers still accounted for 671 of the 741 dunums under plastic houses, and for 4,454 of the 6,015 dunums of row tunnels. The next most popular vegetables grown under plastic were tomatoes, squash, pepper, eggplant, muskmelon and watermelon.

Dr Akram Steitieh concluded from his ongoing research that most of the area cultivated under plastic tunnels has been rented land, with a trend towards the more efficient large plastic houses with drip irrigation, and a relatively slower growth rate in the use of row tunnels.

The overall adoption of plasticulture and drip irrigation continues to spread through the valley at a fast pace. Dr Steitieh's most recent survey showed that owner-operators accounted for 1,379 dunums of plastic and/or drip cultivated land in 1978-79, which rose to 2,400 dunums in 1979-80. Rented land under plastic drip systems increased from 328 dunums to 730 dunums, while sharecropped plastic/drip lands increased from 13,563 dunums to 22,000 dunums. Of the sharecropped land, 15,400 dunums were cultivated by open field drip systems, of which 14,801 dunums, or ninety-six per cent, were in the southern third of the valley, south of Masri Intersection – confirming the trend towards intensive investments in new areas coming into production as a result of the JVA's Phase One irrigation works. The dominant trend is for owner-operators to manage their own plastic houses (given the large investment at stake), while rented land is more commonly turned over to sharecroppers.

The development of the southern portion of the valley reverses the trend of the past 6,000–8,000 years, during which the northern valley was more intensively inhabited and cultivated, while the southern half became increasingly drier and more barren. The East Ghor Canal started the pattern of north-to-south development in the early 1960s; Phase I has extended it to the southern region; and the implementation of Phase 2 will complete it, by taking it all the way down to the very southern tip of the Jordan Rift Valley (the Southern Ghors and Wadi Araba) – thereby capping a 10,000 to 12,000 year-old cycle of rising and ebbing development that was only controlled as mankind has been able to harness and rechannel the valley's indigenous water resources to areas of its own choosing. In some cases, such as in the Ghor Kibid area in the south, commission agents have been renting large tracts of land, fitting them with plastic tunnels or drip irrigation, and turning them over to sharecroppers to operate. The best land rents for JD 30–35 ($100–115) per dunum, and the poorest for JD 15–20 ($50–66) per dunum. A sharecropper pays between JD 20–30 ($66–100) per dunum for the use of a drip system installed by the landowner, but the cost of plastic tunnels and mulch is shared evenly between the two. Landowners generally bear almost the entire cost of the more expensive plastic houses; if a sharecropper pays for a share of the cost of the house, he will take that same share of production. In practice, sharecroppers pay anywhere between thirty to seventy per cent of the cost of plastic houses.

The sharecropping arrangement is generally on a fifty-fifty basis, with the farmer providing the land and the sharecropper the labour. There is considerable debate about whether sharecropping is efficient or socially equitable. In the circumstances of the valley, sharecropping has proved to be the most practical solution to meet the needs of both landowners who could not or did not wish to farm their lands, and peasant farmers who did not own any land.

The system has allowed the landless sharecroppers to make a living by farming, and the landowners (who usually live outside the valley) to generate income from land that would otherwise remain idle. By receiving a percentage of production, instead of a fixed salary, the sharecropper has an incentive to work efficiently and aim for maximum output. And because he usually stays on the same farm for three or four years, he also has an interest in taking care of the land so that it gives him good returns in future seasons. A few sharecroppers stay on one farm all their lives, and other, less efficient, ones move around every year or two. A typical sharecropping family works an average of fifteen to thirty dunums, and brings in hired wage labourers during harvest season. The sharecropper pays all extra labour expenses, which he minimizes by relying on his wife and children to work the land with him. The major drawback of the system in practice is that it has rarely allowed the sharecropper to break out of the subsistence farming category because he could not achieve financial or marketing independence from the commission agents to whom he is contractually bound.

This may be starting to change under the impact of the new technology that is spreading throughout the valley, coupled with the Jordan Valley Farmers' Association's programme of extending credit to small farmers. Sharecroppers using plastic and drip cultivation have been able to increase their net income substantially, despite the higher initial capital expenditure, rising labour costs and the thirty-five to forty-five per cent share of output that a sharecropper normally takes in the case of plasticulture and drip farming. Compare, for example, three sharecroppers who have farmed in the central area of the valley for more than a decade each: Mohammad Kleibi, Abu Ali Nutheem and Abu Nayef Al Ghaleb.

Mohammad Kleibi cultivated twenty dunums in the 1979–80 season, growing one crop only between October and June in open field, furrow-irrigated conditions, on a fifty-fifty sharing basis with the landowner. His first trip to market was on 23 March, 1980 (several cartons of fava beans); on 9 April, he sent his first squash to market, and three days later he picked his first boxes of tomatoes ("the first wound", as it is called in the vernacular of the *ghor*). During the season, between 23 March and 20 June, he made twenty-nine trips to the market to sell his produce, on each trip taking between three and forty-five boxes of vegetables. His total gross sales for the year (after the commission agent had deducted his five per cent and the cost of the boxes) came to JD 900.840 ($2,973). His total expenses that season were JD 333.600 ($1,101), which included ploughing, furrowing, fertilizers, seeds, sulphur compounds, herbicides, pesticides, fungicides, spraying services, strings for the onion bags, nursery preparation expenses, and diesel fuel to drive a water pump. The net income of his 20 dunums was JD 900.840 minus JD 333.600=JD 567.240 ($1,872). Divided in half between himself and the landowner, this left Mohammad Kleibi with a net income of JD 283.620 ($936) – an average performance in view of his income during the three previous years of JD 333, JD 239 and JD 240. He also works as a labourer on other farms, earning JD 30 per month to supplement his income from sharecropping, and therefore makes an average net annual income of over JD 500 ($1,650).

He owns his own two-room concrete home. In the 1979–80 season, he took unusually large cash advances from the landowner and the commission agent (JD 270), to get married.

Abu Ali Nutheem sharecropped eighteen dunums of land in the 1978–79 season, of which twelve were under plastic houses (cucumbers) and six were open field (squash). His total gross sales for the year were JD 3,398 ($11,213), and his expenses were JD 1,513 ($4,993), leaving a net profit of JD 1,885 ($6,220). Because he used plastic housing paid for by the landowner, he took only forty per cent of the profits, or JD 745 ($2,488), while the landowner took sixty per cent, or JD 1,131 ($3,732).

Abu Nayef Al Ghaleb sharecropped twenty-one dunums in

1978–79, of which fifteen dunums were under plastic and six were open field. His gross sales were JD 3,755 ($12,391), while his expenses were an inordinately high JD 2,107 ($6,953), of which JD 947 ($3,125) was for labour. His farm's net income that year was JD 1,647 ($5,435), of which he took thirty-five per cent, or JD 576 ($1,900), and the landowner took sixty-five per cent, or JD 1,071 ($3,534).

The relative profitability of farming with plasticulture and drip systems is also confirmed in a series of surveys conducted by professors at the University of Jordan's Faculty of Agriculture. The main advantage of plasticulture systems is the ability to grow early winter crops without fear of frost damage, and therefore to market produce when both demand and prices are high. Professors Steitieh and Mohammad Falah Abbas found that net revenue per dunum of cucumbers grown by surface irrigated furrows in 1977–78 was JD 28.7 ($95), compared to JD 196 ($647) in surface-irrigated plastic tunnels, and JD 1,118 ($3,689) in drip-irrigated plastic houses. Similar differences obtained with tomato cultivation. Open field tomatoes brought in net returns of JD 47.4 ($157) per dunum, compared to JD 256 ($849) for open field, drip-irrigated cultivation and JD 796 ($2,627) for drip-irrigated plastic houses. A 1978–79 survey by the same two professors found that the net revenue from cucumbers grown in drip-irrigated plastic houses had increased to JD 1,525 ($5,033), compared to JD 1,053 ($3,475) in surface-irrigated plastic houses, JD 426 ($1,406) in drip-irrigated plastic tunnels and JD 303 ($1,000) in surface-irrigated tunnels.

These same surveys also show that farmers have been able to recoup their initial capital investments in drip and plasticulture within one to three years on average, depending on their efficiency, market conditions and crop mixtures. As a rule, the surveys showed, drip irrigation systems can be paid for within two seasons, plastic tunnels within one season and plastic houses in two or three years.

Despite the impressive statistics, sharecropping in the Jordan Valley remains a tough, monotonous and often unyieldingly restrictive system. While farm owners can expect to make substantial profits in a good year (to offset the losses of the bad ones), sharecroppers are locked into a more rigid system that allows them to make a living and support their families – but not much more than this. The provision of social services by the JVA has visibly improved their standard of living, particularly in the spheres of education, health services and water. But the future of sharecropping in the valley is uncertain, given the sharecroppers' own views of how hard their life is, not to mention the trend towards "corporate", hired labour-based farming practices most evident in newly developed areas in the southern half of the valley.

Ali Mahmoud Suleiman Al Fattah puts it most clearly when he says: "Life in the *ghor* is harder than pulling a tooth." He was born in Damiyah, in his father's bedouin tent, either thirty-four or thirty-six years ago; he doesn't know his precise age. His father insists Ali was born on 10 April, 1930, making him over fifty years old, which is probably an over-estimation. Whatever his age, Ali has known nothing but the sharecropper's life in the central Jordan Valley. As a young boy, he started learning to read and write, sitting in the sheikh's tent to be taught by the local *khatib*, who used the Koran as an all-purpose textbook.

After just a few days of studies, he dropped out, and picked up the farming chores with his father that he still practises today. After the age of twenty-five, he set out on his own to sharecrop nearby lands, "to become a man and be responsible for myself while my father is still alive." In 1970 he married. His wife Salwa bore him four boys, all of whom died before the age of one, and one girl, Ghada, who is now

Farm owner (right) and sharecropper (left) discuss the past year's performance

eight years old and attending the new JVA-built primary school at Damiya.

"I want Ghada to learn as much as possible in school," Ali says, "because the best things in this life are for those who know how to read and write." When she finishes secondary school, he wants to send Ghada to university in Amman, where she would live with a cousin in Sweileh. He would like her to study engineering, "above all else."

"Farming is the most noble profession there is," he says, "but today there is no *baraka*, no financial blessing, in the *ghor*. There are no rules. Everybody does what he wants. The retailers charge high prices for their seeds and fertilizers. The commission agents set their own terms for loans and fix the price of vegetables at a level that suits their own interests. In the last five years, I have not saved a fils. If the commission agents were God-fearing, perhaps we could save a bit and build a small house."

Ali Fattah complains about being tied to the commission agents. He pays them 400 fils for every wooden vegetable box, which he says they buy for only 150 fils.

"How am I supposed to make a profit? The agent takes five per cent of my sales, the boxes cost me 400 fils each, I have to pay between 70 and 120 fils to transport my vegetables to Sawalha or Amman, I am obliged to buy fertilizer from the commission agent at prices that reach JD 75 per ton, labourers now cost JD 2 for five hours of work, and the price of seeds has gone up from JD 4 to JD 24 per kilo. Sharecropping is like gambling. Sometimes you win, sometimes you lose. A box of tomatoes may sell for JD 6 at the beginning of the season, but then it drops to JD 1–2. We cannot make a living at that price, but what are we supposed to do?"

He sharecrops a thirty-two-dunum farm unit near Damiyah, on the same farm he has worked for the past five years. The farm owner provides him with a free two-room concrete house. He grows tomatoes, eggplant and squash, and in 1980 started growing cucumbers in drip-irrigated plastic houses, which should increase his earnings significantly. He shares expenses and income on a fifty-fifty basis, but pays all labour costs himself.

The root cause of Ali Fattah's predicament – and potentially the single biggest weak link in the future development of the Jordan Valley – is the marketing system. As it has operated for the last several decades, it is a relatively uncontrolled system based on auctioning off fresh produce at roadside markets in Sawalha, Wadi Yabis or

Karameh via the medium of the commission agents. Some farmers send their produce directly to the wholesale markets in Amman, Zerqa or Irbid, where it is similarly sold by auction by commission agents who usually are also represented in the valley. Some commission agents buy directly from farmers, and some farmers export their produce directly to wholesalers in Syria, Iraq, Saudi Arabia or Kuwait. A few farmers sell directly to wholesalers in Amman. The most common practice, however, is for boxes of fresh produce, carried by pick-up trucks, to be auctioned off by commission agents, which turns the main street in the centre of Sawalha, the biggest market town, into a bustling, noisy trading centre every morning of the week, except for Thursday, the market's day off. The buyer then transfers his goods into a bigger truck, or into refrigerated vans, for the trip to retail outlets, in Jordan, the neighbouring states in the Fertile Crescent (Syria, Iraq, Lebanon) or the Gulf. Until the Arda centre opened in 1980, there had been no grading or sorting of produce. Farmers, like their counterparts throughout the world, filled their boxes with the best produce on top and the less scrumptious variety underneath. The standard box being used in the valley is the twenty-five kilogram apple box that first came into Jordan from Lebanon. It is particularly inappropriate for delicate fruit such as tomatoes, which are badly mauled after a long truck ride.

Buyers include wholesalers in Amman, exporters, government agencies, large retailers and even the commission agents themselves, who export produce on their own account. The commission agents, much maligned though they are by farmers and sharecroppers, serve a vital brokerage function in the present marketing system in Jordan, by channelling the output of many small farmers to the equally small-scale retail outlets in Jordan and beyond. There are some eighty commission agents operating in the country's wholesale markets, with a dozen who dominate business in the valley. They have gradually expanded their operations, and, in fact, have become complete vertically integrated agro-businesses. Besides auctioning off farmers' produce and taking five per cent of gross sales as their fee, they also sell wooden boxes, lend money to farmers and sharecroppers (both seasonal loans and non-farming credits, such as for weddings or education fees for a farmer's children), sell agricultural inputs on credit (seeds, fertilizers, insecticides), buy and export produce, and even rent land and farm it themselves by using sharecroppers. A farm owner usually agrees to market his produce exclusively through one commission agent, and that farmer's sharecroppers also sell through the same agent and secure seasonal loans and inputs from him. Given the rising cost of intensive, irrigated cultivation in the valley, the small-scale farmer quickly falls into debt to the commission agent, and remains contractually bound to him, unable to market his produce via any other agent, until he pays his debts. In practice, debts to commission agents are rolled over from season to season, and from year to year. The farmer goes into debt at the start of the season, and pays off as much as he can at harvest time. Though it is difficult to calculate precisely how much interest the agents charge on their loans and advances of inputs, farmers complain about chronically high interest rates. According to most knowledgeable estimates, the interest rate charged by the commission agents is somewhere around fifteen per cent.

Small farmers and sharecroppers historically turned to the commission agents because of a lack of other sources of credit, though this deficiency is slowly being remedied. The Agricultural Credit Corporation (ACC), the government-owned agricultural bank, specializes in relatively large medium- and long-term loans, leaving most seasonal credit to other institutions. It requires collateral, in the form of land or other capital goods, and therefore tends to lend mostly to big landowners who are investing heavily in irrigation systems, land reclamation, machinery or tree planting. Its average loan in 1979 was JD 6,000 ($20,000), with the few seasonal loans it made averaging JD 1,058 ($3,491). Total loans extended in 1979 were worth JD 3.466 million ($11.438 million), of which just over JD 1.6 million ($5.3 million) went to farmers in the Jordan Valley. Long-term loans for farm machinery are for eight years at seven per cent interest. Loans for drip, sprinkler and plastic systems, land reclamation, orchard planting and small farmer projects are at six to seven per cent interest, for periods ranging between six and twelve years. ACC Director General Dr Sami Sunna' says the ACC's policy is to favour larger capital development projects, such as sheep or poultry farms and large-scale irrigation works, which have been given individual credits of up to JD 400,000 ($1.3 million). "The problem for the small farmer in the valley is collatoral," he says, "but the capital is there for the farmers who need to borrow. There is no shortage of money." He sees a division of responsibility emerging, with ACC credits for big schemes, and small farmers and sharecroppers turning to the Jordan Valley Farmers Association (JVFA) for seasonal loans. To prod the development of the JVFA, the ACC tries to lend only to JVFA members who certify that they have repaid their outstanding JVFA credits.

The JVFA is still coming into its own, after being formally established by a royal decree issued on 9 April, 1974. In theory, all farmers in the valley have to be members, whether they own, rent or sharecrop land. The farmer pays an initial membership fee of JD 2 ($6.60) and annual dues of JD 3 ($10), symbolic amounts intended to show the farmers that the JVFA is there to help them, not to make money, according to JVFA Director General Dr Imad Haddadine. In its first year of formal operation, 1975-76, it had 3,603 members. By August 1980, these had increased to 4,995. As conceived, the JVFA would become the most important farmer-based organization in the valley, responsible for all grading, packing and marketing operations, and providing credit, agricultural inputs, technical services, machinery, transport, storage and food processing plants. In practice, it has developed slowly, reflecting the traditional reluctance of small farmers to become involved in new, large-scale institutional set-ups whose relevance and benefits to them have not been emphatically demonstrated in the field — that is, in their pocketbooks.

Its most important service to date has been to buy wholesale quantities of seeds, fertilizers and insecticides, and sell these to its members at lower than the existing commercial prices. For example, the most popular fertilizer is being sold by the JVFA at JD 107 per ton, compared to the Jordan Co-operative Organization's price of JD 115 per ton and the retail market price of JD 130 per ton. By importing large quantities directly from foreign producers, it aims to undercut the retail market price by twenty to twenty-five per cent. Its plan, Dr Imad Haddadine explains, is to survey farmers before the season starts, determine their needs for the coming year, and import enough agricultural inputs to cover all those needs at a significant reduction from retail prices in Jordan. A three-man JVFA mission made a ten-week buying trip in Europe and the United States in 1978, visiting 120 agricultural products companies in five countries. That year, it bought seventy-five per cent of the needs of its members, sometimes having to channel its purchases through third country dealers to get around the insistence of some manufacturers that imports had to pass through the company's agents in Amman, who would have demanded a higher price than the JVFA secured by direct purchases. With its policy of selling its inputs at six per cent over cost price, to cover its expenses, the JVFA was able to sell seeds for JD 12 per ton, compared with the Amman retail price of JD 18 per ton for the exact same product.

Farid Kamal, an elected member of the JVFA's fifteen-member

board of directors, notes that Jordanian retailers sold 30,000 kilograms of squash seeds in 1979, at an average price of JD 15 per kilo, while the JVFA imported the same seed brand for JD 9 per kilo delivered to Aqaba port in south Jordan. Therefore, he charges, the importer-retailers made a profit of JD 180,000 in one year on one kind of squash seed alone. "They are making excessive profits on imported agricultural items," he says, "and it's the role of the JVFA to counter this by providing farmers with the same products at lower prices."

Dr Imad Haddadine says that "we see ourselves as providing a form of competition with the private sector, geared to serving the farmers. We have started to challenge the pricing structure of the private sector, while showing the farmer that the JVFA is there to serve him, that it is *his* organization."

The second big JVFA programme is to provide seasonal credit to small farmers, tenants and sharecroppers who lack the collatoral to borrow from banks or the ACC, and who may not be members eligible to borrow through the co-operatives. A joint programme initiated in 1978 with the financial assistance of US AID aimed to break the collatoral bottleneck by providing credit against a farmer's prospective output. A $1.5 million US AID loan, an FAO fertilizer donation worth JD 37,000 and Jordanian government funding of JD 576,000 started off the loan programme with total resources of JD 1.078 million ($3.55 million), which sought to meet fifty-eight per cent of the volume of loans to owner-operators with forty dunums or less, sharecroppers and tenants. Between August 1978 and April 1980, the scheme had disbursed JD 260,000 ($858,000) in seasonal credits, ninety per cent of which went to owner-operators, and only ten per cent to sharecroppers or tenants. The nine-month loans carry an interest rate of seven per cent. They are provided through the JVFA, half in cash and half in agricultural materials, mainly seeds, chemicals and fertilizers. In 1979, the programme approved JD 295,000 ($973,000) of credits, and in 1980 it projected over JD 400,000 ($1.32 million). The average loan has been worth JD 513 ($1,693), with the maximum allowed by JVFA regulations set at JD 3,000 ($10,000). Besides its loans, the JVFA's sales of agricultural inputs have also been rising. In 1978, they totalled JD 98,052 ($323,571), which increased to JD 149,587 ($493,687) in 1979, and over JD 200,000 ($660,000) in sales of seeds, chemicals and fertilizers projected for the 1980 calendar year.

The long-term goal is to link the JVFA's seasonal credits with production and marketing operations, and to provide a supervised

Open tomato market at Karameh

loan that is backed by a package of services, with the introduction of technology and credit linked to inputs, farm management, production and marketing; to upgrade the farmer's abilities and get him out of the hands of the commission agents.

Dr Imad Haddadine adds that "we hope gradually to organize the cropping patterns in the valley by a slow process of convincing farmers that they should not all grow the same thing. We might begin by contracting with a few farmers to buy their output at a fixed minimum price, and we could organize the system on a larger scale by tying in our credit programme with production and marketing."

The three grading, packing and marketing centres that will function in the valley at full development are supposed to be owned and operated by the JVFA. The theory now is that the JVFA would extend seasonal credit to a farmer, and then recoup it from his output as it passes through the marketing centres and is sold there on the same auction basis that now takes place informally in Sawalha, Wadi Yabis and Karameh. Until this happens, the JVFA's credit programme will remain as a money-lending operation that complements the efforts of other institutional lenders, mainly ACC and the co-operatives.

The marketing centres themselves are still being built and introduced into service. The first one, at Arda, operated for the first time for one month in the spring of 1980, at the tail end of that season. It includes 40,000 square metres, of which 18,000 square metres is covered area, with a main grading and packing hall, an adjacent box assembly plant, wholesale halls and offices. The main hall has two tomato grading and packing lines with a combined capacity of fourteen tons per hour, and two other vegetable lines with a total capacity of ten tons per hour. At peak demand, 150 workers will operate the lines for sixteen hours a day, packing produce into 15 and 28-centimetre-high wooden boxes produced at the six million boxes per year capacity box assembly line. Delicate fruits such as tomatoes will be packed into the shallower boxes, to protect them during transport, and sturdier produce, such as cucumbers, citrus or eggplant, will go into the bigger boxes. The farmer pays 190 fils for each box and 10 fils for the lids and labels, with their distinct "Jordan Valley Produce" stamp. Ibrahim Areikat, the Agriculture Ministry grading and packing expert who has been seconded to the JVA for two years to help bring the Arda centre into operation, learned the business during fourteen months at similar centres in California. He says, "we want to convince the farmer that passing his produce through the grading centres is in his own interest; we don't want to force people to bring their produce to us," despite the JVFA law's provision for compulsory passage of all valley produce through one of the three centres that will operate at Arda, Wadi Yabis and South Shouneh. Grading is done according to a combination of the produce's size, colour, shape and physical condition (whether or not it is bruised, dirty, and insect-free). Tomatoes and squash will be sorted into three grades and culls (rejects); other fruits and vegetables may have only two grades, depending on the variety of produce that is brought in. Mr Areikat explains that the farmers' habit of including poor quality produce at the bottom of a twenty-five-kilogram box worked against them in the long run, because the retailers throw out the poor and sell the good produce at higher retail prices to consumers, thereby making a profit on the best quality produce that should be shared with the farmer. In the one month's trials grading tomatoes in 1980, a ten-kilogram box of first class tomatoes sold for JD 2 (the low, end-of-season price), or the same price that was paid for a twenty-five-kilogram box of unsorted tomatoes. Sorting produce into specified grades is a boon for exporters, who can guarantee their overseas clients specified quality produce. Given the tastes of the various export markets (Iraqis like their tomatoes very ripe, Lebanese like them more on the pink side, and Gulf palates like them somewhere in between), grading produce in the valley will allow farmers to sell all their different kinds of vegetables and earn maximum profits in the long run. With the profit motive coming into play, grading should also encourage farmers to improve their production techniques, to provide specific produce for target markets in different months of the year. As the production skills of farmers increase, new, more sophisticated and demanding export markets will open up, such as in Europe. Given the valley's unparalleled two-month harvesting advantage, there is no reason why airfreighted quality produce should not compete handsomely in the retail shops of Amsterdam and Frankfurt in the cold European winter months. New export markets will have to be developed in any case, as increased local production in the Gulf states stabilizes the high growth rates for Jordanian exports to those countries.

The key to the coherent future development of the valley in a manner that benefits the farmers and their families, above all others, is the evolution of a strict marketing policy based on disciplined grading and packing, rational cropping patterns and better farm management. The JVFA may be the best suited institution to oversee such a complex effort, but it is still getting on its feet, having been spawned by the JVA in 1974–75. There is some uncertainty, for example, about when the JVFA will take over ownership and operation of the Arda centre, which has been brought into service by the JVA itself. Omar Abdullah Dokhgan says: "It is our policy to set up and support non-governmental institutions such as the JVFA, and then to work closely with them. But we also don't want to overload them as they are growing. The firm policy is to turn over the grading and marketing centres to the JVFA, but we cannot put a date on when this will happen because it depends mostly on the ability of the JVFA itself to assume the responsibility."

Mr Sa'id Ghzawi, Chairman of the Board of the JVFA, has been involved with the organization since its inception in 1974, when he was Under-secretary of the Ministry of Agriculture. "The idea from the very beginning," he says, "was to set up an organization that included all the farmers of the valley, and that was especially geared to overcoming the disadvantages suffered by the small farmers, especially sharecroppers and renters who did not own land. We wanted to free them from the commission agents, and to give them services that they were not getting from other sources or institutions. Eventually, the JVFA will have to become the sole conduit for all produce leaving the valley, auctioning it in the marketing centres and deducting seasonal loans from the farmer's sales. In this respect, the JVFA is designed to replace the commission agents, but this depends on developing a marketing system for the entire valley, which is the most difficult thing to do."

He suggests trying sectoral organization of farmers, such as having the citrus growers jointly export their produce on their own, instead of going through middlemen and exporters. He also thinks that guaranteeing farmers a minimum price for their produce before the season starts is worth examining, the price to be determined by calculating known production costs and adding on a reasonable profit. The JVFA, which would sell the produce itself, could set aside excess money when the market price goes above the minimum price, to compensate farmers when the market price drops below the minimum price. Such a system could be tried with one crop at a time, he proposes, and expanded gradually to cover all fruits and vegetables grown in the valley. He notes:

"You can only impose a crop pattern on farmers if you can also guarantee them a fixed, minimum income at the end of the season. Eventually, this will have to be done, because importers who rely on produce from the valley will soon want to have *guaranteed* prices, quality, and delivery dates. In the long run, if the Jordan Valley is to maintain its export potential, and also profitably sell the added output that will come from new lands and higher yields, it will have to have a disciplined marketing system."

The JVFA will probably emerge as the logical body to manage such a system, but only after its own credibility is firmly established. This will be a function of its internal organization, which is still developing according to the model spelled out in its law. The JVFA Law divides the valley into thirty-three "development areas", each of which has at least 8,000 dunums and 200 farmers, organized into a local "general assembly" with its own council. The number of members on the local council is determined by dividing the total number of farmers by fifty. If a development area has 200 farmers, its council will have four members. All the local council members throughout the valley combine to form the general assembly of the JVFA itself. Local assemblies have been formed slowly. By the start of 1980, they had sent seventy-four local council members to form the JVFA's general assembly; by the end of 1980, the JVFA general assembly had one hundred members, who in turn elect ten of its member farmers to the fifteen-member JVFA board of directors. The other five members of the board are appointed by the government, representing the JVA, the Ministry of Agriculture, the Agricultural Credit Corporation, the Jordan Marketing Organization and the Jordan Co-operative Organization. The board of directors in turn elects a chairman of the board, and appoints a director-general to manage the day-to-day affairs of the JVFA. The theory behind the organizational structure of the JVFA is that its top-level management is elected by, and is ultimately responsible to, all the thousands of farmers who make up its membership. The ten farmer members of the board of directors are elected in two lots; five members serve for four-year terms, and five others for two-year terms, thereby ensuring a continual turnover of members, bringing in fresh perspectives and ideas. The two-tier structure is supposed to give every farmer a direct say in the development areas' affairs, while valley-wide matters are handled from the association's main headquarters at Deir Alla. Four regional offices are located at North Shouneh, Kufrein, Tell Arba'een and Manshiyyeh.

The third lending body in the valley, besides the ACC and the JVFA, is the Jordan Co-operative Organization (JCO), which was established in 1969 on the basis of experience in co-operatives in Palestine and Transjordan dating back to 1933. It continues to stress agricultural co-operatives because of farmers' annual needs of credit and farm services. The JCO has 365 individual co-operative societies as members (with another 540 in the occupied West Bank); 149 agricultural co-ops with over 15,500 members now operate in Jordan, of which thirty-two are in the Jordan River Valley, and four in the Southern Ghors area, totalling over 3,300 members. At least ten people have to get together to form a co-op, which becomes eligible for a loan from the Co-operative Bank, a wholly-owned JCO subsidiary that is also its most important operation. About sixty per cent of farmers in the valley are members of co-ops, which typically have between one hundred and two hundred members. The JCO's credit programme, well established in the valley, historically emanated from the farmers' need for more seasonal credit than was available to them from other sources. The co-ops do not carry out co-operative farming. Rather they provide members with access to seasonal and medium-term loans, which the farmer uses according to his own priorities and needs, such as purchase of seeds, fertilizers, chemicals, spraying machinery, irrigation systems and even small trucks and machinery. Co-op members formulate their season's cultivation plans in advance, and submit an application for credit to the Co-operative Bank. The loan application is reviewed by the local co-op manager before being submitted, to verify whether individual farmers' plans are realistic. The co-op gets a loan from the bank at 5.5 per cent interest, which is re-lent to the farmers at seven per cent, with the difference going into the treasury of the local co-operative society. Seasonal loans are repayable in less than one year. Medium-term loans, for one to six years at seven per cent interest, are extended for big projects, such as land reclamation, large-scale plasticulture and drip systems or poultry farms. Long-term loans of more than seven years are made to co-operative societies themselves, usually for construction of offices.

In 1979, the Co-operative Bank lent a total of JD 4.052 million ($13.37 million), of which half, or JD 2.024 million ($6.68 million), went to farmers in the Jordan Valley.

The JCO's other main service to its farmer members is the sale of agricultural inputs at lower-than-commercial prices, which started in 1975–76 with fertilizer that was sold at about fourteen per cent less than the market price. The JCO has since become the single biggest fertilizer supplier in Jordan, with a storage and distribution network covering the entire country. In 1979, JCO's sales of agricultural supplies totalled JD 1.718 million ($5.669 million), of which the Jordan Valley accounted for sixty-three per cent, or JD 1.083 million ($3.574 million).

The advantage that the co-ops have over other institutional set-ups in the valley is the combination of voluntary association and grass roots peer group pressure (in loan repayments, for example). Most co-ops are based on existing community ties, geographic proximity, family or tribal links or common marketing arrangements. The JVFA's development areas are more randomly arranged, and therefore will take a longer time to generate the kind of group cohesion and sense of shared purpose that has developed more spontaneously in the co-ops.

The Agricultural Marketing Organization (AMO), an autonomous body tied to the Ministry of Agriculture, was established in 1970 to organize and extend the marketing of fresh Jordanian produce inside the country and abroad, but it has played a marginal role to date. It has successfully contracted with some farmers at the start of a season to buy their potatoes at harvest time at an agreed upon minimum price, based on production costs. If the market price goes above this, the farmer is free to sell in the wholesale markets, AMO

Director General Dr Mohammad Lubani explains. The purpose of the exercise is served in either case: a farmer who might not otherwise have done so has grown potatoes, and thereby reduced Jordan's import requirements of that product. In the 1978-79 season, the AMO bought 1,000 tons of potatoes at the minimum price of JD 80 ($264) per ton before the market price reached JD 100 ($330) a ton. A new trial is now in progress by which AMO contracts with farmers to grow bell peppers for export to Europe in the winter months. "If the quality of the produce is assured, there is a huge market in Europe," Dr Lubani says. A ton of peppers delivered to Amsterdam airport fetches $1,000, he says.

The AMO also operates a twenty tons per day capacity tomato paste plant at Zerqa, which consumes one hundred tons of tomatoes a day, but its impact on soaking up excess production in the valley is small. The JVA and the JVFA jointly are discussing establishing a similar plant in the valley itself to can vegetables and fruit juices, with the ownership of the plant's capital offered to farmers.

In the early 1980s, top-level decision-makers in Jordan's agricultural sector must decide on the long-term institutional framework for Jordan Valley farmers, to avoid the kind of duplication of services that is now being allowed to flourish. The JVFA, JCO and ACC are all providing agricultural credit, along with the commission agents, landlords and some commercial banks. Six sources of loans is clearly an extravaganza that could be rationalized. Dr Sami Sunna', head of ACC, thinks it is best to have a single credit body in the valley, such as the JVFA. Dr Imad Haddadine, the head of JVFA, concedes that some duplication of services is perhaps unavoidable at this stage of the valley's institutional development, though in the future a more clear division of responsibility should emerge (such as JVFA handling seasonal loans, and ACC providing bigger, longer-term credits and JCO focussing on its members' inputs and services needs). Already, JCO, JVFA and JVA are separately discussing similar new projects, such as farmer-owned nurseries, loans for non-agricultural purposes and farm machinery companies. Top-level co-ordination and the supportive middle-level management to carry through with closely integrated programmes on the ground is sorely lacking, both in the valley and in the agricultural sector throughout Jordan. For example, as the JVA-JVFA push ahead with their three big agricultural packing and grading centres in the valley, JCO is already grading and packing co-op members' produce in its own small centres. There are some doubts about the ability of JVFA to develop quickly into a really coherent valley-wide body that can impose cropping and marketing systems on the farmers, just as there are doubts about whether the co-ops should be allowed to assume the dominant organizational role in the valley. Dr Sami Sunna' suggests that the JVFA's development areas might emerge as the most practical administrative units through which cropping patterns might be organized; the JVA-JVFA could license crops based on farmers' known water needs, which would be tied into a guaranteed market price for produce at harvest time. Some people say the co-ops are the more logical vehicle for this sort of effort. Others yet suggest a two-tier system of individual co-ops in the valley being loosely co-ordinated by the JVFA, with a division of responsibility on local and valley-wide services, i.e., the co-ops would handle individual farmers' requests for loans, seeds and machinery, while the JVFA would take charge of importing goods from abroad and operating the marketing centres. Whatever system emerges in the end, the pressures are there for the farmers of the Jordan Valley to organize themselves into a system that they control and that directly serves their interests. In the absence of such organization, there is a big danger of the rapid expansion of irrigated farming in the valley simply compounding the erratic swings in production and pricing of produce that are already causing farmers major worries.

This will be even more important given the new trend towards farming as a corporate activity in the Jordan Valley. The completion of the JVA's Stage I projects has suddenly opened many people's eyes to the commercial potential of a piece of land in the valley, given the availability of water, capital, labour and farm services. A new breed of profit-motivated businessmen from Amman has started penetrating the valley purely because of its commercial possibilities, joining the indigenous Jordanian farmers whose presence in the valley has been more related to an ancestral agricultural background. Dozens of companies have been profiting from the valley's needs for agricultural services, such as seeds, chemicals, irrigation systems and plasticulture. More recently, though, some groups have been renting land in the valley to farm on their own account or to manage other people's farms on a contract basis, bringing in the kind of sophisticated management that will increase production and thereby put more pressure on the farmers to organize themselves in such a way as to avoid everyone growing cucumbers and tomatoes that would come on to the market at the same time of year, depress prices violently and send many of them into the poorhouse. Typical of these new entrepreneurs is Dr Abdul Raouf

Dakkak, a Palestinian from Tershiha village, near Acca on the Mediterranean coast, whose family came to Jordan after the 1948 war to settle in Zerqa. He worked as a carpenter while finishing high school in 1954, then obtained a BSc degree in agriculture from Cairo University, upon which he returned to Jordan and joined the Agriculture Ministry in 1961, in the early years of the East Ghor Canal's construction. He spent sixteen years with the Jordanian government, during which he was sent abroad on scholarships to complete an MA degree at Nottingham University in England and then a PhD in civil engineering and irrigation at Belgrade University, Yugoslavia. In 1977, he left the JVA to go into private business, convinced that "there were big possibilities to introduce new technologies into the Jordan Valley, to meet farmers' changing needs from A to Z, without going into direct competition with the big retailers who already had a stranglehold on the market."

In June 1978, he and seven partners put up the JD 315,000 ($1.04 million) capital to form the Dakkak and Partners Engineering Company for Irrigation and Farming, which started by importing new seed varieties from Holland and France, plasticulture and drip irrigation systems, complex fertilizers and systems to provide fully controlled greenhouse environments for optimum growing conditions all year round. In November 1979, they set up their first commercial project in the valley, a JD 100,000 ($330,000) 5.5-dunum greenhouse near South Shouneh producing seedlings that farmers specially order for instant planting in their soil. In the 1979–80 season, it produced 350,000 seedlings. For the 1980–81 season, farmers had ordered 2.5 million seedlings, which they buy for between 8 and 20 fils each, depending on the variety and whether the farmers or the nursery provide the seeds. The project's full capacity is six million seedlings a year. Water-cooling, thirty-six fans, summer and winter thermal screens and automatic thermostats maintain the greenhouse at a constant 20°–25°C, seventy-five to eighty per cent humidity environment throughout the year. The project is run by just six people, using machines to inject the seeds into 2.5 cubic centimetre cubes of compound compost that is imported from Great Britain and the Netherlands. The seedlings are grown for ten to fifteen days before being turned over to the farmers.

The company's newest venture is managing a 1,000-dunum farm in Ghor Al Safi, where it will introduce bananas, grapes, pineapples, avocados and mangoes for the first time even in the southern valley.

Another company that is farming in the valley on a commercial basis is Haj Taher Hudhud & Sons. It has lemon orchards on a 150-dunum farm at Kufrein that has been in the Hudhud family for years. Six large greenhouses are being developed for a twelve-month cropping cycle, producing tomatoes, squash, cucumbers, aubergines, eggplant and beans. The farm is now managed by Dr Taha Hudhud, a medical doctor who has watched over the firm's new agricultural division since it was established in 1979. He will give way to a professional farm manager who will run the valley farm. Mr Angus Cameron, the British director of the parent company, says that "we have been attracted to the valley by the potential that exists there from the combination of climate and land and water resources." The firm is looking into the feasibility of hydroponics, flower cultivation, using miniature sprinklers inside the greenhouses, small-scale machinery, and new water-based ventilation systems. Depending on market demand in Jordan and abroad, Mr Cameron says, the farm might eventually use plasticulture cultivation systems on seventy-five per cent of the land.

Abdulsalam Shaker's experience to date on his small farm may be a

Banana groves in North Shouneh

harbinger of things to come. Using semi-hydroponic and hydroponic systems to grow strawberries, lettuce and houseplants throughout the year, he has turned his 1,152 square metres of greenhouses into a profitable, JD 100,000 a year business operated by just two people working full time. He, too, was attracted to the valley by commercial motives, which in turn have prompted him to devise new cultivation techniques to increase production and quality. One of his innovations has been to apply sulphuric acid in small quantities near the roots of tomato plants to bring down the pH level of the soil, thereby dissolving iron compounds that are naturally available in the earth and eliminating the need to apply bulk iron compounds. He has thus been able to achieve high yields that reached thirty-five kilograms per tomato plant in some cases. He is also in the midst of a trial project to grow asparagus in the open air land between the greenhouses, to test the plants' performance as well as the local and regional market for asparagus.

Both the efficiency and magnitude of production in the Jordan Valley are rising fast under the impact of commercially-minded entrepreneurs and innovators such as these, some of whose techniques will be adopted on a large scale when other farmers witness their successes. The advent of the "corporate agrobusiness", if it can be called that, now poses a far greater challenge to officials and farmers in Jordan than merely installing the infrastructure of the Jordan Valley ever did. Both on the farm level and the valley-wide and nation-wide level, Jordan must make a qualitative leap forward in the business of farming, turning the promise of the JVA's engineering achievements into a rising standard of living for the farmers and residents of the Jordan Valley. The farmers themselves, and their entrepreneurial colleagues in the hill country, have swiftly demonstrated their willingness to make big investments in the future. This is most visible in the amount of plastic in the valley, the number and sizes of new orchards being planted, and the new private construction taking place. Such signs of confidence in a future pay-off are perhaps incongruous in the heart of a region of conflict that has erupted into four major wars in the past thirty-five years. The Jordan Valley is, after all, a war zone, a military frontier whose entrances and exits are ringed by fenced-off mine fields that have exploded into warfare before and may well do so again.

The redistribution of lands coming into production in Stage I areas in the southern part of the valley has followed the pattern originally established for the northern sections of the canal. Stage I lands in the eighteen-kilometre extension were fully redistributed after September 1978, while redistribution is still in progress in the North-East Ghor, the Zerqa Triangle and Hisban-Kufrein. The eighteen-kilometre extension redistribution has brought the average holding size down from 31 to 29 dunums. Before redistribution, there were 1,140 owners holding 35,300 dunums, with twenty-three landowners holding more than 200 dunums each. After redistribution, there were 1,221 land owners, with only two people owning more than 180 dunums each.

One of the few comprehensive analyses of the JVA's work to date was completed in 1980 by a four-man US AID team, headed by Dr Jarir Dajani and including Messrs Jared Hazleton, Richard Rhoda and David Sharry. It concluded: ". . . . the land redistribution programme is being carried out in an efficient manner in accordance with the provisions of the law, and is resulting in: (1) a reduction in the average size of holdings; (2) the creation of a modest number of new holdings, giving ownership of irrigated land to previously landless farmers; and (3) elimination of fragmentation of holdings by consolidating previously dispersed holdings into a single continguous area. Thus, it was concluded that the land redistribution programme is addressing both the efficiency and equity concerns which gave rise to it. One indication of the impact of the programme is that the percentage of farm holdings in the valley of more than forty dunums in size fell from 27.8 per cent in 1975 to 21.7 per cent in 1978."

The programme has not always moved quickly, however, as many farmers bitterly challenged the amount of land they had to relinquish and the compensation terms. In one case, a farmer tried to hold off JVA officials with gunfire, but finally succumbed to the rule of law.

Chapter Ten

The Last Frontier

On 16 May, 1977, Jordan's Official Gazette published the text of the *Jordan Valley Development Law: Temporary Law No. 18 for the year 1977*, thereby giving the force of the law to the Council of Ministers' decision of 20 April to establish a new, all-powerful body to take charge of developing the entire length of the 380-km-long Jordan Rift Valley, from the Yarmouk River in the north to Aqaba in the south. The Jordan Valley Authority (JVA) took over all work in the valley previously done by the Jordan Valley Commission, the Jordan River and Tributaries Regional Corporation, the Natural Resources Authority and the Domestic Water Supply Corporation. Two of the main reasons for expanding the JVC into the JVA were the decision to go ahead with the Maqarin Dam and its irrigation network (known as Stage II), and to develop the southern half of the Jordan Rift Valley, from the Dead Sea to Aqaba. With Stage I work now completed, the JVA has turned its attention to Stage II projects.

Since the early 1960s, the government had thought in terms of fully exploiting the valley's agricultural potential by building two dams on the Yarmouk River – Khaled Ibn Al Walid Dam, at Mukheibeh, and Maqarin Dam. Work on the former was stopped with the outbreak of the 1967 Arab-Israeli War, after which efforts turned to building the King Talal Dam on the Zerqa River. As the JVC was getting started in 1973, it also looked ahead to the 1980s and beyond, which meant reviving the Maqarin Dam project that had been studied a decade earlier. By 1975, Maqarin Dam was formally included in the JVC's new seven-year plan (1975–82). In March 1976, Harza Overseas Engineering Company was awarded the contract for technical and economic feasibility studies for the dam. Fourteen months later, it handed in Phase One of the study, which in turn was distributed to a score of international lending agencies that had been approached about financing the dam. In June 1977, design work for the dam got underway, and the JVC was transformed into the JVA in anticipation of at least ten more years of work to implement the Maqarin project. A series of meetings took place in the late 1970s in

213

Amman, Washington, London and Chicago, at which prospective donors studied all aspects of the new project, including the revived 1950s political problem of regional water rights. The United States Congress authorized $150 million in US AID soft loans to the Maqarin Dam, to be appropriated in three equal sums on an annual basis. Such a multi-year aid commitment is unusual, but is explained by two factors: the importance to the Jordanian economy of developing the valley (which has been heightened by the valley's new role in supplying domestic water to the Amman-Irbid region), and the "regional" aspects of Maqarin's potential benefits, i.e. controlling the Yarmouk River's winter floods to provide irrigation water all year round to Jordan, Syria and Israel. In a post-peace era in the Middle East, Maqarin could become a model of regional co-operation in a sector that is critical to life: water. But that era is still elusive, and the practical challenges of actually building the Maqarin Dam have included their share of political wrangling. The American aid is explicitly contingent on settlement of the issue of riparian rights to the Yarmouk's water. The Israelis have sought assurances from the United States that construction of Maqarin would not affect their share of water that now flows into the Yarmouk Triangle to irrigate farms there. Based on accepted international legal principles and the Yarmouk Triangle's actual requirements, designs for the Maqarin Dam include an allocation of twenty-five million cubic metres of Yarmouk water per year to the Yarmouk Triangle. Syria's agreement is also needed before construction work can start, and this has also been delayed by political differences.

Sixty-two international contractors applied for prequalification for the Maqarin Dam construction contract in early 1980. Twenty-two were shortlisted. The dam alone, according to Mr Zafer Alam, head of JVA's Dams Directorate, will cost at least $650 million, and will require five years to build. If sufficient water is available for use in the valley, the dam would be able to run a new pressure pipe irrigation network covering 219,000 dunums, bringing the total irrigated land in the valley to some 360,000 dunums. In fact, drawing water from the valley to meet domestic needs in Amman and Irbid will reduce the irrigable area in the valley to somewhere between 300,000 and 330,000 dunums, depending on the amount of rainfall, the cropping pattern and the irrigation technology being used.

As designed, Stage II projects include the following main components:
1 Maqarin Dam, a rockfill, clay core dam, 148 metres high, with

Children cool off in the secondary canals, Zerqa Triangle area

live storage capacity of 388 million cubic metres and dead storage of 98 million cubic metres. Twin tunnel spillways will pass an outflow of 2,800 cubic metres/second without reservoir surcharge, and an attenuated probable maximum flood inflow of 6,420 cubic metres/second with the reservoir surcharged to the crest of the dam. Two 11.25 MW hydro-electric generating units at the toe of the dam will transmit electricity to Irbid via a 21-km-long 138-KV high-tension line.

2   Wadi Raqqad diversion works include a four-metre-high concrete overflow weir and a three-kilometre-long channel to divert Wadi Raqqad, in Syrian territory, into Wadi Allan which drains into the Maqarin reservoir. The channel is designed to divert flows up to 300 cubic metres/second before the weir overflows.

3   Addasiyyeh diversion facilities, 250 metres downstream from the existing intake tunnel to the East Ghor Canal, include a ninety-metre-long concrete overflow weir across the Yarmouk River and a rockfill draining dyke along the left bank with a bypass culvert to supply the intake tunnel with a maximum of 20 cubic metres/second and provide controlled releases of water to the Yarmouk Triangle.

4   The East Ghor Canal will be extended 14.3 kilometres to reach near

the northern tip of the Dead Sea, and the existing ninety-six-kilometre-long canal will be cleaned and rehabilitated by repairing cracked lining panels. Seventeen existing radial gate checks along the canal will be converted to electrically-powered hoists with automatic controls.

5 Irrigation networks will include installing twenty-one pipe systems on 115,300 dunums of presently surface irrigated land, and twenty-one pipe systems for 98,200 dunums of new lands.

6 A powerhouse will be installed in the toe of King Talal Dam, with one hydro-electric generating unit of 2–3 MW capacity.

Stage II irrigation works will draw on an average of 416 million cubic metres of water a year, from the following sources:

210 Mm^3 – Yarmouk runoff
84 Mm^3 – Yarmouk unregulated flow
48 Mm^3 – Wadi Raqqad diversion
14 Mm^3 – miscellaneous supplies (wadis Rajib, Kufranjeh and Yabis, and surplus flows from King Talal Dam)
60 Mm^3 – return flow from municipal and industrial water use.

The irrigation works, to cost an estimated $130 million at 1980 prices, will require four years to be built. The contracts for irrigation projects will be awarded one year after the Maqarin Dam contract is signed, with the aim of all Stage II works entering service simultaneously in 1986 or 1987.

The feasibility study predicts JD 26.49 million ($87.4 million) in annual benefits from the irrigation networks, JD 9.6 million ($31.7 million) from municipal and industrial water supply and JD 945,000 ($3.1 million) from power supply, for an estimated internal rate of return of fifteen per cent.

In stark contrast to the attention paid to the Jordan River Valley after the 1967 war, the southern half of the Jordan Rift Valley, known as the Southern Ghors and Wadi Araba, remained until recently Jordan's last frontier. Its inhabitants fell victim to malaria attacks well into the late 1960s. The area was totally cut off from the rest of the country; it lacked a paved road, and was also sealed off as a military area. In any case, few people would have any reason to go there. Tomato farmers in the Southern Ghors, especially Ghor Al Safi, took advantage of their ability to produce the earliest harvest in the country, while the nomadic bedouins of Wadi Araba scraped a bare living from the earth by tending to their herds of goat, sheep and camels.

By 1977, however, things suddenly began to change. A fast, two-

Plastic sheeting installed along sides of dyke at Arab Potash Company project along the south-eastern shore of the Dead Sea

lane paved highway was built, linking Aqaba with Ghor Al Safi, the Lisan Peninsula and the road to Kerak. The Arab Potash Company, reviving a scheme first identified in the mid-1950s, started implementing the $430 million project to extract 1.2 million tons of potash a year from the mineral-rich brine of the Dead Sea. The potash plant, located along a forty-kilometre stretch of the Lisan Peninsula's southern coastline, will start producing in the winter of 1982–83. In the meantime, it has brought jobs, infrastructure and new hope to the area's inhabitants, who have practiced a combination of subsistence farming and livestocking for the past several hundred, if not thousand, years. The Arab Potash Company's arrival promised to induce radical changes into the traditional lifestyle and economy of the Southern Ghors. Wage labour offered the indigenous bedouins an alternative to their erratic farming economy. Services that came into the area with the potash company – electricity, piped water, medical care, a post office, schools – quickly showed up the Southern Ghors and Wadi Araba as the most primitive, poorly serviced part of the country.

The JVA was given the mandate in May 1977 to assess the area's social services needs, and to formulate a plan to meet these, while maximizing local agricultural production. Being the southern extension of the same rift valley that formed the better known and more developed Jordan River Valley to the north, the Southern Ghors and Wadi Araba should enjoy a similar natural advantage in producing winter vegetables. Therefore, Jordan's planners concluded, an integrated development programme for the Southern Ghors and Wadi Araba should be a logical physical and conceptual extension of the work that was well under way north of the Dead Sea.

The Southern Ghors and Wadi Araba are two distinct areas in terms of their geography, economic systems and social make-up, but they have been addressed as one unit by the JVA for planning and implementation purposes. The Southern Ghors, from Wadi Ibn Hammad, at the northern edge of the Lisan Peninsula, to Ghor Feifeh, twenty-five kilometres south of the Dead Sea, average just seventy millimetres of rainfall a year. Local agriculture relies almost totally on irrigation water from the side wadis and some perennial springs. According to a census conducted in October 1978, 11,504 people live in the Southern Ghors: 4,738 in four villages in the northern Mazraa'a area, and 6,766 in six villages in the Ghor Al Safi district to the south.

Wadi Araba, 180 kilometres long and ten to thirty kilometres wide, rises from sea level at Aqaba to 280 metres above sea level just north of Ghrandal, then drops quickly to 400 metres below sea level, at the southern shore of the Dead Sea. The 1978 census only counted 793 people in four permanent settlements in Wadi Araba; the area's total population, including nomadic tribes, is probably closer to 2,000. Thus the total population of the Southern Ghors and Wadi Araba is in the neighbourhood of 14,000, and is rising steadily in the wake of a series of small development schemes and the completion of the potash complex. Agriculture and livestocking are the mainstays of the local economy, with several hundred people working in non-agricultural jobs, such as construction or transport, or commuting to work outside the valley, to Aqaba or Kerak. Employment in the military or police is also an important source of income for local families.

Most farming is done on a sharecropping basis that is less advantageous to the sharecropper than the typical 50-50 arrangement in the Jordan River Valley. In most cases, the sharecropper takes one-third of the season's production and the landowner takes two-thirds, with costs shared on the same basis. According to a 1979 baseline socio-economic survey of the Southern Ghors and Wadi Araba conducted for US AID by Dr Jarir Dajani, Associate Professor of civil engineering at Stanford University, "the sharecropping system [in the Southern Ghors and Wadi Araba] has resulted in the exploitation of the farmers by the owners/financiers, who monopolize both the supply and marketing functions of the small farms. . . . It can be concluded that all farms having a size less than 40 dunums and producing less than one ton per dunum are incapable of generating a bare-subsistence income of JD 400 ($1,300). Farms of 30 and 40 dunums, producing a yield of 1.5–2 tons per dunum, will generate family incomes of between JD 415 and JD 840 ($1,400 and $2,900). For a family of eight, this represents a seasonal per capita income of JD 52–105 ($175–$360). By Jordanian standards, even the upper limit of this income is within the poverty level."

Like the rest of the Jordan Valley, the Southern Ghors and Wadi Araba now produce far less than their potential yields. The JVA has initiated a limited development programme that is a small-scale version of its work north of the Dead Sea. The aims are the same: to meet the basic human needs of the population, install water harnessing and irrigation systems, and implement a land redistribution programme to raise the general socio-economic level of the inhabitants by exploiting the full agricultural potential of the region. The Southern Ghors include 549 agricultural holdings totalling 34,832 dunums, of which only 26,670 dunums are cultivated. Two-thirds of the area is planted with tomatoes – by far the most important crop – with eggplant, sweet peppers, green beans, broad beans and cucumbers next in importance. Most crops are irrigated by traditional open field furrows fed by side wadi base flows. The annual production of the area averages JD 2.3 million ($7.6 million).

The British consultants Binnie and Partners have designed a drip irrigation system covering 50,000 dunums in the Southern Ghors, between Ghor Haditha and Wadi Khanazira. Because the soils are sandier in the Southern Ghors than they are in the Jordan River

Valley, a low-pressure drip system has been chosen as the most appropriate means of irrigation. It will have a pressure of twenty-five metres, compared to thirty to thirty-three metres in the northern part of the rift valley. Water will come from a few springs and nine side wadis (Hassa, Ibn Hammad, Kerak, 'Ain Mughara, 'Ain Sikkin, Draa', 'Isal, Feifeh and Khanazira). At a later stage, another 30,000 dunums will be irrigated with water from Wadi Mujib, providing for a total of 80,000 dunums of drip irrigated farmland in the Southern Ghors.

The JVA at first considered constructing the drip irrigation systems itself in the initial phase, but rejected the idea in favour of awarding construction contracts to local and foreign contractors.

Designs for a 20,000-dunum project in Wadi Draa', completed in the autumn of 1980, were scheduled to be implemented in 1981. Wadi Hassa is the second priority area, also expected to be designed and under construction in 1981. Because of the higher capital cost and greater yields inherent in drip irrigation, the JVA is likely to reduce the standard farm unit size to 30 dunums in the Southern Ghors, Dr Munther Haddadin says. All land transactions and private construction work in the Southern Ghors and Wadi Araba has been frozen, pending JVA approval of any new developments. Land redistribution will commence as soon as the irrigation projects are under way.

Dr Dajani's study estimates that the Southern Ghors irrigation project, "if executed and if coupled with adequate reforms in the land-tenure and farm management systems, and with the introduction of effective alternative institutions for lending, servicing and marketing, could truly revolutionize the life of the people of the Southern Ghors." It predicts that even if the present sharecropping system were to remain in effect, increased yields of up to five tons of tomatoes per dunum could be achieved by better availability of water, drip systems and agricultural extension services. With better management and land-tenure systems, farming families' incomes could rise by about 150 per cent. A farm of 40 dunums could achieve a gross income of JD 12,000 ($40,000) per season, compared with JD 5,000 ($16,500) today.

Farming in Wadi Araba will have to rely more on underground water reserves than on perennial springs or side wadi flows. A thorough survey of underground water resources is now in progress. The JVA's strategy to set up small agricultural pilot projects wherever underground water is struck would provide the indigenous inhabitants with an alternative, settled lifestyle. Groundwater sources

Water well in Ghor Al Safi area in Wadi Arabah

struck to date have provided between 20 cubic metres and 50 cubic metres of water per hour, allowing the establishment of four irrigated farming pilot projects at Wadi Moussa, Rahma, Metla and Qaa' Saa'diyyine, covering 500 dunums each. The Metla scheme was completed in 1980, with the three others scheduled to enter service in 1981. The JVA's initial thinking is to distribute the land in thirty-dunum lots; there is also some thought being given to providing each farming family in Wadi Araba with a fifteen-dunum plot of drip irrigated land and a one-dunum plot fitted with a plastic house and drip irrigation. The five-year plan objective for Wadi Araba is to irrigate 15,000 dunums, though this is only a rough preliminary estimate to be refined according to definitive ground water measurements that will be available by the end of 1981. The little farming that now takes place in Wadi Araba is primitive rainfed cereals cultivation, mainly at Qaa' Saa'diyyine, fifteen kilometres north of Ghrandal.

In line with the poor state of the agricultural sector in the Southern Ghors and Wadi Araba, the few social services available are poor in quality and insufficient to meet local needs. Only one domestic water supply system, installed with the assistance of CARE, the American charity, serves some thirty houses in Mazraa'a. Most others have to fetch their water from the irrigation canals, or buy at commercial rates from roving tanker trucks.

The people live in tents, mud brick houses or metal shacks, with a few scattered clusters of cement block houses. Much housing was destroyed in the Safi and Feifeh regions in the 1968–70 period as a result of Israeli incursions. As happened in the Jordan River Valley, many of the inhabitants in the southern half of the rift valley fled for the safety of the eastern hills leading up to Kerak, and only returned to their villages after security was restored in the early 1970s. A few government housing schemes totalling some 250 units at Safi, Ghrandal and Rahma, provide the bulk of the area's concrete houses.

The first two schools in Wadi Araba were opened in 1973, joining twelve in the Southern Ghors. The only full secondary school is at Safi village. Classrooms are under-equipped and badly overcrowded, with six students per desk in some cases. Total enrolment in the Southern Ghors is just over 3,000 students, representing a ten-fold increase in the past decade. The two schools in Wadi Araba have 130 students.

Health services include a central clinic at Safi and three smaller ones at Mazraa'a, Haditha and Feifeh, visited by a physician on a rotation basis once a week. A patient in need of anything more than rudimentary health services has to make the fifty-kilometre trip to Kerak – reminiscent of the journey that residents of the Jordan River Valley had to make to Salt in the 1930s and '40s if they needed the services of a doctor. There are no electricity systems serving the area, except the Potash company's own power plant.

The JVA, drawing on its practical experience in implementing the integrated development project north of the Dead Sea, tackled the development of the Southern Ghors and Wadi Araba from the perspective of meeting basic human needs as the top priority, even before lining up international financing or determining the final shape of agricultural projects. To wait for irrigation networks to be installed and then for land to be redistributed would mean a delay of at least two years before village development work could start. Therefore the JVA initiated its own studies for a plan to provide basic social services to the most important villages and scattered settlements in the southern portion of the rift valley. Village Development III, as the package of projects was called, formally got under way in June 1979 when a JD 1.7 million ($5.61 million) contract was awarded to

Shin Seung Corporation of South Korea to build the following facilities:
1 Twelve schools (primary through secondary, for both boys and girls) in eight villages: Haditha, Mazraa'a, Safi, Feifeh, Fidan, Bir Mathkoor, Ghrandal and Rahma.
2 One type A health centre at Safi, two type C centres at Ghrandal and Rahma, and four in-school clinics.
3 Fifty housing units for government employees (teachers and health care staff).
4 Four 200 cubic-metre drinking water reservoirs at Safi, Mazraa'a, Haditha and Feifeh, and eighteen wells, to serve a domestic water network that will be built at a later stage. The thirteen wells in Wadi Araba will also be used to provide irrigation water.

Three petrol stations, at Bir Mathkoor, Haditha and Sweimeh, are being built by the Jordan Petroleum Refinery Company but financed by the JVA. The Jordan Electricity Authority, as part of its national power network expansion, is constructing a 32 KV line from Kerak to the Lisan Peninsula, from where the JVA will take over and set up a low-voltage distribution system for home, commercial and irrigation requirements.

The main highway from Aqaba to Ghor Al Safi and Mazraa'a is being extended three kilometres, over a new bridge to reach the northern side of Wadi Ibn Hammad. Along the north-eastern Dead Sea coast, the road from Sweimeh has been extended twenty-four kilometres to the south, to the hot springs at Zara. The last remaining stretch of thirty-three kilometres between Zara and Wadi Ibn Hammad is scheduled to be completed in the present five-year national plan, to provide a continuous, two-lane valley highway linking Addasiyyeh with Aqaba. Engineering challenges and high costs have delayed completion of this new national highway because the thirty-three kilometres pass through rugged cliffs along the eastern shore of the Dead Sea. Initial estimates put the cost of the work at JD 17 million ($56 million). Dar Al Handasah has completed the design work for the road, but contracting procedures have yet to begin.

Until this stretch of road is built, the JVA has filled the gap in the intra-valley transport network by buying two Hovermarine boats to provide a high-speed sea link between Sweimeh and Haditha. The two eighty-six-passenger boats, the *Princess Bedi'a* and the *Princess Sumaya*, cost $1.2 million each, and can make the fifty-kilometre voyage in one hour. Initially, the boats now make regular round-trips only between Sweimeh and Haditha. At a later stage, when touristic facilities are in place, passengers will also be able to get off to visit the entrances to two of Jordan's more spectacular but heretofore inaccessible gorges: Wadi Mujib and Wadi Zerqa Ma'in. Though developing the rift valley's touristic potential is an ancillary benefit of the two hovercraft, their primary aim is to provide a link for farmers, government employees, farm labourers and other travellers using the new highways in the northern and southern halves of the rift valley.

When the last thirty-three-kilometre stretch of highway is completed in the mid-1980s, the boats are likely to stay in service for touristic purposes. By then, the JVA expects to be implementing much of a touristic masterplan developed for the Jordan Rift Valley by a consortium of five French and Jordanian consultants named Groupement d'Études Touristiques Jordan Rift Valley. The JD 25 million ($83 million) plan proposes touristic facilities of assorted sophistication at twenty-one sites, from Mukheibeh-Himmeh in the north to Ghrandal in the south.

The valley's touristic, like its agricultural, potential is vast, and largely untapped, given its mild winter weather, natural wonders (hot springs, the Dead Sea, side wadi gorges), archaeological wealth, and man-made attractions (dams and water schemes). Limited financial resources have forced the government in Amman to concentrate expenditures on the four main touristic centres in the country: Petra, Jerash, Aqaba and Amman. The JVA hopes to develop the valley to complement attractions in the highlands, while providing a major new push to the development of domestic tourism. The valley is already an important, if casual, touristic centre for Jordanians as evidenced by the many hundreds of automobiles that take families there for holiday outings during the five winter months of the year. The completion of the rift valley highway in the mid-1980s should be an important impetus to integrating the valley into Jordan's existing touristic circuit, which includes, most notably, Aqaba, Petra, Wadi Rum, Kerak, Amman, Jerash, Ajlun, the desert castles, Madaba, and the Holy Land sites in the Israeli-occupied West Bank cities of Jerusalem and Bethlehem.

The touristic masterplan for the valley proposes two "action areas" at Mukheibeh-Himmeh and Zara, catering for long-staying visitors, with a basic network of facilities geared to day and weekend visitors throughout the length of the valley. Within a few years, the entire touristic system should be able to handle several hundred thousand visitors a year without detriment to the general agricultural environment or the individual touristic sites.

The two main centres would include hotels, holiday homes, hot spring therapies, clubhouse and sports facilities, camping sites, shops, swimming pools, water sport facilities and a full range of basic services, such as restaurants and snack bars, playgrounds, parking areas and resthouses. The nineteen other sites throughout the valley (including Tabaqat Fahl, Wadi Yabis, Deir Alla, King Talal Dam, Wadi Shu'eib, Sweimeh, Wadi Mujib, Mazraa'a, Safi-Feifeh, Feinan and Ghrandal) would have different combinations of these facilities, depending on their particular attractions. Two initial basic touristic complexes have been established at Sweimeh and Haditha – the hovercraft terminals – and are expected to induce fast, but limited, expansion of domestic tourism in the area.

One of the more unusual aspects of the JVA's work related to the area's touristic potential has been its care to preserve the valley's many archaeological sites. Its early awareness of the magnitude of the potential problem impelled it in 1974 to ask the Jordanian Department of Antiquities to survey the valley, to identify all archaeological sites that should be protected. The survey was conducted in two stages in 1975 and 1976, jointly by the Department of Antiquities, the University of Jordan and the Amman-based American Center of Oriental Research (ACOR). It identified 224 antiquities sites, which all consultants working on JVA projects were instructed to avoid at all costs. Whenever a JVA construction project was about to get under way, the Department of Antiquities and ACOR were called in again to double check the site. A similar survey was conducted in the Southern Ghors and Wadi Araba, which resulted in shifting the site of two new schools that would have disturbed some ancient cemeteries. All the archaeological sites that will be submerged underneath the Maqarin Dam are being identified, and salvaged artifacts will be displayed in a small museum at the dam's township.

At the end of the day, the JVA and the Jordanian government will be assessed according to their own twin criteria of "development" in the Jordan Valley: maximizing agricultural output, and raising the standard of living of the people. The first objective can be quantified and objectively measured. The second is more elusive. How does one measure the quality of life? The relative well being and happiness of an individual? The future prospects and aspirations of a schoolchild?

Dr Munther Haddadin explains the JVA's underlying philosophy: "Social services just touch the skin of what we are trying to do in the Jordan Valley. It's easy to build new buildings. What's more difficult is social engineering, and the objective of social development is the betterment of the human being. How do we zero in on this? Above all, it's a person's well being, environment and way of thinking. Is it social development when a man who has always ridden a donkey one day buys a Mercedes? What about his way of thinking? How he raises his family? It's a slow process, but it can only start by providing people with the most basic social services, like schools, clinics, roads, electricity, water and houses. Then, maybe in a year or two, they add a cultural centre, or a small sports complex. Things begin to change. Young people study new ideas. The entire village structure starts to loosen up. A rigid society starts to change. . . .

"Social development is people's attitudes, and it's not easy to change attitudes quickly. How do we speed this up? The only thing we can do is plan and implement to provide the services that in turn give people the ability to decide about their own lifestyle. They begin to have a choice."

The 1980 US AID interim evauation of the Jordan Valley development effort since 1973 concluded: "Available information suggests that the quality of life in the Jordan Valley has improved considerably since 1973. It appears that agricultural as well as non-agricultural real incomes have increased rapidly. Improvements in access to schools, health clinics, improved water, electricity and other public services have been dramatic. In addition, improvements have also been made in access to private services. Literacy rates and levels of educational attainment have increased very considerably since 1973."

However much progress has been registered in providing social services, the fate of the Jordan Valley is directly tied to its farming performance. Farid Kamal, one of the more successful and adventurous farmers, states: "I farm to make money. If you want to help me, you can help me make money by finding me a market, assuring me a fixed price at the end of the season and providing me with cheaper inputs. When people see that there is money to be made in the valley, they will come down here on their own. The profit motive alone will develop the Jordan Valley. A farmer who makes a profit will improve his standard of living by himself, whether or not the government steps into the picture."

There are as many viewpoints about the developments now taking place in the valley as there are people living or working there. To attempt to summarize the scope and intensity of the changes taking place in the valley today would be presumptuous. To value judge the developmental effort now under way would be equally impertinent.

The overriding point is that forces have been unleashed, incentives created, resources harnessed, ingenuity sparked and hope stimulated – in an area that has tried unsuccessfully to do these things for at least the past 10,000 years. It would be appropriate, indeed, if the valley that gave birth to human civilization proved to be the site of an experimental rural development strategy that helped sustain the same civilization more than ten centuries later.

Bibliography

AWWAD, ABDUL WAHHAB JAMIL, *Agricultural Production and Income in the East Ghor Irrigation Project: Pre- and Post-Canal*, Amman, US AID, 1967

BAKER, MICHAEL JR, and HARZA ENGINEERING COMPANY, *Yarmouk-Jordan Valley Project: Master Plan Report* Chicago, Illinois, July 15, 1955

——— *Yarmouk-Jordan Valley Project: Appraisal Report* December 1953

BLAKE, G.S., *Geology and Water Resources of Palestine* Jerusalem, 1928

BURCKHARDT, JOHN LEWIS, *Travels in Syria and the Holy Land* London, Association for Promoting the Discovery of the Interior Parts of Africa, 1822

DAJANI, JARIR S., *A Baseline Socio-Economic Study of the Southern Ghors and Wadi Araba*. A report to the US Agency for International Development, Amman, Jordan, 20 April, 1979

DAJANI, JARIR S. and MURDOCK, M.S., *Assessing Basic Human Needs in Rural Jordan*. A report to US AID, Amman, Jordan, September 1978

DAJANI, JARIR S.; HAZLETON, JARED; RHODA, RICHARD; and SHARRY, DAVID, *An Interim Evaluation of the Jordan Valley Development Effort: 1973–1980*. A report prepared for US AID, Amman, Jordan, August 1980

DAR AL HANDASAH CONSULTING ENGINEERS and NETHERLANDS ENGINEERING CONSULTANTS [NEDECO], *Jordan Valley Project: Agro and Socio-Economic Study* Amman, April 1969

DAVIS, URI; MAKS, ANTONIA E.L; and RICHARDSON, JOHN, "Israel's Water Policies," *Journal Of Palestine Studies*, Vol. IX, No. 2, Winter 1980

DEPARTMENT OF STATISTICS, *The East Jordan Valley: A Social and Economic Survey* Amman, 1961

——— *1973 Social and Economic Survey of the East Jordan Valley* Amman, June 1973

——— *Agricultural Sample Survey in the Ghors*, Amman, November 1973, October 1978 and February 1980

——— *Agricultural Statistical Yearbook and Agricultural Sample Survey 1979* Amman, August 1980

DOHERTY, KATHRYN B., *Jordan Waters Conflict, International Conciliation No. 553*, Carnegie Endowment for International Peace Boston, May 1965

FRANCO-BRITISH CONVENTION OF DECEMBER 23, 1920 *On Certain Points Connected with the Mandates for Syria and the Lebanon, Palestine and Mesopotamia* London, 23 December 1920

GROUPEMENT D'ETUDES TOURISTIQUES *Jordan Rift Valley*, Jordan Rift Valley

Tourism Development Project, Interim Report, Amman, March 1979
HARDING, LANKESTER G., *The Antiquities of Jordan.* Jordan Distribution Agency, Amman, 1959
HARZA OVERSEAS ENGINEERING COMPANY, *Jordan Valley Irrigation Project, Stage II Project Overview* Chicago, September 1979
—— *Feasibility Study for Stage II Development of the Jordan Valley* Chicago, 1978
HAZLETON, JARED E., *The Impact of the East Ghor Canal Project on Land Consolidation, Distribution and Tenure* Royal Scientific Society, Amman, 1974
HENRIQUES, CYRIL Q., *Irrigation and Water Supply* Reports of Experts Submitted to the Joint Palestine Survey Commission, Boston, 1928
H.M. KING HUSSEIN, *Uneasy Lies the Head* Heinemann, London, 1962
HOWARTH, FRED, *The Organisation of Jordan Valley Farmers* a memorandum submitted to the Jordan Co-operative Organisation, May 1978
IONIDES, M.G., *Report on the Water Resources of Transjordan and their Development* Amman, 5 March, 1939
HATEM, M. ABDEL-KADER, *Land of the Arabs* Longman, 1977
JORDAN CO-OPERATIVE ORGANIZATION, *A Brief History and Outline of Main Activities in 1979* Amman, June 1980
JORDAN DEVELOPMENT BOARD, *Five-Year Program for Economic Development 1962–67* Amman, December 1961
JORDAN ELECTRICITY AUTHORITY, *Jordan Valley Rehabilitation and Development Plan: Jordan Valley Electrification Project* September 1973
JORDAN RIVER TRIBUTARIES AND REGIONAL CORPORATION, *Jordan Valley Project Agro and Socio-Economic Study: Comments on Messrs Nedeco and Dar Al Handasah's draft report* Amman, July 1968
JORDAN VALLEY AUTHORITY, *Status Report: Jordan Valley Development Stage I* Amman, October 1979
JORDAN VALLEY COMMISSION, *Rehabilitation and Development Plan of the Jordan Valley (East Bank) 1973–1975* Amman, October 1972
—— *Economic Analysis of Yarmouk-Dead Sea Road* Amman, 14 March, 1974
—— *Housing in the Jordan Valley* Amman, 30 March, 1975
—— *Jordan Valley Development Plan 1975–82* Amman, November 1975
MAVROMATIS, E., *Irrigation of the Jordan Valley* London, October 1922
MAZUR, MICHAEL P., *Economic Growth and Development in Jordan* Croom Helm, London, 1979
MCCREERY, DAVID W., *Initial Report of the archaeological survey of the Southern Ghors and Wadi Araba* American Center of Oriental Research, Amman, 23 May, 1979
MERRILL, S., *East of the Jordan* American Palestine Exploration Society, 1881
NATIONAL PLANNING COUNCIL, *A Plan for Rehabilitation and Development of the Jordan Valley (Report)* Amman, June 1972
—— *Three-Year Development Plan 1973–75* Amman, November 1972

ODEH, HANNA S., *Economic Development of Jordan 1954–71* Amman, Ministry of Culture and Information, 1972

OFFICIAL GAZETTE NO. 2488, MAY 1, 1974: *Jordan Valley Farmers Association Law No. 19 for the Year 1974*

OFFICIAL GAZETTE NO. 2700, MAY 16, 1977: *Temporary Law No. 18 for the Year 1977 Jordan Valley Development Law*

PATAI, RAPHAEL, *The Kingdom of Jordan* Princeton University Press, 1958

PLANNING AND DEVELOPMENT COLLOBORATIVE (PADCO), *Preliminary Evaluation and Recommendations for East Ghor Regional Settlement Pattern* Washington, D.C., April 1973

—— *Settlement, Planning and Housing Recommendations for the East Ghor Valley* Washington, D.C., November 1973

——, —— *(Appendices I–VII)*

REIGNER, CLAUDE and WARREN, SIR CHARLES, *Survey of Western Palestine* Committee of the Palestine Exploration Fund, London, 1884

A Survey of Palestine, Prepared in December 1945 and January 1946 for the information of the Anglo-American Committee of Inquiry, Vols, I and II 18 February, 1946

TROPICAL PRODUCTS INSTITUTE, *Report of the Jordan Valley Marketing Mission* October–November 1977

SHARAB, HISHAM, *Agro-Economic Aspects of Tenancy in the East Jordan Valley* Royal Scientific Society, Amman, 1975

STEITIEH, AKRAM; BEQAEEN, AKRAM; HABBAN, SAMEER; and ABBAS, MOHAMMAD FALAH, *A Manual for the Main Vegetable Crops Grown in the East Jordan Valley* Faculty of Agriculture, University of Jordan, Amman, 1978

STEITIEH, AKRAM and ABBAS, MOHAMMAD FALAH, *A Preliminary Economic Analysis of Returns from Producing Cucumber and Tomato Under Plastic Covers and Drip Irrigation* Faculty of Agriculture, University of Jordan, Amman 1978

STEITIEH, AKRAM and MUSA, ABDULE HAMEED, *Vegetables Grown Under Plastic Covers and Drip Irrigation Systems in the East Jordan Valley* Faculty of Agriculture, University of Jordan, Amman, 1980

UNITED STATES DEPARTMENT OF STATE, AGENCY FOR INTERNATIONAL DEVELOPMENT (AID), *Capital Assistance Paper: Proposal and Recommendations for the Review of the Development Loan Committee – Jordan, Village Development* Washington, D.C., 18 June, 1975

US AID, *Project Paper: Jordan, Village Development III* Washington, D.C., 14 August, 1979

US AID, *Project Paper: Jordan, Sprinkler Irrigation* Washington, D.C., 17 September, 1976

URS CORPORATION, *Planning for the Development of the Jordan River Basin* San Mateo, California, June 1967

WHEELER, JOSEPH C., ACTING ADMINISTRATOR, US AID, *Statement before subcommittee on Europe and Middle East,* United States House of Representatives Foreign Affairs Committee Washington, D.C., 28 January, 1980

WOLF, DONALD G., *Summary Report: Review of present marketing practices for vegetable crops in Jordan and the Jordan Valley and suggested policy for operating the El Arda Marketing Centre* Amman, December 1979

Index

Abbas, Prof. Mohammad Falah, survey by 194
Abbasid rule 39
Abdullah, King, assassinated 65
Abdullah, Abu (Mohammad Abdullah Salem Maher) 155–6
Abu Dhabi fund loans 138, 145
Addasiyyeh: Bahais at 79; proposed diversion dam 68, 70, 76, 215
administrative centres 120
Adnan, Abu, 134–5
afforestation 116
Agricultural Credit Corpn (ACC) 116, 198, 207
Agricultural Marketing Organisation (AMO) 96, 206; tomato paste plant 207
agriculture: earliest 26–7; advance (1940–60) 76, see also Kamal, Fayez; increase from East Ghor Canal 91–3; school of 121; survey (1973) 138; farm services 165–6; corporate farming 208–11; see also irrigation, Jordan Valley Farmers Assocn, marketing and plasticulture
Alam, Zafer 214
Al'Imad, Abdul Hamid 166–7
All Israel Plan (1951) 71
Amer Building and Contracting Office (Amman) 151
American Center of Oriental Research (ACOR) 21
American Naval expedition 46
American Palestine Exploration Society 47
American School of Oriental Research 26
Amman: ancient Citadel 33: population (1948) 65; water for 17–18
Amman, Greater (region): development plans, population 19
Aqaba region, development plans for 19
Arab Contractors (Egypt) 87
Arab League and Johnston plan 71–4; see also pan-Arab
Arab Potash Co. 217–18
archaeology 21; earliest history 23–4;

pottery 28, dolmens 28; early animals, seeds, 28, 30; frescoes 28–9; ancient trade 33; preservation of sites 225
Arda marketing, packing and grading centre 173, 202; costs 130, 151
Areikat, Ibrahim 202
Awwad, Abdul Wahab 92
Azar, Wasef 137
Azraq, cattle farm at 8

Bab Al Dthraa' 29–30, 30–1
Bahais, the 79
Baker, Michael, Jr Inc. 72
Baker-Harza report 72, 74–6, 84; and small farms 88; forecasts validated 93; see also Harza Overseas Engineering Co.
Banias River diversion 74, 85
bedouin: ancient use of Valley 41; in 19th cent. 44–8; agriculture (1930s, 1940s) 64; farmers 134, 156–7; see also sharecroppers
Binnie and Partners 219
Blake, G. S. "Geology and Water Resources of Palestine" report (1928) 54
Boyle Engineering Corp. 17
British mandate 50
British Naval expeditions 45–6; and bedouin 46–7
British Royal Commission recommends irrigation survey 56
Bunger, Mills, plan 68–70
Burckhardt, John Lewis (explorer) on bedouin 44–5

Cameron, Angus 210
CARE (USA) 222
Central Ghor University Graduates' Club 174–5
Central Water Authority (CWA) 114
cereals: research into varieties 180
Cho Suk Construction Co. (S. Korea) 140, 141, 145–6, 147, 149, 151
clubs 174–5
Commercial centres 120

232

commission agents 191-4, 195; and
  marketing 196-8; credit facilities 197
communications difficulties with residents
  163
community and social development centres
  152
Co-operative Bank 205-6
Cotton, Joseph, plan 71, 73
Covell Matthews Partnership (GB) 151
crops, ancient 28, 30

Dajani, Dr Jarir 212, 220
Dakkak, Dr Abdul Raouf, Dakkak and
  Partners Engineering Co. for Irrigation
  and Farming 208-209
Damiyah self-help housing scheme 129, 134
Dar al Handasah Consulting Engineers,
  studies by 104, 141, 145-6, 151
David defeats Philistines 34
dawaleeb 178
Dead Sea 23; shrinking 24; water level
  (1913) 49; and tourism 139
Decapolis 34, 35, 37
Deir Alla 33; agricultural research station
  180; club 174; girls' school 173
DeLeuw Cather International 127, 150
Dept of Irrigation and Hydro-electric
  power 83; and canal plan 84
Dept of Lands and Surveys, irrigation
  section 82, 83
deserts, formation of 26; Jordan 28
doctors and clinics: (1950s) 158-9; (1980)
  168; *see also* health centres
Dokhgan, Omar Abdullah (Min. of
  Agriculture) 108, 114, 126, 131-3, 136,
  144; *quoted on*: "integrated development"
  concept 114; writing JVC Law 124-5;
  village settlement 162; JVFA 203
dolmens 28
Domestic Water Supply Corpn 213; *see
  also* water, domestic
drainage, sub-surface 147-8

East Ghor Canal 17, 21, 22, 70, 74; planned
  links with "West Ghor Canal" 76;
  building of (1960s) 84-5; raising sides 86;
  and land redistribution 90-3; production
  increase 91-3; War (1967) 99-103, 115;
  work on 156; extension 7, 11, 139, 141,
  142, 145, 215-16; administration by
  JVC, later JVA 144; *see also* NRA
East Ghor Canal Authority (EGCA) 85, 113
electricity: Bunger plan 68, 69; JVC plan
  119, 127, 148-9; from Maqarin Dam
215; from King Talal Dam 216; southern
  valley 223
Elektrim (Poland) 149
Energoprojekt (Yugoslavia) 112; study of
  Yarmouk dams 85-6
exports: ancient 21, 30, 40; (1972+) 16, 17,
  197, 202-3

farming *see* agriculture
Fattah, Ali Mahmoud Suleiman Al (bedouin
  sharecropper) on hard life 195-6
fertilisers: production of 16, 17; "no need
  for" 82; and drip irrigation 183; supplies
  by JCO 206
flower cultivation 210
Franco-British agreements on water 50-2
Franghia, Georges: development plan
  (1913) 48-50
frescoes at Ghassul 28-9
frost 194; (1948) 80
full bed mulch system 187

German Capital Aid loan 153
Germany, Federal Republic of, loan from
  139
General Contracting Co. of Jordan 149
Ghaleb, Abu Nayef Al (sharecropper) 193-4
Ghani, Fahd Abu (Fahd Mreiwid Khaled)
  94-8
Ghassul 26, 28; frescoes at 28-9
ghor meaning 15, 27
Ghor Al Safi, fruit farm at 209
Ghor Kibid area and commission agents
  191
Ghrandal, health centre at 223
Ghzawi, Mr Sa'id, on JVFA 203
Glueck, Nelson: exploration of Valley 43-4
Greek occupation 34
Groupement d'Études Touristiques Jordan
  Rift Valley 224

Haddadin, Dr Munther, *quoted on*: early
  JVC problems 126; marketing centre
  130; consultations with Valley residents
  133; formation of JVA 144;
  communications 160-1; village
  settlement 162; social development
  problems 225-6
Haddadine, Dr Imad (Dir. Gen. JVFA)
  199, 200; on cropping programmes 201;
  on loans 207
Hadidi, Dr Adnan, on bedouin 42
Harza Overseas Engineering Co. 72, 147,
  213; *see also* Baker-Harza

Hasbani River: dam/diversion 70, 74, 86; and Litani River 73
Hassan, Crown Prince 18, 123, 130-1; and planning council 107; *quoted on*: visits to World Bank (1971) and loan credibility 108-10; Jordan Valley plans 110; consultations with Valley residents 133; and plastic houses 181
Hays, James B., development proposals 63, 71, 73
Hazleton, Jared 212
Health centres (clinics) 120, 152, 159; at Safi 222, 223; in southern valley 222, 223
Hennessy, Basil 34
Henriques, Cyril Q.: irrigation report (1928) 54-5
highways *see* roads
Hijaz railway 48
housing: self-help in Damiyah 129, 134; for govt employees 152; village plans 121-3, 143, 152-61 *passim*; and individuals 156-67 *passim*; southern valley 223
Hovermarine boats 223-4
Hudhud, Haj Taher, and Sons: farm 210
Huleh swamps, drainage of 61-2, 69, 70, 73
Hussein, King: accession (1953) 65; *Uneasy Lies the Head* on Bunger plan failure 69
Hweirim, Miss Khadeeja 175
hydro-electricity *see* electricity
hydroponics 5-7, 210

Ibrahim, Afaf Ameed (teacher) 172
illiteracy 137
imports (1972-9) 16, 17
Imprese Vanete wins canal contract 85
International Development Assocn (World Bank) 138, 146
International Labour Organization (ILO) and 10-year plan for Jordan 109
Ionides, M. G. (Director of Development) 55; *The Water Resources of Transjordan and their Development* (1939) 57-61, 67, 70, 83
Irbid region: development plans for 19; electricity for 215; water for 17
irrigation: Bronze Age 21; Roman 39; under Mamluks 21-2, 22-3, 39; Negev 71; simple 1947 scheme 82-3; survey (1973) 138; gravity system converted to overhead 138
irrigation, drip 15, 18, 183; and fertilisers 183; compared with sprinklers 184-6; for Southern Ghors 219-20

Islam, conquest by 38
Israelis: and Bunger plan 69, 70; and Johnston plan 71; and Maqarin Dam 214; unilateral diversion of Jordan river 73; *see also* Wars

Jamil, Sa'id (farmer, businessman) 175-7
Japan International Co-operation Agency 146
Jenkins, Charles 187
Johnston, Ambassador Eric, and "Johnston Plan" 69, 70; "Unified Plan" 72-3; negotiations 74
Jordan: ancient history (922-63 BC) 34; poverty (1950s) 67; *see also* Transjordan
Jordan Co-operative Organisation (JCO) 116; credit facilities 205-6, 207
Jordan Dept of Statistics: socio-economic survey (1973) 136-8
Jordan Electricity Authority: designs JVC project 127, 149; and southern valley 223
Jordan Engineering Consortium 151, 153
Jordan Petroleum Refinery Co. 223
Jordan Rift Valley *see* Jordan Valley
Jordan River and Tributaries Regional Corpn (JRTRC) 86, 143-4, 213
Jordan Valley: climate 13; river system 13-15; statistics 20; (1930s, 1940s) 158; tourism 224-5;
 southern part: dries up (10,000-5,000 BC) 27; *see also* Southern Ghors and Wadi Araba
 see also archaeology *and* Jordan Valley, Plan
Jordan Valley Authority (JVA): founded (1977) 213; in Lowdermilk plan 62; survey of ancient sites by 31; and land redistribution procedure 90; modifies irrigation systems 184; starts own housing programme 153-61 *passim*; works jointly with US AID 190; analysis of work to 1980 211-12; *see also* Jordan Valley Commission *and* Jordan Valley Plan
Jordan Valley Commission (JVC) 109; formed 124; expansion of staff 126; writing law, publication (1973) 124-5; extension of responsibilities 131; and self-help housing 134; incorporated into JVA (1977) 144, 213; *see also* Jordan Valley Plan
Jordan Valley Committee: (six-man) 107, 110-13; (three-man) 114

Index

Jordan Valley Farmers' Assocn (JVFA): credit facilities 192, 198, (seasonal) 200, 201; compulsory membership 199; activities 177, 199, 204; marketing centres 201–3; Law (development areas) 204; electoral system 204–5; future development and loans 207–8

Jordan Valley: *Plan for Rehabilitation and Development of the Jordan Valley* (East Bank): NPC report (June 1972) 110; finalised plan for 1973–5 (Oct. 1972) 9–11, 109, 114ff: agriculture, veterinary services 115–16; marketing, credit 116, co-operative development 116; erosion, soil conservation, afforestation 116; social services 116–21, *see also* housing; feasibility study for loans 126; cost escalation 128, 129–30; problems with contracts 129–30;

7-year Jordan Development Plan (1975–82) 138; details 139–40; production targets 15, 16; investment 19–20; irrigation 141–2; Stage II completion 141; projects completed (1980) 145–54; forecasts for 1982 141–2; *see also* JVA, JVC, NPC

Jordanian Dept of Antiquities 21, 29, 34, 42

Jordanian Dept of Statistics: *East Jordan Valley, a Social and Economic Survey (1961)* 91, 92

Jordanian Ministry of Public Works 150

Jericho, archaeological finds 23, 25, 26

Kabelmetal (W. Germany) 149
Kamal, Farid (Dir. JVFA) 199–200; and plastic houses 181–2; on farming 226
Kamal, Fayez 76–80
Kamal, Nabil 158
Kamal, Raji, on pests 188
Karameh: battle of (1968) 102, 173; farm near 7; girls' school at 171; population 137
katar meaning 15
KFW (W. Germany) loans 147, 148, 149, 151
Khalaf, Abu (labourer) 1–4, 6, 8, 11
Khaled, Fahd Mreiwid (Abu Ghani) 94–8
Khaled Ibn Al Walid Dam at Mukheibeh planned 85–6, 87; suspended 112, 213
Khayyat, Mrs Baheeji (teacher) 171–2
Khayyat, Khalil 99
khatib meaning 94
King Talal Dam 86, 115; construction (1973–4) 136, 138, 142, 213; completed 145; generators at 139
Kleibi, Mohammad (sharecropper) 193
Kreimeh, community and social development centre at 152
Kufrein *see* Wadi Kufrein
Kuwait Fund for Arab Economic Development loan 138, 145; King Talal Dam 112

Lahmeyer International (W. Germany) 127, 149
land leasers and land redistribution 90
land redistribution: programme (1962) 88; laws (1968, 1973, 1977) 89–90; procedure 90; cost of land 91; and Abu Ghani 95–8; and housing 97; communications problems 160–1 (1978–9) 191; Stage I areas 211; southern valley 220
Lawzi Ahmad (Prime Minister) 123
Lina, Abu (bedouin) 134
Lisan: "lake" 23; peninsula 24; potash plant 217–18
local administration complexes 152
Lowdermilk, Walter Clay: development plan (*Palestine: Land of Promise*) 62–3, 71, 73
Lubani, Dr Mohammad 207

Macdonald, Sir Murdoch, and Partners: report 65, 70; consultants 147
McNamara, Robert 108
Maher, Mohammad Abdullah Salem (Abu Abdullah) and housing 155–6
Main, Charles T. (consultants) 70
malaria 48, 55, 67, 216
Mamluk rule, irrigation and sugar production under 21–2, 22–3, 39–40
Maqarin Dam: design stage 17, 18; Bunger plan 68, 70; Baker-Harza 76; JVC plan 139, 141, (generator) 139; JVA 144; Stage II irrigation works 142, 213–16
marketing: centres 96, 201–3, 206; at Arda, cost 130; and commission agents 196–8
Marlowe, Dr George 186–7, 188–9
Mashare' and tourism 139
Mavromatis, E: development plan 52
Mazraa'a, domestic water in 222
Merrill, S. 47
Metla project 221
Min. of Agriculture research stations 180
Min. of Social Development 175
Mukheibeh: dam at, *see* Khaled Ibn Walid dam; hot springs, tourism 139
mulch system 184, 187

235

Musa, Abdul Hameed 181

Nabataeans 34, 42; and water storage 21
Nagai Engineering Co. 146
National Planning Council (NPC): and water shortage 17; planning (1971) 104–7; report (1972) 110, 113; taken over by JVC 123–4; *see also* Jordan Valley: Plan
National Savings and Loan League (USA) loans 153
National Water Carrier scheme (Israel) 69, 71, 73
Natural Resources Authority (NRA): established (1965) 101, 113, 114; canal maintenance during War 99–103, 213; repair to main canal (1973) 136; works taken over by JVC 143–4
Negev, irrigation of 71
Netherlands, grant from 151
Netherlands Engineering Consultants (NEDECO), study by 104
Nippon Koei 146
North-east Ghor complex 146
North Shouneh: population 137; and tourism 139
Nutheem, Abu Ali (sharecropper) 193

Obeid, Farhi (Budget Director) 114
Odeh, Dr Hanna (Sec. Gen. NPC) 104–7; *quoted on:* concept of integrated development 110, 113; JV Committee 114; lack of statistics 116; and search for foreign aid 128
Omeirat, Sweileh Al 'Abed Al 157
OPEC: 1973–4 decision on price rises 128; special fund loan 146
Osman, Osman Ahmad 87
Ottoman rule 23, 40; control of Valley 48
Overseas Development Administration (GB) loan 151
Overseas Economic Corpn Fund of Japan loan 146

Palestine Electric Corpn 55
Palestine Land Development Co. 61
Palestine Partition Commission 56–7
Palestinian refugees 65, 80, 82, 103; clash with Jordanians 103; as sharecroppers 95; *see also* UNRWA
pan-Arab and Johnston plan 71–4; later plans 84, 86
Pella 33, 34, 35–8, 39, 42
pests and viruses, plasticulture and 188–90

petrol stations 223
Philistines invade 33, 34
phosphates 16, 17
Plan see Jordan Valley: Plan
Planning and Development Collaborative International (Padco) 129, 134
Planum Zemun (Yugoslav contractors) 112
plasticulture: hothouses and tunnels 15, 18, 180ff; yield increase 183, 190; and drip irrigation 183; types, tunnels 183; costs and profits 177, 183, 193–4; mulch 184, 187; and pests 188–90; seedlings grown for sale 209
population: Greater Amman 19; Transjordan (1939) 61; Amman (1948) 65; Valley (1973) 136–7; (1979) 20, 167
potash 16; plant 217–18
potatoes, growing (1940s) 158

Qaa' Saa'diyyine project 221
Qheiwi, Dr Jamil, on plastic experiments 180–1

Radwan, Abu (bedouin), and housing 156–7
Rahma: project 221; health centre 223
"regional development", "regionalism" 18
Rhoda, Richard 212
roads: ancient Roman 35–6; Rehabilitation Plan 119, 139, 140, 150, (farm) 142, 150–1; main highway (feasibility study) 126, (improvement and construction) 127; Addasiyyeh–Dead Sea 142; Aqaba-Ghor al Safi-Lisan Peninsula 217–18, 223
Roman: irrigation 39; roads 35–6
Royal Scientific Society 107, 109
Rushdi, Dr Yousef M.: surveys on yields 190
Rutenberg, Pinhas 55, 62

Saleh Al Din (Saladin) 39
Salt: Ottoman provincial seat of govt 48; *and passim*
schools 19, 120, 159; agricultural 121; Education Ministry and 127; survey (1973) 137; development (1973–8) 170–3; sports 173; sewing and embroidery 174–5; (1979–80) 151; in southern valley 222, 223
seasons 179
Serbinovitch, V. 57
Shahin Engineering Co. (Amman) 140, 150

Shaker, Abdulsalam 4–8, 11, 210
sharecroppers 79; and land redistribution 90, 160; and commission agents 191–4, 195; economics 193–4; life of 195–6; in southern valley 219
Sharry, David 212
Sheikh, Saleh Abu (truck operator) 165–6
Shin Seung Corpn (S. Korea) 129, 153, 223
Shneikat, Dr Mustafa 168–70
Simansky, Nikolai 82, 83; canal plan 84
slaughter houses 121
Smith, Prof. Robert Houston 34
Smithsonian Institution 26
social services: (before 1967) 117; Valley Plan 119–23, 151–2, 162; southern valley 221–3; *see also* housing *and* villages
South Shouneh marketing centre 151, 202
Southern Ghors and Wadi Araba ("southern valley") 216; statistics: rainfall, population, etc. 218; farms, crops, irrigation 219
Stanley Consultants 17
Steitieh, Dr Akram M: surveys 182, 183, 191, 194
sugar production under the Mamluks 21–3, 39–40
Sunna' Dr Sami 198; on loans 207, 208
Syria: agreement to Bunger Plan 69; negotiations with 84

Talal, King 65; *see also* King Talal Dam
telecommunications, telephone 120
Tell Deir Alla 33; *see also* Deir Alla
Tell Handakook 31
Tell Mazar 33
Tell Nimrin 33
Tell Saa'adiyyeh 31, 33; 19th cent. cultivation 47
Tennessee Valley Authority (TVA) plan for Jordan Valley 70
Tiberias, Lake: formation of 23; and water storage 65, 69, 70, 71–2; Ionides plan 61; Baker-Harza plan 76; and East Ghor canal 84
tishriniyyeh (autumn season) 179
tomatoes: research into irrigation systems 186–7; full bed mulch for 187–8; varying national tastes for 202–3; past plant 207
training personnel (JVC) 139
tourism, JVC plans for 139, 224–5
Transjordan, Emirate, later Hashemite Kingdom of: hydrographic survey (1937) 56–7; population (1939) 61; independence (1946) 65

Trans-Orient Engineering Co. (Amman) 153
Tropical Products Institute (GB) 151
truck operation 165–6

Ummayad rule 38–9; reservoirs and canals 21
"Unified Plan" 72–3; *see also* Johnston
UNRWA (United Nations Relief and Works Agency): and Bunger Plan 68; Palestinian resettlement in Valley 70; *Jordan Valley Agricultural Economic Survey (1953)* 91, 92
University of Jordan: archaeological survey 21; Faculty of Agriculture 181–3, 190, 194
University of Sidney 34
US Agency for International Development (AID): report on Jordan (1962) 66; memo. on canal effects 92; review of plans (1972) 113, 125; evaluation (1973) 226; analysis of JVA work (1980) 212; joint research with JVA 186–7, 190; Water Management Technology Project 187; socio-economic survey of Southern Ghors 219
loans 84–5, 138–9, 140, 141, 145, 150, 151, 152, 153; Maqarin Dam 214; seasonal, to farmers, with JVFA 200
US Geological Survey (USGS) (1978) 24
US Point Four Programme 68

VBB (Sweden) 149
vegetables, most successful 191
villages: planned types 113, 119, 129; streets and parking areas 121; local consultations over 133–4; development projects (JVC) 139; preferred to farms 162–3; construction 142–3, 151–2; Village Development III in southern valley 222; *see also* housing

Wadi Allan, diversion into 215
Wadi Arab: concrete canal 83; dam 87, 115, 139, 142, 146
Wadi Araba: copper in 34; Nabataean water storage 21; ground water projects 220–1; *see also under* Southern Ghors
Wadi Draa' irrigation 220
Wadi Hassa irrigation 220
Wadi Hisban *see under* Wadi Kufrein
Wadi Jurum 146
Wadi Kufrein: archaeological finds 23; first settlers in 27; dam 87; Kufrein-Hisban

237

project 139, 142, 146–7
Wadi Moussa project 221
Wadi Raqqad diversion 215
Wadi Shu'eib: first settlers in 27; dam 87
Wadi Telah, Nabataean dam in 42
Wadi Yabis: agricultural research station 180–1; marketing centre 151, 202
Wadi Ziglab dam, 87, 107, 146
War (1947–8) and refugees 65
War (1967): effect of 9–10, 99, 104, 115–17; and Yarmouk project 87; refugees 103; post-war bombardments, incursions (1967–70) 93–4, 96, southern valley 222; check to research 180
water: resources of Jordan 17; Nabataeans store 21; underground, in Wadi Araba 220
water, domestic 213; for Amman and Irbid 17–18; trucked in 98; Valley Plan 119, 149; southern valley 221–2, 223
West Bank, loss of 103
"West Ghor Canal" 76
wheat, tractor and combine harvester for 81

World Bank 146; and loan credibility (1971) 108, 109–10; on small farms 88
Wooster College (Ohio) 34

Yarmouk River 13–15; Ionides plan 60; Bunger Plan 68–9; diversion tunnel 84, 85; plans (1963–7) 85–7; (suspended) 87, 112, 213; *see also* Khalid dam *and* Maqarin dam
Yarmouk triangle 214

Zerqa, tomato paste plant at 207
Zerqa River 13–15; pollution 17; Ionides plan 60; dam on 87
Zerqa River Project 112, 115, 142; completed 145; *see also* King Talal Dam, East Ghor Canal extension *and* Zerqa Triangle
Zerqa Triangle project: feasibility study for 126; JVC and 140, 142; completed 145–6; farming and life in 157–60
Ziglab *see* Wadi Ziglab
zor meaning 15, 27